ONLY IN PR.

Duncan J. D. Smith

ONLY IN PRAGUE

A Guide to Hidden Corners,
Little-Known Places
and Unusual Objects

Photographs by Duncan J. D. Smith

CHRISTIAN BRANDSTÄTTER VERLAG

I dedicate this book with love and thanks to Roswitha,
without whom the following pages could not have been written,
as well as to my loving parents Mary and Trevor,
brother Adrian and auntie Catherine
– and not forgetting those who work tirelessly to maintain and protect
Prague's many churches, museums and cemeteries

Above: A quiet back street in Hradčany's New World (Nový Svět) (see no. 14)

Page 2: Tesla advertisement in the Světozor pasáž, *Nové Město (see no. 65)*

CONTENTS

Vyšehrad, Smíchov & The Southern Suburbs
(Prague 2, 4, 5, 11, 12, 13, 16, 17)

Appendices

Introduction

"When I search for another word for magic,
the only word I can find is Prague."
Angelo Maria Ripellino, Magic Prague (1973)

Prague is surely one of the most beautiful, magical and beloved capital cities in Europe. Straddling the North Sea-bound River Vltava, with Prague Castle on the west bank and Old Town on the east, it is also one of the most fascinating. The many guidebooks available in the city's myriad bookshops offer the undemanding visitor an amazing (and effortlessly accessible) array of museums, churches, historic buildings and eateries, reflecting the history of the city from prehistoric and medieval times, via the Soviets and the Velvet Revolution, up to the present day.

However, for those with a little more time on their hands, and who want to *discover* something of the place for themselves, this new guide has been expressly written. It only takes a few minutes of planning, and a glance at a decent street map*, to escape the crowds and the orchestrated tours and discover a different Prague.

Based on personal experience, and footslogging all 22 of the city's districts (*obvody*), the author will point the explorer in a new and unusual direction. This is the Prague of hidden medieval cellars, quiet Gothic cloisters, authentic Bohemian beer-halls and pre-revolutionary canteens; secret gardens and historic river islands; little-known museums brimming with fascinating objects; forgotten cemeteries and wild, unspoilt valleys; Cubist houses and old fashioned house signs; not to mention the abandoned British sewer system now open to the public and the Soviet-era printing works converted into an art gallery. It is also a city with a turbulent past, its windows used by the Hussites to *defenestrate* Catholics, its abandoned Jewish cemeteries witness to Nazi genocide, and its walls bearing plaques to the city's liberation in 1945 and the anti-Communist revolutions of 1968 and 1989.

As would be expected, many of these curious locations, all of which are both visible and visitable, are to be found in the ancient alleyways of the castle district (Hradčany) and the Lesser Quarter (Malá Strana) on the west bank, as well as in the relatively flat Old Town (Staré Město) and Jewish district of Josefov on the east (all lying in Prague 1). Equally interesting are the broad streets of New Town (Nové Město), laid out by Charles IV (1346–1378)** in 1348 and stretching southeastwards beyond Národní třída. However, a considerable number lie *outside* these long-established areas of occupation, for instance in Holešovice

(Prague 7) on a bend in the Vltava to the north, in Střešovice (Prague 6) amongst the gentle hills to the west, as well as in Vyšehrad (Prague 2) and Smíchov (Prague 5) to the south. Meanwhile to the east, beyond the divisive Wilsonova ring road, are ranged the city's sprawling outer suburbs, including fascinating Žižkov (Prague 3).

By walking around Prague's relatively compact city centre and using the integrated transport network of underground trains (*metro*), trams (*tramvaje*) and buses (*autobusy*) to venture into the suburbs, the explorer can quite quickly reach all the places described – and that's without detracting whatsoever from the sense of personal discovery that each of these places has to offer. Indeed, directions have been kept to a minimum so as to leave the visitor free to find their own particular path. Whether exploring the newly restored Baroque Palace Gardens of Malá Strana, searching Vyšehrad for Prague's ancient foundation myths, getting lost amongst the tombstones of Žižkov's Olšany Cemetery, or uncovering Romanesque cellars beneath the bustling streets of Old Town, it is hoped that the visitor will experience a sense of having made the discovery for his or her self.

In embarking on these mini-odysseys in search of Prague's tangible historical legacy the author would only ask that telephones are switched off in places of worship (which must not be visited during services), and that due respect is shown in the quiet city courtyards and backstreets that are home and workplace to many Czechs. Other than that, treat Prague as a giant oyster containing many precious pearls – I just hope you enjoy finding them as much as I did.

Duncan J. D. Smith, Prague, Czech Republic and Vienna, Austria

* Prague is divided into 22 administrative districts (*obvody*), the most important of which, together with transportation routes, are covered by the Freytag & Berndt City Map of Prague. Many of Prague's old buildings carry two numbers, a blue one showing the modern street number and a red one as recorded originally in the Prague land registry; the lower the red number the older the building. Addresses given within the text are the blue ones.

** The dates given after the names of Bohemia's various monarchs are the actual years they reigned for, whereas those given after important non-royal personalities relate to their birth and death.

Statue of John of Nepomuk (Jan Nepomucký) on Charles Bridge (Karlův most)

1.   Of Saints and Sinners

Prague 1 (Malá Strana), Charles Bridge (Karlův most) between Karlova
and Mostecká
Metro A to Malostranská; Tram 12, 20 from náměstí Kinských, 17,18
along eastern riverbank, 22, 23 from Národní třída

For many visitors to Prague the Czech capital's two great architectural icons are St. Vitus's Cathedral (chrám sv. Víta) and Charles Bridge
(Karlův most). Whilst this guidebook is for those attempting to escape
the tourist hordes that regularly throng both of these historic locations,
no visit to Prague would be complete without seeing them. However, as
with several other 'must see' locations in the city that legendary British travel writer Bruce Chatwin dubbed "one of the most curious places
in the world", there is a way of escaping the crowds, albeit cerebrally,
by immersing oneself in the alternate histories of the city, supplant-
ing hard fact with fanciful legend – and vice-versa. Thus, Prague is the
ultimate Kafka-esque urban experience, enabling insightful visitors to
transport themselves to another plane in even the most populous tourist hotspots, the city's cathedral and bridge being cases in point.

Holy Roman Emperor Charles IV of Luxembourg (King Charles I
of Bohemia) (1346–78) founded St. Vitus's Cathedral whilst still prince
regent, after securing an archbishopric for the city in 1344. Although
the 23 year old German Swabian architect Peter Parler commenced
work on the building in 1352, it was not completed until 1929 by the
architect Kamil Hilbert, almost exactly a thousand years after the murdered Christian Duke Wenceslaus (Václav) I (921–935) of Bohemia's
first dynasty, the Přemyslids, had been buried on the same spot (see
no. 18). Today, Parler's bejewelled Chapel of St. Wenceslaus (Svatová-
clavská kaple) occupies the site of a 10th century rotunda that once contained his tomb. A door in the corner of the Chapel, locked with seven
keys held by seven different officials (after the seven seals of the Biblical
Revelations), leads to a chamber containing the Czech Crown Jewels,
protected by Papal bull since 1346 and carrying a curse on those unau-
thorised to don them (see no. 69).

Amidst Parler's late Gothic pomp and splendour – not to mention
all the visitors – it is easy to forget that the cathedral's location had
been an important and potent pre-Christian site, where Svatovít, the
Slavic god of fertility had been worshipped in pagan times (as recently
as the 18th century young women and worried farmers still made offer-

ings here). When the Slavs were converted to Christianity during the 9th century the name Svatovít was changed to the nearest-sounding saint's name, svatý Vít (St. Vitus). Vitus was a Sicilian peasant who was thrown to the lions during the persecution of the Christians by the Romans in 303 AD and he is counted as one of the Fourteen Helpers of the Roman Catholic Church.

Equally rich in history and folklore is the Charles Bridge. Commenced in 1357 and again commissioned by Charles IV to a design by Peter Parler, it replaced the old Romanesque Judith Bridge (Juditin most) that had been destroyed by a flood (see no. 2). For the next 500 years Charles Bridge was Prague's only way across the Vltava, its resilience allegedly the result of mortar mixed with egg yolks; even electric trams once ran across it (see no. 36). However, long before either bridge was built the riverbed was littered with naturally flat stones, or sills (*práh* in Czech), attracting early settlers to what was effectively a ford across the river and possibly giving rise to the Czech name *Praha*.

Since the reign of the Czech King George of Poděbrady (Jiří z Poděbrad) (1458–71), Charles Bridge was part of the so-called Royal Route (Královská cesta), the coronation path established by the Přemyslids and taken by Bohemian kings from the Royal Court (Králův dvůr) in Republic Square (náměstí Republiky) up to Prague Castle (Pražský hrad) (see nos. 9, 15 & 77). A rare benefit of the endless crowds of tourists crossing the bridge today is that it allows one to imagine the scene in 1836 when the Austrian Emperor and King of Bohemia Ferdinand V (1835–48) came this way with a retinue of 3400 horses and four camels!

The 16-arched sandstone bridge was originally unadorned, except for a large crucifix, until a statue of John of Nepomuk (Jan Nepomucký) was added in 1683. Such was its popularity that the Catholic Church commissioned further statues for the bridge, most of which are now housed in the National Gallery's Lapidarium in Holešovice, where they are protected from the ravages of time and pollution (see no. 35); the statues seen on the bridge today are copies. The Baroque statues continue in their original role as a Jesuit-inspired reminder to passers-by to pray. Worth looking out for as one crosses from Lesser Quarter (Malá Strana) to Old Town (Staré Město) – two of the five originally separate towns that make up old Prague is Duke (later Saint) Wenceslaus (Václav) I (first on the right), St. Vitus (second on the left), St. Ludmila (8th on the right; wife of the first Přemyslid duke and grandmother of Saint Wenceslaus) (see no. 18), and Saints Cyril and Methodius (11th on the left); the latter are credited with devising the Glagolitic alphabet in order to translate the Bible for Slavic audiences (see nos. 70 & 71).

Of all the thirty statues that line the bridge today, it is the bronze statue of Nepomuk (8th on the left) that is most popular with tourists, who line up to touch it for good luck; nowhere in Prague is fact and fiction so intertwined as here. According to legend Nepomuk was confessor to the queen of King Wenceslaus (Václav) IV (1378–1419) of the Luxembourg dynasty. When in 1393 he refused to divulge details of the queen's confessionals the king had him placed in a sack and thrown off the Charles Bridge, five stars appearing in the sky as he hit the water. Subsequently, Nepomuk became a popular national saint of Bohemia, the first martyr of the seal of confession and a patron saint against floods, hence his star-haloed statue being found on bridges across Central Europe. However, there is a more prosaic version of the Nepomuk story, set against the run-up to the Hussite Wars (1420–36). It is based on the life of one John of Pomuk, a town in the Plzeň region that was renamed Nepomuk in 1384. In 1393 John was made vicar-general to the Archbishop of Prague, a non-radical, staunch supporter of the Pope in Rome. By contrast, the ruling monarch King Wenceslaus IV backed the Avignon papacy – reflecting what historians call the Great Schism – and sought to protect the Protestant religious reformer Jan Hus against demands for his suppression as a heretic by the Catholic Church. Matters came to a head when John and the Archbishop opposed the king's candidate for a new abbot of the wealthy Benedictine Monastery of Kladruby (the monastery's resources were crucial to the king in his struggles against the nobles); again Nepomuk meets a watery end at Charles Bridge.

Today, John of Nepomuck is seen by Catholics as a martyr to the

The controversial Baroque Calvary on Charles Bridge (Karlův most)

cause of clerical immunity (he was canonized by Pope Benedict XIII in 1729 as part of the Counter Reformation), by Czech nationalists as a martyr to imperial interference, and by historians as a victim of the longstanding power struggle between secular and religious powers in medieval Europe. Some commentators even suggest there were two Nepomuks, whilst others claim that he never existed at all; however, there is no doubting the presence of his incredible Baroque silver tomb in St. Vitus's Cathedral, the object on a nearby platter said to be his discreet tongue!

When the queue to touch Nepomuk's lucky statue grows too long, visit instead the bridge's Calvary (13th on the left). Most visitors will be quite unaware that this statue, with its Hebrew inscription arching above, is a fascinating illustration of the ethnic symbiosis of old Prague, whereby Bohemians, Jews and Germans lived and worked side-by-side, sometimes in harmony and sometimes not. According to legend, a Jew was ordered to finance the placing of the inscription here in the 17th century, as punishment for spitting in front of the statue. The actual story is rather more complex and dates back to the period after the Thirty Years War (1618–48) and the Peace of Westphalia, when the Habsburgs set about restoring Catholicism to heretical Bohemia. For the sake of good order they divided Bohemia's self-governing Jews into Prague Jews and rural Jews, the council leaders of these groups gaining considerable prestige and financial gain. In 1693 one of the powerful rural Jews, Abraham Aron Lichtenstadt, denounced another, Elias Backoffen, for blaspheming against the Holy Cross in an encoded Yiddish message the latter had sent to a friend in Vienna. Lichtenstadt was already in prison, having been accused previously by Backoffen of embezzlement, and now Backoffen joined him, where each attempted to destroy the other's reputation. Backoffen denied the charge but in order to gain an acquittal from the local authorities he was asked to reveal the code. Claiming to have destroyed it, his guilt could not be demonstrated and so, instead of facing the executioner, he was made to pay a large fine. In 1696 the money was used to finance the Hebrew inscription on the Charles Bridge Calvary, an angelic utterance taken from Isaiah chapter 6, verse 3, and an important credo in the Jewish liturgy: "Holy, holy, holy, is Jehovah of hosts". Below is another inscription, in Latin, German and Czech, which reads: "Three times holy, holy, holy in honour of Christ on the Cross, from a fine ordered by the most praiseworthy Royal Court of Appeal to be paid by a Jew who defiled the Holy Cross". Three hundred years later, following an outcry from Jews who felt that the court proceedings against Backoffen were improper, and that the inscriptions were an attempt to humiliate the Jewish community, a modern explanation in Hebrew, Czech and English was added to the right of the Calvary; it stresses the importance of tolerance and humility, explaining that when Jews recite the verse they are not referring to Jesus.

Other places of interest nearby: 2, 3, 4, 5, 23

2. A Tale of two Towers

Prague 1 (Malá Strana), Judith's Tower (Juditina věž) on Mostecká
Metro A to Malostranská; Tram 12, 20 from náměstí Kinských, 22, 23
from Národní třída

It was the German poet, scientist and thinker Johann Wolfgang von Goethe (1749–1832) who described Prague as "the most exquisite gem in the world's stone crown". The city has also been dubbed 'the golden city of a hundred spires', although the actual number is somewhere between five hundred and a thousand. Many of these spires, towers, turrets and belfries (*věž* in Czech) are famous, although the majority are less well-known: this is the tale of two of the latter.

The famous Lesser Quarter Bridge Tower (Malostranská mostecká věž) gives access to Lesser Quarter (Malá Strana) for those seeking out this beautiful Baroque district. Converted from an older, possibly Romanesque structure in 1464 by Czech King George of Poděbrady (Jiří z Poděbrad) (1458–71), this Gothic tower guards one end of Charles Bridge (Karlův most) (see no. 1). The model for its construction was undoubtedly the Old Town Bridge Tower (Staroměstská mostecká věž), constructed in 1373 on Křižovnické náměstí at the opposite end of the bridge (Peter Parler's original sculptures still survive on its eastern side, as does a protective Latin palindrome and a rare statue of a 14th century watchman inside).

The enigmatic Judith's Tower (Juditina věž) stands at one end of Charles Bridge (Karlův most)

Connected to the Lesser Quarter Bridge Tower, however, is the shorter and less well-known Judith's Tower (Juditina věž). Erected in the early 12th century as part of the fortifications of the left bank, it was later joined to the west end of Prague's first stone bridge, the Romanesque Judith Bridge (Juditin most), built between 1160 and 1172 by the Přemyslid Duke Vladislav II (1140–72). Named after his wife this bridge was swept away by floods in 1342 and replaced fifteen years later by the Charles Bridge, although traces of it still remain underground (see no. 49). On the first floor of the tower is the carving of a young man kneeling; open to interpretation it dates from c. 1170 and is Prague's oldest secular sculpture.

Another less well-known tower is the Henry Tower (Jindřišská věž) near the Main Station (Hlavní nádraží) in New Town (Nové Město). It was originally built as a detached bell tower for the Church of Sts. Henry and Kunhuta (kostel sv. Jindřicha a Kunhuty), founded in 1352 in the square known today as Senovážné náměstí. The square's original name was Senný trh, meaning 'hay market', and it was one of three market places established in 1348, when Holy Roman Emperor Charles IV of Luxembourg (King Charles I of Bohemia) (1346–78) laid out New Town (Nové Město); the other two were Horse Market (Koňský trh), now Wenceslas Square (Václavské náměstí), and Cattle Market (Dobytčí trh), now Charles Square (Karlovo náměstí). The church originally had a wooden tower built in 1475 that was replaced in 1599 by the Gothic-style stone tower seen today (at 66 metres high it is the tallest of Prague's freestanding belfries; another can be seen at the Church of St. Peter (kostel sv.

The Henry Tower (Jindřišská věž) in New Town (Nové Město)

Petra na Poříčí) on Biskupská). The tower contained ten bells, the oldest of which, called St. Maria, still survives.

Within the last few years the tower has been ingeniously adapted for use as a café, restaurant and retail outlet. So as not to damage the ancient fabric, a self-supporting ferroconcrete tower has been carefully erected *inside* the old tower. As such it is the only Gothic tower in Central Europe to have been re-used in this way. The 7th and 8th floors of the tower now contain the Zvonice (meaning 'Belfry') Restaurant, where customers sit amongst giant timber roof trusses. On the 6th floor there is a museum of spires, whilst on the 10th floor, atop a huge truss from 1879, there is a viewing gallery offering stunning views. Also located here is a modern set of ten bells that chime hourly between 9 am and 6 pm from a selection of 1152 pre-set melodies.

About midway between the towers described above, at Rytířská 16, there is the last of several Early Gothic tower houses that once had a defensive function but which were later hidden behind Baroque façades and turned over to domestic accommodation.

Other places of interest nearby: 1, 3, 4, 5, 23

3. Little Venice and the Devil's Stream

Prague 1 (Malá Strana), Kampa Island
Metro A to Malostranská; Tram 6, 9, 22, 23 from Národní třída, 12, 20
from náměstí Kinských

One of central Prague's unexpectedly peaceful and romantic locations, even during busy August when visitors pour across nearby Charles Bridge (Karlův most), is Kampa Island. Approaching Lesser Quarter (Malá Strana) from Old Town (Staré Město) the island's northern tip is reached via a staircase near the end of the bridge, on the lefthand side.

The largest island on the river, Kampa is actually a flat swathe of riverbank made into an island by means of an artificial canal, cut in the late 12th century in order to provide power for a series of medieval watermills. Two of the mills still retain their wooden waterwheels, namely the Smeltery Mill (mlýn Hut') at the southern end of the island and the Grand Prior Mill (Velkopřevorský mlýn) in the north, first recorded during the 13th century when the Knights of St. John owned it (see no. 5). The resulting landscape of historic buildings and canal has given rise to the modern name of 'Little Venice'.

The canal itself is called Čertovka, meaning Devil's Stream, although the reason is unclear. One legend tells of an evil woman who lived in Maltézské náměstí in a house called At the Seven Devils (Dům U sedmi čertů), although only six were depicted on the wall. It was assumed that the woman herself was the seventh and because she did her washing in the canal the waterway was named after her. Whatever the truth, the canal has been used for washing down the ages, indeed at the southern end of the island there is the Gothic Church of St. John, known as the Laundry Church (kostel sv. Jana na Prádle), since that is what it became after being closed down by Habsburg Holy Roman Emperor and King of Bohemia Joseph II (1780–90) in 1784 (it re-opened as a church in 1935).

As for the name Kampa, used officially from 1770 onwards (it was originally called simply *ostrov*, or island), several explanations exist. The word might be derived from the Latin *campus*, meaning a flat field, or else possibly from the name of Tychon Gangsel of Camp, who made his fortune growing tulips and built a house on the island in the 17th century. Additionally, the Italian word *campo* means 'island garden' and Kampa certainly has a long history of gardens, providing peace and inspiration for writers, poets and artists. Potters first came here in 1599

The Grand Prior Mill (Velkopřevorský mlýn) on Kampa Island

when plague broke out in the castle district of Hradčany and the name of the charming square, Hrnčířský plácek, means 'Potters' Place'.

Other places of interest nearby: 1, 2, 4, 6, 7, 8

4. The John Lennon Wall

Prague 1 (Malá Strana), the John Lennon Wall on Velkopřevorské náměstí
Metro A to Malostranská; Tram 12, 20 from náměstí Kinských, 22, 23 from Národní třída

In front of the Main Station (Hlavní nádraží) on Wilsonova is a park containing a statue called *The Brotherhood*. It was erected shortly after the Red Army's liberation of Prague from German troops on May 9th 1945 and depicts a tall Russian soldier embracing a tellingly smaller Czech soldier. It remains one of the few Communist-era statues still standing in the city today.

With the close of the Second World War, Czechoslovakian President Edvard Beneš (1884–1948) returned from self-imposed exile and on April 3rd 1945 reestablished a government on his native soil; he entered Prague on May 16th to an enthusiastic welcome. Beneš's pre-war fears over the union of Austria and Germany, which he had deemed a threat to Czechoslovakia's continued existence, had been more than justified (see no. 69).

Although the government of Beneš was the only eastern European government in exile to be allowed to return to power after the war, Beneš still had every reason to feel abandoned by his allies. With his faith in liberalism severely knocked he now saw Czechoslovakia's future as a bridge between democratic capitalism and Stalinist Communism. The Soviets and Czech Communists were widely seen as war heroes and in the 1946 elections they won the largest share of the votes. Realising that Czechoslovakia now had to cooperate closely with the power that had officially liberated it, President Beneš appointed the Communist Klement Gottwald as prime minister of a coalition government. The Communists quickly established workers' militias in factories, placed Communist loyalists in the police force, and infiltrated the army. By 1947, with the approval of the allies, the Government had expelled 2.5 million Germans from Czechoslovakia; in the same year Stalin turned down the American brokered Marshall Plan. With elections looming, Gottwald ordered the militias onto the street and on February 28th 1948 forced Beneš to consent to an all-Communist government. Shortly after, from a balcony of the Golz-Kinský Palace (palác Golz-Kinských) in Old Town Square (Staroměstské náměstí), Gottwald announced the glorious Communist victory. Feeling unable to sign the new constitution Beneš resigned, making way for Gottwald as Czechoslovakia's

Graffiti covers the John Lennon Wall on Velkopřevorské náměstí

first Communist president and heralding the dawn of the single-party state. Purges and deportations of resistance fighters, Jews and any party members under suspicion followed, resulting in several show trials and a deep sense of paranoia (a group of statues by Olbram Zoubek unveiled in 2002 near the lower station of the Petřín Funicular Railway (lanová dráha na Petřín) commemorates these victims).

Despite the death of both Stalin and Gottwald in 1953, the latter embalmed in a mausoleum on Vítkov Hill in Žižkov, the Communist Party kept a firm hold on the reins of power (see no. 56). Whilst the Politburo met to discuss their five-year plans behind a reinforced steel door in the glittering Spanish Hall (Španělský sál) of Prague Castle (Pražský hrad), the lifestyle of the average Praguer was lacklustre (see no. 45). The utopian dreams and grim realities of the period are well illustrated in Prague's unusual Museum of Communism (Muzeum komunismu), located somewhat ironically between McDonald's and a casino at Na příkopě 10 in New Town (Nové Město). By the early 1960s, against the backdrop of a downward-spiralling economy and the continued use of fear to suppress protest, voices on the fringes of the Czech Communist Party began suggesting that traditional Stalinism may have had its day. Things came to a head on January 5th 1968 when party reformists replaced the incumbent president, Antonín Novotný, with a Slovak reformist Communist called Alexander Dubček. "Socialism with a human face" was the stated aim of the so-called Prague Spring and for the next eight months the world watched as Dubček abandoned press censorship, rehabilitated political prisoners and attempted to democratise the country. It was a shortlived experiment and on August 21st half a million Warsaw Pact troops entered Czechoslovakia and occupied Prague Castle. The National Museum (Národní muzeum) at the top of Wenceslas Square (Václavské náměstí) still bears the scars of shelling when tank crews mistook the grand building for the Parliament! Despite considerable resistance on the streets of Prague during which 90 protesters were killed, and the self-immolation on January 16th 1969 of the young philosophy student Jan Palach (1948–69), Communist orthodoxy was gradually reimposed under new hardline president Gustáv Husák.

For the next twenty years, until the Velvet Revolution in 1989 and the collapse of Czech Communism, tortures, arrests and show trials were replaced by apathy, demoralisation and totalitarian consumerism (see no. 64). Protests against the regime now tended to be intellectual ones, centred on groups such as Václav Havel's dissident Charter 77 and its defence of civil liberties. However, the man in the street could still have his say, albeit at the risk of being arrested, at the so-called John Lennon Wall, tucked away opposite the Buquoy Palace (Buquoyský palác), now the French Embassy, on Velkopřevorské náměstí. After the peace-loving Beatle's death in 1980, a fan painted the musician's face here encouraging dissidents to embellish it with anti-government slogans. Despite the secret police repeatedly whitewashing the wall the face was always repainted. After the Velvet Revolution the wall was handed back to the Knights of Malta, of whose nearby Grand Prior Palace (Velkopřevorský palác) it is a part. At the instigation of the French Ambassador, the wall was renovated and the face reworked by the artist František Flasar; graffiti here is today officially sanctioned and even Yoko Ono added her name during a visit in 2003.

Jan Palach Day on January 19th – the day the student succumbed to his burns – is a public holiday in the Czech Republic, marked by the laying of tributes at his grave in the Olšany Cemetery (Olšanské hřbitovy) in Žižkov (Prague 3), as well as the Victims of Communism Memorial (Obětem komunismu) at the top of Wenceslas Square, where he set himself alight (see no. 57). Another holiday is Labour Day on May 1st, which coincides with the much older *Majales*, a spring festival dating back at least two centuries. Until the Second World War, students celebrated *Majales* regularly but the Nazis suppressed it; it was revived in the 1960s only to be suppressed by the Communists after 1968, and then revived once again in 1997. Today, it is marked with a parade from Jan Palach Square (Náměstí Jana Palacha) in front of the Rudolphinum via Kaprova to Old Town Square (Staroměstské náměstí) and on to the Carolinum.

Other places of interest nearby: 1, 2, 3, 5, 6, 7

5. At the Inn of the Maltese Knights

Prague 1 (Malá Strana), the Knights of Malta Restaurant (U Maltézských rytířů) at Prokopská 10
Metro A to Malostranská; Tram 12, 20 from náměstí Kinských, 22, 23 from Národní třída

Prague offers visitors and locals alike a surprising array of different food, from hearty traditional platters of roast pork with sliced bread dumplings and sauerkraut (Vepřo, knedlo, zelo) to exciting menus featuring world cuisine. Equally surprising is the array of unusual venues in which such culinary delights can be experienced, from ancient vaulted cellars to a pair of converted trams in the centre of Wenceslas Square (Václavské náměstí)!

A fine example is the Knights of Malta Restaurant (U Maltézských rytířů), situated in an atmospheric candlelit cellar in Lesser Quarter (Malá Strana). Dating back to the 12th century the building was once a part of a brewery malt house belonging to the Knights of St. John of Jerusalem (later called the Maltese Knights) and was used by them as a tavern and hospice. Their monastery, rebuilt in the Baroque period and known today as the Grand Prior Palace (Velkopřevorský palác), can be found in nearby Grand Prior Square (Velkopřevorské náměstí). Rising above the square are the twin towers of the unfinished Church of the Virgin Mary Beneath the Chain (kostel Panny Marie pod řetězem), built in the late 12th century but only partially Gothicised due to the outbreak of the Hussite Wars (1420–36).

During the late 13th century the Vltava flooded many times and the low-lying streets of Lesser Quarter, as well as Old Town, were repeatedly submerged. The level of the streets was thus deliberately raised by one storey and many vaulted medieval chambers, including the knights' tavern, became cellars in the process (see no. 51). The Knights of Malta Restaurant is also noteworthy for its unique double figurative house sign featuring a Maltese Madonna and a later Baroque black horse.

Farther uphill, in Hradčany, is the Peklo Restaurant at Strahovské nádvoří 1, occupying the former wine cellars of the Strahov Monastery (Strahovský klášter) (see no. 11). In the 14th century Holy Roman Emperor Charles IV of Luxembourg (King Charles I of Bohemia) (1346–78) introduced French vines to Prague and the Premonstratensians of Strahov were quick to produce fine wines from their fruits, so much so that the king granted them a crest that can be seen hanging over

The subterranean Knights of Malta Restaurant (U Maltézských rytířů) on Prokopská

the bar. The name Peklo means 'hell', in deference to the Paradise Gardens that lie above (for other subterranean restaurants, see no. 51).

Also in Hradčany is the U Ševce Matouše ('At the Shoemaker Matthew') Restaurant at Loretánské náměstí 4, serving steak and Czech *Pilsner* beer at rustic tables in what was once a shoemaker's workshop. Utilitarian in origin too is the U Tří housliček (At the Three Fiddles) Restaurant at Nerudova 12, back down in Lesser Quarter, dating from the time of Habsburg Holy Roman Emperor and King of Bohemia Rudolph II (1576–1611); from 1667 it belonged to the widow of a lute-maker in whose courtyard was once the workshop of three successive families of violin makers.

Down on the riverbank near Kampa Island is the fashionable Hergetova cihelna Restaurant at Cihelná 2b, in what was once the Herget family's brick factory built in 1830. The restaurant's opening was delayed when it was flooded during the Vltava's one-in-a-thousand year flood in 2002 (see the high water mark inside the entrance). For understated grandeur visit the Pálffy palác Restaurant at nearby Valdštejnská 14, hidden away in a first floor room of the former late Baroque Palffy Palace, which served latterly as the dining room for the music conservatory that still owns the building.

Across the river on Jindřišská in New Town (Nové Město) is the Zvonice, the only restaurant in Europe that occupies a Gothic belfry (see no. 2). Finally, by way of a complete contrast to the above, try one of the city's few remaining pre-revolutionary workers' canteens in which communal seating, cheap soup and sliced bread dumplings evoke a more recent age (see no. 45).

Other places of interest nearby: 1, 2, 3, 4, 6, 7

6.　A Concealed Baroque Garden

Prague 1 (Malá Strana), the Vrtba Gardens (Vrtbovská zahrada) at Karmelitská 25
Tram 12, 20 from náměstí Kinských, 22, 23 from Národní třída

Prague's Lesser Quarter (Malá Strana) is today a fascinating tangle of alleyways filling the space between the Vltava River and Prague Castle (Pražský hrad). The area was founded as a market settlement during the 9th century and chartered in 1257 by the Přemyslid King Otakar II (1253–78), when German merchants were invited to conduct business in the lee of the castle walls. During the second half of the 17th century the Catholic aristocracy transformed this medieval settlement into a glittering Baroque district, having been given large tracts of land during property redistribution following the Thirty Years War (1618–48) (see no. 23). Although the Habsburg court and its nobles in time relocated to Vienna, the ornate Baroque churches and palaces remain. The palace gardens remain too, hidden from view behind high walls and sturdy wooden doors.

One of the most beautiful is undoubtedly the Vrtba Gardens, entered through an inconspicuous gateway at Karmelitská 25, via a dark and narrow courtyard flanked by Renaissance buildings, the one on the left built in 1575 and the one on the right in 1591. Between 1619 and 1620 the latter was home to Kryštof Harant of Polžice and Bezdružice, a gentleman and diplomat, who led the artillery during the rebellion of the Czech Estates against the Habsburgs. In 1621, a year after the Battle of White Mountain (Bílá hora) at which the Habsburg army crushed the insurgency, Harant became one of the 27 Protestant rebels beheaded in front of the Old Town Hall (Staroměstská radnice) by order of Habsburg Holy Roman Emperor and King of Bohemia Ferdinand II (1619–37) (see no. 26). In 1631 Sezima of Vrtba, a supporter of the Emperor acquired both properties and created the palace seen today (Vrtbovský palác).

In 1715–20 the Prague-born Baroque architect František Maximilian Kaňka created the palace garden for Count Jan Josef of Vrtba. It is a wonderful example of Italianate aristocratic gardening, a form that reached its apogee in the Baroque period, having been born during the preceding Renaissance. Such gardens are typically laid out across sloping terrain, in this case the eastern flank of Petřín Hill, along a strict axial system necessitating the use of terraces and steps. The Vrtba Garden is especially unusual in that the architect managed so ingeniously to

The hidden Vrtba Gardens (Vrtbovská zahrada) on Karmelitská

include all the required structural and decorative elements within a steep and restricted space of just 0.31 hectares (3100 square metres).

At the foot of the garden, beyond a gateway topped by a statue of Atlas carved by Matyáš Bernard Braun, there is a pond with a *putto*-adorned fountain and a ground floor room *(Sala Terrena)* decorated with a fresco of Venus and Adonis by Václav Vavřinec Reiner. Double staircases then rise to the first and second terraces, supported by typically Baroque curved retaining walls, crowned by a *gloriette* pavilion decorated with mermaids and seashells. Unfortunately, Reiner's fresco on the front of the pavilion has been lost to the elements. Finally, a staircase within the pavilion rises up to a viewing platform marking the highest and narrowest point of the garden, from where there is not only an overview of the garden's layout, punctuated by further examples of Braun's Baroque statuary, but also a stunning view of neighbouring palaces and churches, notably the dome and tower of the Cathedral of St. Nicholas (chrám sv. Mikuláše) in Malostranské náměstí.

Standing here today it is hard to imagine that the Vrtba Palace had become a semi-derelict tenement by the early 19th century and eventually a children's playground; equally, it is easy to understand why the painstaking restoration of the garden during the 1990s took five years to complete.

Other places of interest nearby: 2, 3, 4, 5, 7, 8

7. The Prague *Bambino*

Prague 1 (Malá Strana), the Church of the Virgin Mary Victorious (kostel Panny Marie Vítězné) at Karmelitská 9
Tram 12, 20 from náměstí Kinských, 22, 23 from Národní třída

Prague's very first church to be constructed in the Baroque style was the Church of St. Trinity (now the Church of the Virgin Mary Victorious) on Karmelitská at the foot of Petřín Hill (see no. 50). However, this fact has today been all but overshadowed by an unusual object contained inside the church, known as *Il Bambino di Praga* (Pražské Jezulátko). This 400-year-old wax effigy of the Infant Jesus draws pilgrims from around the world looking for cures and Divine intervention. The hundred or so stone votive plaques hanging on the walls are proof of the effigy's healing powers, so much so that it has been granted official miracle-working status by the Catholic Church.

In the 14th century similar effigies were made of wood but by the Baroque period it was more usual to model them from wax, ivory or bronze and to dress them. The right hand is usually raised in the act of blessing whilst the left carries a bird, an apple, a book, a cross, a bunch of grapes – or in the present case a golden orb, signifying the worldwide kingship of Christ.

The 47 centimetres high Prague effigy was made in Spain in the late 16th century, where the tradition of venerating the Infant Jesus was especially strong. The artist is unknown although tradition insists that he was a blind monk working in a convent between Cordoba and Seville and that the statue was a copy of a much-venerated wooden one. It was acquired by Doña Isabela Manrique de Lara a Mendoza and then brought to Bohemia as a wedding gift by her daughter Maria Maximiliana Manrique de Lara, who had married the prominent Czech nobleman Vratislav of Pernštejn. She then gave it as a wedding gift to her daughter Polyxena who, after the death of her second husband, donated it to an order of White Friars (a Mendicant Carmelite Order) based near the Church of the Virgin Mary Victorious in Lesser Quarter (Malá Strana). German Protestant Lutherans had built the church in 1611–13, dedicating it to St. Trinity, but Habsburg Holy Roman Emperor and King of Bohemia Ferdinand II (1619–37) donated it to the White Friars after the defeat of the Protestants at the Battle of White Mountain (Bílá hora) in 1620 (see no. 26). They rebuilt it with a tower and re-dedicated it to the Victorious Virgin in memory of the Catholic military triumph

Reproductions of the Prague Bambino for sale on Karmelitská

(above the High Altar hangs a copy of a miraculous painting of the Virgin Mary carried by the Carmelite commander of the Catholic forces during the battle).

When King Gustavus Adolpus of Sweden invaded Prague in 1631 during the Thirty Years War (1618–48) the monastery was ransacked and the effigy was lost for several years. With peace restored in 1635 the monks returned and re-discovered the effigy in debris dumped behind the High Altar. Once again it became the object of worship and several miracles are recorded from this time, including the successful protection of the city from the Swedes. In 1655 the bishop of Prague gave the effigy its golden crown, a coronation still celebrated by a special mass on the feast of the Ascension. In 1784 Habsburg Holy Roman Emperor and King of Bohemia Joseph II (1780–90) abolished the monastery and the church became a parish administered by the Maltese Knights.

By the 19th century the fame of the little miracle-working figure had spread far and wide, especially in traditionally Catholic regions such as Italy, South America and even Asia, giving rise to the name *Il Bambino di Praga*. Eventually, in 1993 the Discalced (Barefoot) Carmelite Friars returned from Italy once more to the Church of the Virgin Mary Victorious, where they remain to this day giving pastoral care to anyone who needs it.

The ritual of dressing miraculous statues is a Baroque custom, the dressing of the Prague effigy having been undertaken for the past two centuries by the Order of English Virgins. The effigy's wardrobe contains seventy or so magnificent, richly embroidered capes, many of which have been donated from as far away as the Philippines and Vietnam. The first to be donated came from the Habsburg Empress and Queen of Bohemia Maria Theresa (1740–80) and the oldest dates back to 1700; several examples are on permanent display in the Museum of the Infant Jesus. The capes are changed for different liturgical events, being placed over a series of undergarments whilst the effigy is held carefully by means of a protective silver canister that reaches up to its waist.

Other places of interest nearby: 3, 4, 5, 6, 8

8.   A Great Photographer's Little-Known Studio

Prague 1 (Malá Strana), the Josef Sudek Atelier at Újezd 30
Tram 12, 20 from náměstí Kinských, 22, 23 from Národní třída

Tucked well away in the courtyard of an apartment building at Újezd 30 in Lesser Quarter (Malá Strana) can be found a simple wooden bungalow with an unusually large window. Now a small museum and gallery, this modest building was from 1927 until 1958 the main studio of Josef Sudek (1896–1976), the father of Czech photography.

Sudek was born in 1896 in Kolín on the River Labe (Elbe) and as a boy learned the art of bookbinding. He was drafted into the Austro-Hungarian Army in 1915 and was wounded in his right arm whilst serving on the Italian front. Surgeons were forced to remove the arm at the shoulder when gangrene set in. It was during his convalescence that Sudek first showed a serious interest in photography by taking portraits of his fellow patients, ghostly souls in soft focus surrounded by haloes of light. The figures appear closed off and distant and perhaps represent how Sudek himself felt at the time.

Following his discharge, and seemingly unperturbed by his physical limitations, Sudek pursued a two-year photography course in Prague, scraping a living from his disability allowance and occasional work as a commercial photographer. In 1926 he returned to Italy, this time in the company of the Czech Philharmonic Orchestra (Sudek was a great

The Josef Sudek Atelier is well concealed on Újezd

aficionado of classical music). The trip was to prove something of a watershed in that the sudden urge to 'find' his missing arm, and the final acceptance that it was indeed gone forever, produced a dramatic change in Sudek's photographic style. Sudek now turned his artistic attention away from people towards the inanimate fabric of Prague itself in what would become one of the most important photographic records of a city. Working from his Lesser Quarter studio the figure of the one-armed Sudek carrying his camera around the city soon became a common sight. Between 1924 and 1928 he undertook an extended study of the reconstruction of the Cathedral of St. Vitus (chrám sv.

A bust of the photographer Josef Sudek at Újezd 30

Víta) that formed the basis of his first book. Many commentators have claimed that the work was a metaphor for the rebuilding of Sudek's own life.

An increasingly important part of Sudek's style from the late 1920s onwards is his distinctive personification of the inanimate, perhaps as an alternative to real intimacy with other people. This is best represented by his thought-provoking series of photographs of specific objects undertaken in and around his studio (e.g. *The Window of my Studio* (1940–54) and *A Walk in my Garden* (1944–53)). However, both his urban landscapes and his still life work share the same melancholic romanticism; perhaps Sudek's way of reaching out to humanity.

In 1940 he came across a 30 × 40 cm photograph of a statue at Chartres that was not an enlargement but rather one lifted directly from a large plate negative by the so-called contact process. The rich diversity of tonal variation offered by such large format negatives made a deep impression on Sudek and from then on he carried with him only the bulky cameras that were capable of producing such negatives. It has been said that Sudek became such a technician that he came closer than any other photographer to portraying light as substance. It is also worth noting that his use of silver halide papers when printing photographs enhanced the distinctive subtle grey palette he so favoured. Using an 1894 Kodak Panorama camera with a sweeping lens capable of producing 10 × 30 cm negatives Sudek produced a wonderful series of Prague panoramas that provided the material for his 1959 book *Praha panoramatická* (*Prague Cityscapes*). In the same year he moved his studio to a house at Úvoz 24 in Hradčany, now the Josef Sudek Gallery, but he continued to use his old studio in Lesser Quarter as a dark room until his death in 1976.

A third venue in Prague that now bears the Sudek name is the Josef Sudek House of Photography at Maiselova 2 in Josefov, a gallery focussing on the work of young documentary photographers. However, to get a true impression of Sudek the man and Sudek the photographer it is his Lesser Quarter studio that should be visited. Lovingly restored in 2000 after a fire, it comprises just four rooms, namely an entrance hall, library, dark room and studio, the latter with its large window overlooking a tiny fenced garden. It is not too difficult to imagine the one-armed photographer returning here after a day's work on the streets of Prague, perhaps preparing to welcome a few friends to one of his famous musical soirées featuring excerpts from his large record collection.

Other places of interest nearby: 3, 4, 5, 6, 7

9. The Hunger Wall and Other Fortifications

Prague 1 (Malá Stravna), the Hunger Wall (Hladová zed') on Petřín Hill
Tram 12, 20 from náměstí Kinských, 22, 23 from Národní třída then by
funicular from Újezd

By the end of the reign of Holy Roman Emperor Charles IV of Luxembourg (King Charles I of Bohemia) (1346–78), much of what is now considered central Prague had been fortified. Walls encompassed Lesser Quarter (Malá Strana) and the castle district (Hradčany) on the west bank of the Vltava, and Old Town (Staré Město), New Town (Nové Město) and Vyšehrad on the east, the whole forming an area somewhat similar in outline to the continent of Africa. It is perhaps not surprising that the border of today's Prague Conservation Area (Pražská památková rezervace) follows approximately the line of these medieval defensive walls. However, as is the case with Vienna and Budapest, only fragmentary evidence now remains of these ancient walls and it makes for an unusual expedition to trace where they once stood.

First to be fortified was Prague Castle (Pražský hrad) itself, constructed in c.870AD by the founder of the Přemyslid dynasty Bořivoj I (c. 870–888/9), first Duke of Bohemia. The location chosen was perfect, being a steep-sided, easily defended, rocky bluff overlooking the river, around which timber bulwarks were raised. Immediately to the south lay a natural basin crossed by communication routes where a trading settlement, the Lesser Quarter, would be built. During the 10th century a stone wall was built around the Castle pierced by three gates, and a Royal Palace (Starý královský palác) was erected on the southern side. Although the Přemyslids de-camped briefly to Vyšehrad during the reign of Vratislav II (1061–92), Prague Castle soon regained its pre-eminence under Soběslav I (1125–40), who added a series of Romanesque ramparts along the northern and southern flanks, as well as the so-called Black Tower (Černá věž) to the east. Additional fortifications were added to the castle later on, notably the trio of Late Gothic cannon towers along the northern wall, on the edge of the natural ravine called the Stag Moat (Jelení příkop) (see nos. 19 & 20). They were built around 1484, when the Polish Jagiellon King Ladislaus II (1471–1516) settled at the Castle.

In contrast, Prague's Old Town was laid out as a commercial centre on flat terrain during the 12th and early 13th century, after Holy Roman Emperor Frederick II (1194–1250) had made the Přemyslid Duke Otakar I (1197–1230) hereditary King of Bohemia. The east-west axis of Old Town was and still is Karlova and Celetná, the latter named after the plaited rolls *(celty)* produced in bakeries that once lined the street. From the time of the Přemyslids the two streets comprised the so-called Royal Route (Královská cesta), a ceremonial approach to the castle taken by Bohemian rulers during their coronations. The route crossed the river by means of the fortified Romanesque Judith Bridge (Juditin most), Prague's first river crossing erected in 1160–72 and replaced in 1373 by the Charles Bridge (Karlův most) (see no. 2).

The Royal Route commenced at Mountain Gate (Horská brána), an entrance through the Old Town walls in Republic Square (Náměstí republiky), so-called because the road led out to the silver mining town of Kutná Hora. In the 1230s early Gothic walls were built northwards from here as far as the Vltava, along what is now Revoluční; southwards they ran along Na Příkopě, meaning 'on the moat', to the Havel Gate (at the southern end of Na Můstku), so-named because it led into a contemporary German settlement called Gallus Town (Havelské město). From this point the walls continued westwards along Národní třída, ending again at the riverbank. Although nothing remains above ground of these walls, the contemporaneous Church of St. Martin in the Wall (kostel sv. Martina ve zdi) on Martinská, which once backed onto them, is still standing. It was here in 1414 that 'Communion in both kinds' was first celebrated, that is the taking of bread and wine by the entire congregation, one of the central tenets of the Hussite faith. In the cellars of the Platýz building next door some fragments of the old walls were discovered during recent renovation work.

In 1348 Holy Roman Emperor Charles IV of Luxembourg (King Charles I of Bohemia) (1346–78) established New Town *beyond* the Old Town walls, and built a new wall around it. He also laid out what is today Wenceslas Square (Václavské náměstí) – then called Horse Market (Koňský trh) – which connected the Old Town Havel Gate with the new Horse Gate, where the National Museum now stands. The walls of Old Town had now been robbed of their original defensive function and Mountain Gate was left marooned. Alongside it was built the palace of King Wenceslaus (Václav) IV (1378–1419) of the Luxembourg dynasty, called Royal Court (Králův dvůr), where the Municipal House (Obecní dům) stands today. To complement it, Mountain Gate was rebuilt in 1475 as a ceremonial entranceway, inspired by the Old Town Bridge Tower (Staroměstská mostecká věž) on Charles Bridge. The work was never completed because the palace was abandoned during the reign of the Polish Jagiellon King Ladislaus II (1471–1516), when he moved back up to Prague Castle around 1484. During the 18th century the re-built Mountain Gate served as a gunpowder store, giving rise to its present name of Powder Gate (Prašná brána), although its appearance dates from Joseph Mocker's neo-Gothic makeover in the 1870s. Also now marooned were several early Gothic tower houses that once had a defensive function but which were later concealed behind Baroque façades and turned over to domestic accommodation (the last extant example is at Rytířská 16).

Of the New Town walls themselves, running approximately north-south down Wilsonova and Sokolská, little remains although there is a good stretch running from Karlov Church (Na Karlově) on Ke Karlovu, southwards across the valley of the River Botič in Folimanka Park, towards Vyšehrad (see no. 74). Here the walls reach their southern extremity and take in the rocky outcrop of Vyšehrad. However, only the ruinous medieval Špička Gate and the guardhouse on the cliff edge date from this period (see no. 75).

The third great phase of Prague fortifications occurred in the 1360s, again during the reign of Charles IV, when walls were thrown up around Lesser Quarter (Malá Strana). The most significant survival from this era is the so-called Hunger Wall (Hladová zed'), running up Petřín Hill westwards from Újezd. It was built in 1360–62 and so-named because it is said the Emperor ordered its construction during a bad harvest to provide employment for the poor and save them from starvation. According to the 12th century Czech chronicler Kosmas, the word Petřín comes from the Latin *petra*, meaning a rock, boulder or shaped building stone; the name is a reminder that Petřín Hill was once quarried for much of the city's Gothic and later architecture. The crenellated wall is 8 metres high and 2 metres wide, with towers each set a crossbow shot apart. Despite falling into disrepair during the 19th century, the Hunger Wall has been thoroughly restored and with a length of 1179 metres it is the longest remaining stretch of Prague's medieval fortifications.

Finally, during the Habsburg era between 1653 and 1727, Prague's walls were modified by the addition of massive, brick-built prismatic bastions, pierced by monumental stone gateways. Imposing remains of these walls can be found at Vyšehrad, as well as around the north-eastern corner of Hradčany, where modern street names containing the words 'Na Baště', signifying the former site of bastions, flank the Písecká brána gate. Most fascinating of all are the imposing bastions hidden away in an unnamed park off Hládkov, west of Keplerova, their brickwork pockmarked with the gravestones of Habsburg military per-

Part of the curiously-named Hunger Wall (Hladová zeď) on Petřín Hill

sonnel. Several fascinating old engravings of the bastions as they once appeared can be found in the Museum of the City of Prague (Muzeum hlavního města Prahy) at Na Poříčí 52 in New Town (Nové Město).

Other places of interest nearby: 6, 7, 8, 10

10. Up Petřín Hill by Funicular

Prague 1 (Malá Strana), the Petřín Funicular Railway (lanová dráha na
Petřín) up Petřín Hill
Tram 12, 20 from náměstí Kinských, 22, 23 from Národní třída to the
lower funicular station on U Lanové dráhy off Újezd

More than fifty cities around the world claim to be founded on seven
hills, including Amman, Athens, Bergen, Brisbane, Brussels, Cam-
bridge, Istanbul, Jerusalem, Kampala, Moscow, Rio de Janeiro and San
Francisco. Prague is also a seven-hill city, and Petřín Hill above Lesser
Quarter (Malá Strana) is its highest (318 metres). With its gardens,
parks and stunning views over Prague it is little wonder that at the end
of the 19th century the Czech Hikers' Club earmarked Prague's largest
green space as the ideal location for an observation tower. Club members had been very impressed by the Eiffel Tower during a visit to Paris
in 1889 and envisaged a similar structure on Petřín, as an eyecatcher for
the Centennial Bohemian Exhibition planned for 1891 (see no. 35).

Consequently, the Petřín
Observation Tower Asso-
ciation was established and
František Prášil and Julius
Souček, from the Bohemi-
an-Moravian Engineering
Company (Českomoravské
strojírny), were employed as
engineers. In just five months
and six days the 60 metre-high
Petřín Observation Tower
(Petřínská rozhledna), exactly
five times smaller than the
Eiffel Tower, was erected using 175 tonnes of iron girders.
Its observation balcony was
made accessible by a flight of
299 steps and a gas-powered
lift.

In order to reach the tower itself another engineering
feat was conjured up to im-

*The Petřín Funicular Railway (lanová dráha na Petřín)
making its 3-minute descent*

press exhibition visitors, namely the Petřín Funicular Railway (lanová dráha na Petřín). It was opened on 25th July 1891, just three days before the unofficial opening of the tower, whose grand unveiling occurred on August 20th.

Invented in the 15th century a funicular railway (from the Latin word *funiculus* meaning 'thin rope' or 'cord') is an ingenious combination of hoist and inclined railway track used in especially steep locations where traditional railways, relying solely on the friction between wheels and track, would not be effective. The Petřín Funicular Railway worked by means of a so-called 'water overbalance system'. The two cars, positioned at either end of the line, were equipped with water tanks that were emptied at the bottom and filled at the top: as the heavier car descended so the lighter car was pulled upwards. A sixteen strand steel wire was used to haul the cars on their six-minute journey, wound around a 2.8 metre-diameter pulley wheel at the top. Halfway along the 396.5 metre-long single line railway – which covered a vertical height of 102.2 metres – the track had a short double section to allow the cars to pass each other. The Ringhoffer Company in nearby Smíchov manufactured the cars themselves, which were 6 metres long and 2 metres wide, each capable of holding fifty passengers.

As part of the same exhibition, another water-powered funicular was built in the Letná Gardens (Letenské sady) (Prague 7) at the top of which the city's first electric tramway, built by the renowned Czech electrical engineer František Křižík, ran to the Exhibition Grounds at Holešovice. Operation of both funiculars was eventually terminated in 1916 due to the First World War and only the Petřín Funicular Railway ran again, on 5th June 1932, by which time it had been taken over by the Electric Company of the Capital City of Prague and electrified.

The new line was extended both at the top, through a hole in the so-called Hunger Wall to a new engine hall near the observation tower (see no. 9), and at the bottom, to a new station inside a converted Baroque house. With an intermediary station at the snailshell-shaped Nebozízek Restaurant the track now reached just over half a kilometre in length giving a vertical rise of 130.45 metres. New Ringhoffer rolling stock consisted of carriages double the length of the old ones that were capable of carrying a hundred passengers each. The electric funicular ran successfully for the next three decades until a storm on 7th July 1965 swept away part of the track, the hill being riddled with old mine workings.

Almost exactly twenty years later the damaged section was repaired with a concrete bridge and on 15th June 1985 the funicular ran once again using two modified cars. Visitors taking the three minute funicular ride today will find several interesting places awaiting them at the summit, including the Štefánik Observatory (Štefánikova hvězdárna) (see no. 48), the Baroque pilgrimage Church of St. Lawrence (kostel sv. Vavřince) built in the 1770s surrounded by the Stations of the Cross, and the Mirror Maze (zrcadlové bludiště). The latter is made of cast-iron and is based on the Gothic Špička Gate of medieval Vyšehrad, its creators having been impressed by a similar pavilion at the Paris Exhibition in the form of the Bastille. Built as the Czech Hikers' Club pavilion for the 1891 Centennial Bohemian Exhibition it was brought to Petřín a year later (see no. 35). In 1893 a hall of mirrors was installed inside as well as a diorama entitled *The Battle between Praguers and Swedes on the Charles Bridge in 1648.*

A miniature, single-car funicular has recently been constructed to connect two hotels on Mozartova in Smíchov (Prague 5). Those who enjoy funicular railways might also like to travel on the Prague Zoo Chairlift (sedačková lanovka) opened in 1977 (see no. 37). Rising just over 50 metres and with an inclined length of 105.9 metres, the chairlift welcomed its three millionth passenger in July 1999.

Other places of interest nearby: 6, 7, 8, 9, 11

11. An Extraordinary Monastery

Prague 1 (Hradčany), the Strahov Monastery (Strahovský klášter)
at Strahovské nádvoří 1
Tram 22, 23 from Národní třída; Bus 143, 149, 217 from Vítězné
náměstí

Crowning the summit of Petřín Hill and surrounded by long-established orchards is the extraordinary twin-towered Strahov Monastery (Strahovský klášter). The Přemyslid Duke Vladislav II (1140–72) founded the monastery for the Premonstratensian Order in 1140, the Order itself having been established in 1120 near Laon in France by St. Norbert (the monastery church's painted ceiling depicts scenes from his life). The mortal remains of both ruler and saint can be found in the monastery to this day.

Much remains of the original monastery complex, ranged around a huge cloistered garden forty metres square, although its Romanesque walls are now concealed beneath layers of plaster added during the Baroque period. When first built it was considered one of the most sophisticated monasteries in Europe. The triple-naved church dedicated to the Assumption of the Virgin Mary (chrám Nanebevzetí Panny Marie) still retains its Romanesque basilica-style floor plan of 1182, although it now boasts a neo-Classical façade by Anselmo Lurago, son-in-law of the great Baroque architect Kilián Ignáz Dientzenhofer. The fashion for neo-Classical architecture was largely a political one, its relatively austere lines deemed more acceptable by Habsburg Emperor and King of Bohemia Joseph II (1780–90) during his campaign to close down religious institutions. Strahov Monastery claimed exemption from closure by virtue of being an educational institution, having amassed Bohemia's largest collection of books. The monastery library now holds 130 000 volumes, with a further 700 000 in storage, the oldest dating back to the 9th century and the smallest being a prayer book in seven languages that measures only six millimetres square! Those on display are contained within two extraordinary halls concealed behind a modest neo-Classical façade broken only by a series of shallow pilasters.

The first of the rooms, the Philosophical Hall (Filozofický sál), was created in 1782–84 to house an influx of books from a recently dissolved monastery in Moravia. The room glows with the patina of its huge Baroque bookcases, enhanced by the leather bindings of the books themselves. The barrel-vaulted ceiling carries a fresco by Viennese painter

Franz Anton Maulbertsch called *The Struggle of Mankind to Know Real Wisdom* (1794).

By contrast the second room, the Theological Hall (Teologický sál), is a more intimate space, decorated with a series of stucco-framed frescoes undertaken by one of the monks. Several fascinating 17th century globes imbue the room with a studious atmosphere. It is little wonder that the room was used as a backdrop for the meeting of the legendary African explorer Allan Quatermain (Sean Connery) and Jules Verne's Captain Nemo in the fantasy film, *The League of Extraordinary Gentlemen*, as well as for Anton Salieri as he plots the downfall of Mozart in Miloš

Strahov Monastery (Strahovský klášter) is surrounded by orchards

Forman's *Amadeus* (see no. 82). The real Mozart demonstrated his prodigious musical talents in the monastery by performing an impromptu version of what would become his *Organ Fantasy* during a visit in November 1787.

In 1950 the Communists nationalised the monastery, expelled the monks and reused the buildings as a Museum of National Literature (Památník národního písemnictví). The monks returned in 1990 although the museum still resides here, as do several more unusual collections. The antechamber to the libraries, for example, contains a series of 200-year-old curiosity cabinets bulging with sea creatures, ancient manuscripts and even a dried Dodo! Equally strange is the Miniatures Museum (Muzeum miniatur) in the monastery grounds in which tiny works of art, such as a portrait on a poppy seed, a prayer written on a human hair, and a camel train on a grain of millet, can be seen through microscopes. Nearby there is the Strahov Gallery (Strahovská obrazárna), containing the monks' collection of religious art.

Other places of interest nearby: 10, 12, 13

12. Beer at the Black Ox

Prague 1 (Hradčany), the At the Black Ox (U Černého vola) beer hall
at Loretánské náměstí 1
Tram 22, 23 from Národní třída; Bus 143, 149, 217 from Vítězné náměstí

The Czech Republic boasts a proud brewing heritage stretching back a thousand years to a time when its monasteries first experimented with locally grown hops to produce beer (*pivo*) for their own consumption. The earliest written record of brewing comes from Prague's Břevnov Monastery (Břevnovský klášter) and dates back to 993 AD (see no. 25). Another early brewery (*pivovar*), once part of a Gothic monastery of Augustinian friars, stands alongside the Church of St. Thomas (kostel sv. Tomáše) at Letenská 12 in Lesser Quarter (Malá Strana). Beer was brewed here from 1352 until 1951, when the Baroque building became a restaurant called U Svatého Tomáše (At the Holy Thomas). Throughout the Middle Ages beer drinking became very popular with commoners and royalty alike and streets such as Dlouhá, running north out of Old Town Square (Staroměstské náměstí), once contained as many as 13 breweries!

Despite the recent emergence of stylish bars and cafés, the traditional, smoky Bohemian beer hall (*pivnice*), with its benches, long tables and gruff waiters, is still popular. Longstanding favourite beers, still brewed traditionally using Czech barley and hops and served in foaming half-litres direct from the keg, include the five classic 12-degree brews: *Pilsner Urquell* (from Plzeň, hence its local name of *plzeňské*), *Budvar* (from České Budějovice), *Kozel, Radegast* and *Krušovice*; *Staropramen* and *Gambrinus* are also popular. It is commonly remarked that the Czech Republic has the highest *per capita* annual consumption of beer in the world (around 160 litres). Fortunately, some of this national beverage is consumed together with hearty Czech drinking food, such as pungent *pivní sýr* (beer cheese), smoked meat platters, and roast pork with sliced bread dumplings and sauerkraut (*vepřo, knedlo, zelo*).

Prague's most famous beer hall is U Fleků at Křemencova 11 in New Town (Nové Město), named after its owner Jakub Flekovský. A justifiably famous 13-degree smoked black beer has been brewed here since 1499 in what is Prague's smallest brewery, its former malt-house now a fascinating museum (Pivovarské muzeum). These well-advertised facts account for the vast numbers of tourists that flock here to imbibe in U Fleků's leafy courtyard and dark, vaulted alcoves.

It is better perhaps to head up to the castle district of Hradčany and the less well-known U Černého vola (At the Black Ox). Despite its relative youth – it was not opened until after the Second World War – the historic location gives it the feel of having always been here. Credit for this must go to the defiant staff and regulars, who have held out against the not inconsiderable powers that have commercialised so much of the surrounding area since 1989. They achieved this by founding in 1992 an association whose main premise has been to donate a share of the takings to a nearby music academy for the blind in return for the town council agreeing that the Black Ox is never privatised. Uniquely

Beyond this doorway is the Black Ox (U Černého vola) beer hall

for Prague, the Black Ox is thus a non-commercial, non-state operation, which not only guarantees an ongoing and affordable service to its regular artisan clientele but also provides a little-known national treasure in the process.

Other places of interest nearby: 11, 13, 14, 16

13. The Legend of Loreto

Prague 1 (Hradčany), the Loreto (Loreta) at Loretánské náměstí 7
Tram 22, 23 from Národní třída; Bus 143, 149, 217 from Vítězné náměstí

The 25th of March is an important date in the Christian calendar being the day when the Annunciation is celebrated, that is the announcement by the Archangel Gabriel to the Virgin Mary that she would conceive a child with the Holy Spirit that would be born the Son of God; the date is exactly nine months before the feast of the Nativity of Jesus, or Christmas. The little house in Nazareth in which the Annunciation had occurred, and where Mary lived until the death of Christ, was subsequently venerated and a church eventually built over it by the Crusaders. In 1263 the armies of the Sultan Baybars destroyed the church, although the house itself was miraculously preserved. However, following the departure of the Crusaders from Palestine, the safety of Mary's house could not be guaranteed and so pilgrims dismantled it in 1291. Under the patronage of the Greek Angeli family the stones were taken by ship to Tersatz in Dalmatia (modern Croatia), giving rise to the legend that angels had removed the building. In 1294 it was transferred to an Italian olive grove, the *'Lauretanum'*, later called Loreto, near Ancona on the Adriatic coast of Italy. As the Shrine of Loreto it soon became a major place of pilgrimage, as a result of which copies of the shrine (known as the *Santa Casa*) were erected all across Europe.

During the Counter Reformation, initiated by the Catholic Church to reconvert the masses in response to the rise of Protestantism during the Thirty Years War (1618–48), the Loreto legend was heavily promoted and in Bohemia and Moravia alone some fifty Loreto shrines were erected. The grandest of them all is the Loreto Chapel (*Loreta*) in Prague, which has been one of Bohemia's most important sites of pilgrimage since its construction on the site of a pagan cemetery in 1626–27.

The Prague Loreto was designed by the Italian architect Giovanni Battista Orsi of Como as a commission from the wealthy Lobkowicz family. In 1664 Italian craftsmen smothered it in stucco depictions of biblical scenes, including one on the eastern wall that depicts the angelic transfer of the *Casa*. Inside the chapel there are two wooden beams and a brick, said to be from the original building in Italy, as well as a crack in the wall made by a thunderbolt that struck down a disbeliever.

Today, the Loreto, surrounded by a cloister where pilgrims once sheltered, is reached through an ornate High Baroque façade added in

1721–23 by the famous father-and-son team of architects, Kryštof and Kilián Ignáz Dientzenhofer. Most prominent is the doorway carrying statues of St. Joseph and St. John the Baptist, above which rises a tower containing a 27 bell carillon; cast in Amsterdam in 1694 the bells chime hourly.

Prague's Loreto has been an important pilgrimage site for almost four centuries

The Dientzenhofers are also responsible for the Church of the Nativity (kostel narození Páně) built at the back of the cloister in 1734–35, using donations from wealthy female pilgrims. Flanking the altar are the robed skeletons of two female Spanish saints, Felicissimus and Marcia, with wax masks covering their skulls, as well as a sculpture of the martyr St. Agatha the Unfortunate, who offers up her severed breasts on a plate. Additionally, in the Chapel of Our Lady of Sorrows, in the righthand corner of the cloister there is a statue of the Spanish martyr St. Wilgefortis (known also as St. Starosta), the patron saint of unhappily married women. When faced with the prospect of marrying the pagan King of Sicily she sought help from God, who made her grow a beard overnight causing her suitor to flee; her father had her crucified as a result.

Other places of interest nearby: 12, 14, 16

14. A Charming New World

Prague 1 (Hradčany), the New World quarter around Nový Svět
Tram 22, 23 from Národní třída; Bus 143, 149, 217 from Vítězné náměstí

The district known as Hradčany, clustered around the west gate of Prague Castle (Pražský hrad), became a town in its own right in 1320 and about forty years later was incorporated into the town fortifications. Before being made a borough of Prague in 1598 the area suffered heavy damage, both during the Hussite Wars (1420–36) and in the great fire of 1541, when 197 buildings in Hradčany, Prague Castle and Lesser Quarter (Malá Strana) were destroyed. Despite these calamities the area was re-built, especially during the Catholic Counter Reformation building boom following the defeat of the Protestants at the Battle of White Mountain in 1620 (see no. 26). Consequently much of the area is filled with ornate palaces and religious buildings, such as the Schwarzenberg Palace (see no. 16) and the Loreto (see no. 13).

However, hidden away on sloping ground behind the Loreto, there remains a charming piece of old workaday Hradčany, a quiet quarter known as *Nový Svět*, or New World. It was built after the great fire for staff working in the nearby castle, their modest abodes now some of modern Prague's most sought after dwellings. Strolling around the area, especially in the evening when most tourists have departed, gives one the feeling that the modern world is far away and that each of the quaint buildings has a story to tell.

The area's main axis is a cobbled street called Nový Svět, once the main throroughfare of Hradčany and still lined with idiosyncratic buildings that were restored during the 18th and 19th centuries. The ensemble has been enlivened by the buildings being brightly painted in the manner of nearby Golden Lane – but without the throngs of tourists (see no. 19).

The first house encountered, at number 1, is called the Golden Griffin, where Tycho Brahe, court astronomer to Habsburg Holy Roman Emperor and King of Bohemia Rudolph II, lived intermittently during the last years of his life (1546–1601) (see no. 48). House number 3, the Golden Acorn, was once home to the Santini family, stonemasons who emigrated to Bohemia from Italy in the 17th century, Giovanni Santini becoming a renowned Czech Baroque architect. The oriel window at number 5, the Golden Grape, is one of several quirky architectural details the street has to offer. A left turn here leads onto Kapucínská that is dominated by the Domeček (Little House) at number 10, once home to the Communist Defence Ministry's counter-intelligence unit known as the Fifth Department. The street itself is named after the nearby Capuchin Monastery, a typically modest structure built in 1602 that has been the venue since 1765 for a unique recreation of the Nativity, us-

Unhurried Nový Svět (New World) has given its name to the surrounding peaceful area

ing forty-three life-sized figures made of wood and paper. The cannon-balls embedded in the monastery walls date from the siege in 1757 by Frederick of Prussia during the Seven Years War.

Meanwhile, farther along Nový Svět at number 25, the House of the Golden Plough is where violinist František Ondříček was born, respon-sible for premiering Dvořák's *Violin Concerto* in Vienna and London in 1883. Nový Svět reaches an abrupt finish in the lee of the Habsburgs' 17th century ramparts with one of Prague's smallest houses, at the junc-tion of Nový Svět with Černínská (see no. 9).

Our tour of the New World ends on Černínská, named after the nearby Baroque Černín Palace (Černínský palác) that now contains the Foreign Office. House number 5 is home to the eccentric Galerie Gam-bra, which specialises in Surrealist art, above which lives film animator Jan Švankmajer, a Prague-born poet, artist, sculptor and member of the Group of Czech and Slovak Surrealists.

Other places of interest nearby: 12, 13, 16

15. The House Signs of Nerudova

Prague 1 (Malá Strana), house signs along Nerudova
Metro A to Malostranská; Tram 22, 23 from Národní třída, 12, 20 from
náměstí Kinských

Prague's Royal Route (Královská cesta), the traditional coronation road used by Bohemian kings for centuries, makes its final approach towards Prague Castle (Pražský hrad) by means of a street called Nerudova (see no. 1). Needless to say, it is often choked with tourists making their ascent to the Castle. A quieter approach is either via the dappled shade of the Stag Moat (Jelení příkop), which runs along the north side of the Castle from a doorway in Na Opyši at the top of the Old Palace Steps (Staré zámecké schody), or else up from Karmelitská via Třziště, Břetislavova and Jánský vršek. However, something special that Nerudova *does* offer is a fascinating collection of one of Prague's most idiosyncratic architectural details, namely its old house signs.

Using figurative signs to identify individual buildings is a practice dating back to the mid-14th century, when literacy was not widespread. Created from carved stone, painted wood or wrought iron such signs depicted animals, fruits, guild emblems, heavenly bodies and religious symbols. The practice continued until 1770, when the Habsburg Empress and Queen of Bohemia Maria Theresa (1740–80) introduced a continuous house numbering system based on the Prague district land registry. These numbers ran well into the hundreds and can still be seen on red wall plaques today, the lowest numbers indicating the oldest buildings. In modern times the system was overhauled and sequences of numbers on blue plaques were allocated to individual streets. Fortunately, Praguers retained their old house signs with the result that today some buildings feature all three numbering systems on their façades (e.g. the Knights of Malta Restaurant (U Maltézských rytířů) at Prokopská 10 in Lesser Quarter (Malá Strana) (see no. 5)).

The Baroque houses of Nerudova rise step-like towards the Castle, each façade unique from the one before, and many still carry their colourful house signs and names. Number 4, for example, is the House at the Devil's, number 6 is the House at the Red Eagle, and number 12 is the House at the Three Fiddles (U Tří housliček), a restaurant that between 1667 and 1748 was home to three successive families of violinmakers (see no. 5). Thereafter is a series of buildings whose names include the word 'gold', probably reflecting the fact that the road was once home to several craftsmen and artists. Thus, number 16 is the House at the Golden Cup, number 27 is the Golden Key, and number 28 is the Golden Wheel (U Zlatého kola).

Continuing up Nerudova can be found the House at the Red Lion (U Červeného lva) at number 41, the Green Lobster at number 43, the Golden Star (U Zlaté hvězdy) at number 48, and the White Swan at number 49. Of special interest is the House at the Two Suns at number 47,

The sign of the House at the Three Fiddles (U Tří housliček) at Nerudova 12

for it was here that Czech Realism writer Jan Neruda (1834–91) lived as a boy and after whom the road was later named. Neruda's father had a grocer's shop on the ground floor, where the young Jan eavesdropped on conversations that would later be used in his popular *Povídky malostranské* (*Tales of the Lesser Quarter*). After his father's death he moved across the road to the House at the Three Black Eagles, working as a teacher and then a free-lance journalist before eventually relocating to Konviktská in Old Town (Staré Město). It is interesting to note that the Chilean writer Pablo Neruda (real name Neftalí Reyes Basoalto) took his pen name from the Czech author he so admired.

Other places of interest nearby: 16, 17, 18, 20

16. The Art of Wall Scratching

Prague 1 (Hradčany), the Schwarzenberg Palace (Schwarzenberský palác) on Hradčanské náměstí
Metro A to Malostranská; Tram 22, 23 from Národní třída, 12, 20 from náměstí Kinských

Sgraffito adorns the Schwarzenberg Palace (Schwarzenberský palác) on Hradčanské náměstí

Like most cities in the world, Prague has its fair share of modern graffiti, daubed on walls, vehicles and other public spaces. Usually consisting of political slogans, unofficial advertising, personal signatures, artistic motifs and obscene curses, graffiti has existed since the time of the ancient Greeks and Romans. The word *graffiti* is the plural of *graffito*, an Italian word most likely descended from *graffiato*, the past participle of *graffiare*, meaning 'to scratch, incise or etch lightly'. These words in turn were derived from the Greek γραφειν (graphein), meaning to write. The graffitists of the ancient world scratched their work onto walls in the same way that their modern counterparts use spray paint.

It was in Italy, during the Renaissance period of the 16th century, that wall scratching was elevated to a fine art, known by the term *sgraffito*, a now obsolete variant of *graffito* taken from the past participle of *sgraffire*, again meaning 'to scratch'. The word is used to describe a decorative process whereby parts of a wet surface layer, either wall plaster or ceramic clay, are scratched away in order to expose contrasting coloured layers beneath. In so doing, decorative surfaces can be created, from simple geometric motifs to large-scale figurative scenes. The direction and form of the scratching is often used to impart a three-dimensional effect to the flat surface thereby creating the illusion of solid forms.

When the Renaissance style arrived in Prague the *sgraffito* style came with it (see no. 21). It was used to decorate many of the city's buildings and, whereas other architectural styles subsequently came and went, *sgraffito* remained popular in Prague for several centuries. As a result, Prague now boasts a collection of *sgraffitoed* buildings unique for a city in Central Europe.

Pride of place usually goes to the Schwarzenberg Palace (Schwarzenberský palác) on Hradčanské náměstí, built between 1545 and 1563 outside the main gateway to Prague Castle (Pražský hrad). It is one of several Renaissance palaces erected by Catholic aristocrats as part of the reconstruction of the castle district of Hradčany after the great fire of 1541, and today contains the National Gallery of Prague's Baroque in Bohemia exhibition. The architect was the Italian Agostin Galli, nicknamed Augustin Vlach, the word 'Vlach' being Old Czech for an Italian. The palace is made all the more impressive by means of a *sgraffittoed* façade, taking the form of staggered rows of diagonally divided rectangles, each coloured so as to give the impression of monumental masonry. The resemblance of each rectangle to a sealed envelope has given rise to the term 'letter *sgraffito*', a further example of which is Hradčany Town Hall (Hradčanská radnice), where Hradčanské náměstí joins Loretánská; it is a building that survived the great fire of 1541 and was *sgraffitoed* in the late Renaissance (1604) (see no. 66). Completing this *sgraffitoed* ensemble is the Martinic Palace (Martinický palác) at Hradčanské náměstí 8, its early 17th century façade adorned with figurative *sgraffito* scenes depicting the Biblical story of Joseph and his escape from Potiphar's wife. One of the palace's owners was Jaroslav Bořita of Martinice, one of the two Catholic imperial governors 'defenestrated' from the palace windows by angry Protestants in 1618 (see no. 26).

Another Renaissance painting technique is *chiaroscuro*, from the Italian *chiaro* (meaning light) and *scuro* (meaning dark), whereby the two are contrasted to create the effect of modelling. A fine example can be found on the Granovský Palace in Týn courtyard off Malá Štupartská. Quiet unspoilt courtyards are a rarity in central Prague, although one exists at nearby Týnská 7, its cluttered antique shops and pretty balconies offering a welcome moment's respite from the area's busy streets; there is another between Michalská 16 and Melantrichova 15.

Other places of interest nearby: 15, 17, 18, 20

17. A Superlative Portal to the Past

Prague 1 (Hradčany), the Matthias Gate (Matyášova brána) between the First and Second Courtyards of Prague Castle (Pražský hrad)
Metro A to Malostranská; Tram 22, 23 from Národní třída, 12, 20 from náměstí Kinských

Occupying more than 18 acres, Prague Castle can lay claim to being the largest castle complex in the world. Its numerous architectural elements, ranged around four internal courtyards, include the towering Cathedral of St. Vitus, the Old Royal Palace (Starý královský palác), the Romanesque Basilica of St. George (bazilika sv. Jiří), and the tiny, former artillerymen's houses on Golden Lane (Zlatá ulička) (see nos. 1, 18, 19 & 39). The castle's size is certainly an advantage when it comes to absorbing the endless tour groups that visit during the hours of daylight. However, for those longing for a more intimate sense of personal discovery, the castle grounds should be visited after nightfall, long after the castle buildings themselves have closed and when the ghosts of Hradčany make themselves known.

Paradoxically, and somewhat typically for a Kafka-esque city like Prague, where nothing is quite as it seems, the portal to all this history rarely gets more than a passing glance from tourists as they pour headlong towards the Cathedral. This is a pity, because the so-called Matthias Gate (Matyášova brána), situated at the back of the First Courtyard, where the boisterous Changing of the Guard occurs since being instigated by Czech President Václav Havel, is Bohemia's oldest secular Baroque monument. Originally a freestanding arch when first erected in 1614, the gate with its Habsburg double-headed eagle is the work of the Italian artist Giovanni Maria Filippi. It is named after the Holy Roman Emperor and King of Bohemia Matthias (1611–19), who ordered its construction.

Emperor Matthias was the brother of melancholic and eccentric Emperor Rudolph II (1576–1611), who when he wasn't indulging alchemists or playing with his pet lion was a staunch supporter of the Catholic Counter Reformation. By contrast, the policies of Matthias were dominated by his chief advisor Melchior Khlesl, Bishop of Vienna, who dreamt of a compromise between Catholic and Protestant states within the empire in order to strengthen it. Even before his accession in 1611 Matthias had been making efforts to circumvent Rudolph's policies and in 1606 he had concluded the Peace of Vienna, which guaranteed religious freedom to the Protestants of Hungary; the latter had revolted when Rudolph attempted to impose Roman Catholicism on them. Rule over Hungary was ceded to Matthias in 1608, together with Austria and Moravia, to whom Matthias again granted religious concessions; Bohemia followed in 1611. However, the more intransigent Catholic Habsburgs, especially Matthias' brother Archduke Maximilian, who hoped to secure the succession for the inflexible Catholic Archduke Ferdinand, opposed his conciliatory policies. In 1618, with Bohemian Protestant unrest on the increase, angry Protestants 'defenestrated' two Catholic imperial governors from Prague Castle (see no. 26). It was the first violent

The historic Matthias Gate (Matyášova brána) leads into Prague Castle (Pražský hrad)

act of the Thirty Years War (1618–48) and the now ailing Matthias was succeeded as Emperor by Ferdinand II (1619–37).

Other places of interest nearby: 15, 16, 18, 20

18. Exploring the Basilica of Saint George

Prague 1 (Hradčany), the Basilica of St. George (bazilika sv. Jiří) on Jiřské
náměstí in Prague Castle (Pražský hrad)
Metro A to Malostranská; Tram 22, 23 from Národní třída, 12, 20 from
náměstí Kinských

For many visitors, a trip to Prague Castle (Pražský hrad) begins with
the midday Changing of the Guard in the First Courtyard, followed by a
visit to the Cathedral, and then onwards to visit the tiny houses of Gold-
en Lane at the far eastern end. Of the numerous buildings passed along
the way, one that is worth taking the time to explore is the Basilica of
St. George (bazilika sv. Jiří), facing the rear of the cathedral. Despite its
deceiving red-and-cream early Baroque façade, much of the building is
Romanesque and predates the cathedral itself. The building is one of
Prague's few examples of extant Romanesque architecture, most having
been concealed by the raising of ground levels in the late 13th century as
a precaution against flooding (see nos. 51 & 75).

The basilica was founded in 921 AD by the Přemyslid Duke Vratislav I (915–921) and remodelled fifty years later when a Benedictine convent was established next door. Both basilica and convent were rebuilt
in 1142 following a fire after which Italian masons added the pair of
distinctive square Romanesque towers to the rear of the building.

During the reign of Holy Roman Emperor Charles IV of Luxembourg (King Charles I of Bohemia) (1346–78) parts of the building were
modified and in the early 16th century a columned portal was added on
the south side, above which is a lively relief depicting St. George slay-
ing the dragon. Finally, in c. 1670 the pinnacled and pilastered Baroque
façade seen today was added.

In contrast to the ornate façade, the basilica's interior is starkly Romanesque. During an early 20th century restoration most of the Baroque
additions were peeled away, revealing chunky stone columns, round-
arched arcade windows, and fragments of 13th century wall paintings.
One Baroque feature that remains is the unusual curved staircase leading from the nave up to a semi-circular apse containing the High Altar.
In the crypt below can be seen a curious statue called *Brigida* depicting
a female corpse in an advanced state of decay; her visible innards alive
with snakes, frogs and lizards! Legend states that during the reign of
Holy Roman Emperor and King of Bohemia Rudolph II (1576–1611)
an Italian artist called Bernardo Spinetti killed his mistress, Brigida,

and threw her body into the Stag Moat (Jelení příkop) that runs along the north side of the Castle. When the decaying body was eventually discovered Spinetti was arrested and sentenced to death. He managed to stave off his execution temporarily by asking to carve an effigy of Brigida in the condition in which she had been found. Only then did he meet his Maker.

The colourful Baroque façade of the Basilica of St. George (bazilika sv. Jiří)

The Basilica also contains several Přemyslid-era tombs, notably the two-storied chapel and tomb of St. Ludmila (860–921), erected next to the apse in 1228. Widow of the founder of the Přemyslid dynasty Bořivoj I (c. 870–888/9), first Duke of Bohemia, Ludmila was a Christian murdered by her pagan daughter-in-law Drahomíra, who was jealous of the possible influence Ludmila might have over her son, Duke Wenceslaus (Václav) I (921–935). Wenceslaus himself was murdered in the same year by his brother, the pagan Duke Boleslaus I the Cruel (935–972), whose tomb is also here. Wenceslaus's promotion of Christianity and conciliatory moves towards his German neighbours upset many of the pagan nobles of Bohemia; it also resulted ultimately in his canonisation (his feast day on September 28th is now a public holiday called Czech Statehood Day and he is also memorialised in J. M. Neale's Christmas carol, *Good King Wenceslas*). The tomb of Ludmila's own son Duke Vratislav I, husband of Drahomira and founder of the basilica, is notable for being just a simple wooden casket.

Other places of interest nearby: 17, 19, 20, 21, 22

19. Tiny Houses on Golden Lane

Prague 1 (Hradčany), Golden Lane (Zlatá ulička) at the top of Old Castle Steps (Staré zámecké schody) in Prague Castle (Pražský hrad)
Metro A to Malostranská; Tram 22, 23 from Národní třída, 12, 20 from náměstí Kinských

One of the most visited streets of Prague – and also one of the most unusual – is Golden Lane (Zlatá ulička), running along the northeastern ramparts of Prague Castle (Pražský hrad). The area began life as a narrow strip of land no more than eight metres wide, created around 1484 when the 12th century Romanesque walls of the castle were strengthened by means of a second wall, built farther out along the edge of a natural ravine called the Stag Moat (Jelení příkop) (see no. 9). Three cannon towers punctuated this new wall, namely the Dalibor Tower (věž Daliborka) at the eastern end, the White Tower (Bílá věž) in the middle, and the Powder Tower (Prašná věž) to the west (see no. 20). Between the Dalibor Tower and the White Tower the wall was buttressed on the inside by a row of twelve archways supported on sturdy columns, above which ran a wooden projecting gallery with loopholes for bowmen. This stretch of wall was serviced by the piece of land that would later become Golden Lane.

Even before the great fire of 1541, which destroyed many buildings in the castle district, it seems likely that these archways, 600–660 centimetres wide and c. 120 centimetres deep, were being used as simple dwellings. The first documentary evidence for them dates from the 1560s, when the lane was called Zlatnická ulička, or Goldsmiths' Lane, suggesting its residents were lesser goldsmiths escaping the guild laws being enforced elsewhere in Prague.

Between 1591 and 1594, during the reign of Habsburg Holy Roman Emperor and King of Bohemia Rudolph II (1576–1611), the outer wall was repaired and the surface level of the lane raised to the top of the archways. From this level sprang a new arcade of twenty-one archways, each 400 centimetres wide and 220 centimetres deep, above which ran a walled defensive passage that replaced the earlier wooden gallery. In 1597 the 'artillerymen at the gates of Prague Castle' gained the Emperor's permission to build houses against these archways. These houses were modest too, consisting of little more than an entrance hall with stove and earth floor, leading into a single room with one tiny window.

Some of Prague's smallest houses are on Golden Lane (Zlatá ulička)

In time they were sold on to other castle employees, such as gatekeepers, guards and bell-ringers.

Habsburg Holy Roman Emperor and King Josef II (1780–90) disbanded the artillerymen's brigade in 1784 and new residents began extending the houses out into Golden Lane itself, reducing it to only a metre wide in parts. Sanitary conditions were poor – the first water pipe was not laid until 1877 – and in 1864 it was decided to clear the lane of all wooden sheds and other unofficial extensions, leaving only those houses along the north wall permitted originally by Emperor Rudolph. The earth floors were gradually covered by wooden ones, tiled stoves and new furniture installed, and the walls painted. As word of the 'restored' Golden Lane spread, so the residents attempted to outdo each other in decorating their little homes as a means of attracting visitors.

With the departure of the last occupant in 1952 the final arangement of the tiny street as a fully-fledged tourist attraction was decided upon, each house being uniquely painted and renovated so as to display its diverse and idiosyncratic history. Thus, house number 24 remains the only one with a water supply, number 23 has a stairway up to the defensive passage, number 22 belonged to Franz Kafka's sister and is where the author wrote *Ein Landarzt* (*A Country Doctor*) in 1916–17, number 20 has its façade stripped back to reveal its timber framework, number 19 has a cellar and a tiny fenced-off front garden, numbers 18 and 16 occupy two archways each, number 14 was home to the clairvoyant Madame de Thèbes and still retains its house sign with playing cards, an owl and a crystal ball, number 13 is the only building to occupy a single archway (as such it is probably Prague's smallest house), and number 12 fronts the Dalibor Tower, access to which – via the defensive passage above – had been lost when the top two storeys were struck by lightning.

Both the Dalibor Tower and the White Tower served as prisons for the aristocracy, with the artillerymen of Golden Lane acting as their guards. The White Tower was so-named because prisoners were transferred here from an earlier Romanesque White Tower in the castle proper. Its most famous inmates were alchemist Edward Kelley, jailed for fraud in 1591, and the Protestant noblemen who led the Estates' rebellion against the Habsburgs during the Thirty Years War (1618–48) (see no. 26). The Dalibor Tower was named after Dalibor of Kozojedy, a knight imprisoned in 1496 for sheltering outlawed serfs. He taught himself to play violin whilst awaiting execution, drawing admirers to listen beneath his window and inspiring Josef Wenig's libretto for Smetana's opera *Dalibor*. The towers ceased being used as prisons following the Judicial Reform of Emperor Joseph II in 1781, which abolished the old provincial court and the court of the Burgrave (supreme governor of Bohemia).

Other places of interest nearby: 18, 20, 21, 22

20. The Alchemists' Tower

Prague 1 (Hradčany), the Powder Tower (Prašná věž) off Vikářská in the
Third Courtyard of Prague Castle (Pražský hrad)
Metro A to Malostranská; Tram 22, 23 from Národní třída, 12, 20 from
náměstí Kinských

In 1583 the Habsburg Holy Roman Emperor and King of Bohemia
Rudolph II (1576–1611), fearing a second Ottoman invasion, moved his
imperial court from Vienna to Prague and for the next twenty years the
city became the capital of an empire for the first time in two centuries.
Despite growing dissension from Protestants within Bohemia in the
run-up to the Thirty Years War, Prague experienced a dazzling golden
age. Rudolph was an eccentric and melancholic ruler but he also pos-
sessed an open and inquiring mind, together with a fascination for eso-
terica. By means of his generous commissions he surrounded himself
with a colourful assortment of talents, including not only artists and
scientists but also astrologers, mystics and alchemists (see no. 20 & 48).
As author Angelo Ripellino wrote in his book *Magic Prague*: "When
Rudolph II moved his court to Prague ... the city became an academy
of the occult".

Scholars are still entranced by the work of the alchemists, those
proto-scientists who believed that all matter was composed of the four
elements (earth, water, fire and air) and
whose work took them into the realms of
mysticism, magic and the occult. Their
two intertwined goals were the Philosopher's Stone, a mythical substance that
would enable the transmutation of base
metals into gold, and the Elixir of Life, a
remedy that would cure all disease and
prolong life indefinitely. Although open
to abuse in the hands of charlatans, its elements of physics, medicine, metallurgy
and religion have made alchemy a colourful precursor to the modern science of
chemistry.

A passageway running off Vikářská
in the Third Courtyard of Prague Castle
(Pražský hrad) gives access to the north-

*The Powder Tower (Prašná věž) at Prague
Castle (Pražský hrad) once housed an
alchemists' laboratory*

An alchemist at work on a wall in Old Town Square (Staroměstské náměstí)

ern ramparts, built around 1484 when the Polish Jagiellon King Ladislaus II (1471–1516) moved up to the castle from Royal Court (Králův dvůr) in Old Town (see no. 9). Here can be found the Powder Tower (Prašná věž), the largest and westernmost of a trio of cannon towers projecting from the ramparts and so-named because it was later used to store gunpowder (see no. 19). The tower was also once home to a number of fishtanks from which the castle kitchens were supplied, hence its alternative name of Mihulka after a species of small fish.

An equally intriguing name is the Laboratory Tower, dating to the reign of Emperor Rudolph II when his royal alchemists were employed here. The most famous alchemists of the day were undoubtedly the Englishman John Dee (1527–1608) and his assistant Edward Kelley (1555–97). Dee was an outstanding mathematician, astronomer and geographer, as well as scientific advisor to Queen Elizabeth I of England. It should be remembered that during the Renaissance the natural sciences and the occult were not so distinct as today and so it is unsurprising to discover that Dee was also an alchemist, astrologer and student of Hermetic philosophy. However, by the early 1580s Dee was increasingly dissatisfied in his quest to learn the secrets of the universe and with his lack of recognition. Instead he turned towards the supernatural as a means of acquiring knowledge and attempted to contact angels by crystal gazing (crytallomancy). To do this Dee needed a 'scryer', or crystal gazer, to act as intermediary between himself and the angels; the man Dee found was Edward Kelley, a spirit medium who had already been pilloried for counterfeiting and who claimed to hold the secret of converting base metals into gold.

Needing patronage to continue their partnership, in 1583 Dee and Kelley accepted an offer from nobleman Prince Albert Łaski to go to Poland. After discovering him to be bankrupt the pair travelled through Central Europe and had audiences with King Stephen of Poland in Kraków and Emperor Rudolph II in Prague. Although neither monarch was impressed, in 1586 they were offered the patronage of wealthy Bohemian Count Vilém of Rožmberk. Kelley rapidly grew wealthy from his promises of manufacturing gold, whereas Dee was less sought after and became embittered, especially after Kelley told him that the angels said he should share his wife with him! Dee returned to England in 1589 and never saw Kelley again, dying there in poverty in 1608.

By 1590 Kelley owned several estates and even Emperor Rudolph had made him a baron in return for the promise of gold: none was to come nor any elixir of life. Indeed, Edward Kelley's life probably first gave rise to the notion of the charlatan alchemist and it is little wonder that his house in Prague is named after Faust, another scholar doomed by his own vanity (see no. 70). Rudolph imprisoned Kelley for fraud in May 1591 in the White Tower of Prague Castle, not far from the alchemists' Laboratory Tower, after which he was transferred to the prison at Křivoklát Castle, west of Prague. Released in 1594 he again failed to produce gold and eventually died in 1597 whilst a prisoner at Hněvín Castle in Most.

Many works of fiction have subsequently tapped the rich seam of alchemy for inspiration, including the novel *Der Engel vom westlichen Fenster (The Angel of the West Window)* by Gustav Meyrink and Christopher Marlowe's play *The Tragical History of Doctor Faustus*, both of which use the life of John Dee as their framework (see nos. 42 & 70).

Before the alchemists the Powder Tower was the workshop of Brno ironmaster and bell founder Tomáš Jaroš. In 1549 Prague's largest bell ('Zikmund') was cast here for the adjacent Cathedral of St. Vitus (chrám sv. Víta) and in 1564 Jaroš cast the so-called Singing Fountain (Zpívající fontána), to be found in the garden of the nearby Belvedere summer palace (see no. 21); its tinkling sound made originally by water dripping into a bronze basin.

Other places of interest nearby: 17, 18, 19, 21, 22

21. From Anna's Palace To Bílek's Villa

Prague 1 (Hradčany), the Belvedere (Belvedér) in the Royal Garden
(Královská zahrada) north of Prague Castle (Pražský hrad)
Metro A to Malostranská; Tram 22, 23 from Národní třída, 12, 20 from
náměstí Kinských

With the death of the Polish Jagiellon King Louis II (1516–26) at the
Battle of Mohács against the Ottoman Suleiman the Magnificent, Ferdinand I (1526–64) of Austria inherited the crown of Bohemia, heralding the start of nearly four centuries of Habsburg rule. After the violence of the Hussite Wars (1420–36) and prior to renewed violence in
the run up to the Thirty Years War (1618–48), Prague experienced an
era of relative calm.

The city's architects, having exhausted the medieval canon of Gothic architecture, now turned to the blossoming Italian Renaissance style
for inspiration (see no. 39). Based on the rediscovery and reinterpreta-
tion of the architecture of Classical Greece and Rome, the Renaissance
style seemed less lofty in concept than the Gothic, being typified by
light and airy palaces with graceful portals rather than overbearing
cathedrals hoary with sculpture. Examples of the Renaissance style
in Prague include the magnificent doorway of the House at the Two
Golden Bears (dům U Dvou zlatých medvědů), added in 1590 to an existing Gothic house at the corner of Melantrichova and Kožná, and the
doorway of the House at the White Lamb (U Bílého beránka) at Old
Town Square (Staroměstské náměstí) 17, also added to an older building, where Albert Einstein would later play violin.

Politics, fire and finances would mean that the Renaissance style
never really became widespread in Prague, indeed only very few purely
Renaissance buildings exist in the city, namely the House at the Golden
Lion (U Zlatého lva) at Lesser Quarter Square (Malostranské náměstí)
10 and the *sgraffitoed* Schwarzenberg Palace (Schwarzenberský palác)
on Hradčanské náměstí (see no. 16). However, there is one further example that is equal to anything found in Italy. The Royal Summer Palace (Královský letohrádek), known today as the Belvedere (Belvedér),
can be found at the east end of the Royal Garden (Královská zahrada),
laid out in the 1530s by Emperor Ferdinand I in a former vineyard on
the north side of Prague Castle. The Belvedere is the purest Renaissance building north of the Alps and is based on a design by the Ge-
noese Paolo della Stella, who was responsible for its Ionic arcade in-

terspersed with mythological scenes. Construction on the building was halted in 1541, due to fire in the castle nearby, after which the architect Bonifác Wohlmut, responsible for completing the upper section of the Great Tower of St. Vitus's Cathedral, continued the work with the addition of an extraordinary copper roof in the shape of an upturned ship's hull. Ferdinand commissioned the palace as a love token for his wife Anna, daughter of Polish Jagiellon King Ladislaus II (1471–1516), but she was long dead by the time the building was eventually completed in 1564. The Habsburg Holy Roman Emperor and King of Bohemia Rudolph II (1576–1611) installed part of his extensive

The Renaissance Belvedere (Belvedér) was commissioned by Emperor Ferdinand

art collection here, after which Emperor Joseph II (1780–90) used it as a military college; later, the Communists bricked up the first floor windows to prevent assassins using it to shoot the president. The Communists were also behind an unusual addition made to the *sgraffitoed* façade of the nearby Ball Game Court (Míčovna), again the work of Renaissance architect Wohlmut and completed in 1569: during restoration in 1952 the woman seated next to the figure of Justice, tenth from the right, was given a hammer and sickle!

Another building that is unusual for Prague, indeed for the entire world, is the curious Villa Bílek (Bílkova vila), situated a couple of streets north of the Belvedere at Mickiewiczova 1. It was built in 1910–1911 to a design by the artist, sculptor and religious thinker František Bílek (1872–1941), for use as a home-cum-studio. Whilst studying art in Paris, Bílek discovered himself to be partially colour-blind and so turned to sculpture and graphic design as a way to express and explain the substance of the world around him. He created his own artistic language, quite independent of traditional 19th century Czech sculpture,

The curious Villa Bílek (Bílkova vila) is a building without parallel

in which he uniquely connected the symbolism of Art Nouveau with Christian and Oriental spiritual traditions. For his villa in Prague, Bílek used the motif of a cornfield – one of the artist's recurring themes – in order to symbolise spiritual fertility. This accounts for the rhythmically articulated brick walls, broken up at intervals by Egyptian-style columns representing sheaves of corn, and the ears of corn carved onto the doorframes and hinges. Even the arc-shaped plan of the villa represents a giant scythe harvesting Bílek's own creative work. Today, the villa contains several pieces of period furniture, as well as an extensive collection of his works, including the group of carved oak figures known as *The Future Conquerors* (1931–37). Most intriguing is his plaster model for an unrealised National Monument commemorating the Czech defeat at White Mountain (see no. 26). (The villa is closed for renovation until 2009.)

Other places of interest nearby: 18, 19, 20, 22, 23

22. Palatial Gardens

Prague 1 (Malá Strana), the Palatial Gardens (Palácové zahrady) at
Valdštejnské náměstí 3
Metro A to Malostranská; Tram 22, 23 from Národní třída, 12, 20 from
náměstí Kinských

In the northeastern part of Lesser Quarter (Malá Strana), behind the
well-concealed garden of General Wallenstein, the great hero of the
Thirty Years War (1618–48), there runs a street called Valdštejnská (see
no. 23). This elegant street is lined with former palaces built by wealthy
aristocrats from the 16th century onwards. Although the buildings
themselves are of architectural note, it is what lies hidden behind them
that merits the greatest attention, namely one of the finest ensembles
of Baroque garden design anywhere in Europe.

During the 1990s this stunning series of five Italianate gardens, each
built for an individual palace, was restored back to something like its
original appearance having been abandoned to the ravages of nature for
years. It is now possible to appreciate both the tastes and sensibilities
of the 18th century Baroque aristocracy who commissioned the gardens
and to appreciate the skill and vision of the craftsmen who built them,
on land previously used only for vineyards.

The gardens are laid out across precipitous terrain beneath the Old
Castle Staircase (Staré zámecké schody), the differences in elevation
turned ingeniously to good advantage by means of a series of stepped
terraces and graceful stairways, finished off with balustrades, arbours,
fountains and statuary. The tiny pockets of horizontal ground that such
designs permitted were used for formal plantings of ornamental shrubs,
climbers and fruit trees. Since the gardens are today interconnected, the
modern visitor is afforded the luxury of being able to make a tour of all
five gardens in one journey.

It is best to begin at Valdštejnské náměstí 3 with the so-called
Ledebour Garden (Lederburská zahrada), the most westerly of the gardens, and named after Adolf, Earl of Ledebour, who bought the adjacent palace in 1852. The garden had been first laid out in the early 16th
century but then modified in 1787–97 by Ignác Jan Palliardi to the Baroque design seen today. At the bottom is a splendid five-arched *Sala
Terrena* designed by Giovanni Battista Alliprandi, with Pompeiian-
style frescoes by Václav Vavřinec Reiner depicting ancient mythological
scenes.

Looking up into the Small Fürstenberg Garden (Malá Fürstenberská zahrada) in Malá Strana

Adjacent to the sloping part of the Ledebour Garden lies the Small Palffy Garden (Malá Pálffyovská zahrada), a strictly utilitarian garden with terraces of fruit trees and small lawns first put down in 1751. Laid out contemporaneously is the third garden, the Great Palffy Garden (Velká Pálffyovská zahrada), re-designed in the early 19th century in the Classicist style (although historical records mention a garden here as early as 1681). On the highest of its seven terraces, reached via a tunnel and arch constructed through the thickness of the parapet walls, there is a loggia bearing a plaque recording the part played in the restoration of the gardens by the Prague Heritage Fund under the auspices of former Czech President Václav Havel (1989–2003) and His Royal Highness Charles, the Prince of Wales.

Like the Small Palffy, the next garden, the Kolowrat Garden (Kolovratská zahrada), is also utilitarian in nature and planted with fruits trees, although there is a fountain at the bottom of its seven terraces. In front of this is a wrought iron gateway leading out onto Valdštejnská created in 1858 by Maximilian Egon of Fürstenberg, who tore down a house that once stood here.

Next is the Small Fürstenberg Garden (Malá Fürstenberská zahrada), which like the Ledebour Garden was designed anonymously and then modified later by Palliardi, this time in 1784–88 in the late Baroque (Rococo) style. From the fountain and frescoed loggia at the bottom a long staircase runs up the axis of the garden, past a pair of orangeries to a *gloriette* pavilion and observatory tower at the top, offering an excellent overview of the gardens. The tower itself acts as a gateway to the Southern Gardens, which are strung out below the southern ramparts of Prague Castle (Pražský hrad).

Finally, to the east of the Small Fürstenberg Garden lies the currently inaccessible and wholly overgrown Great Fürstenberg Garden (Velká Fürstenberská zahrada). It was established in the 18th century for a former palace now occupied by the Polish Embassy and named after the Fürstenbergs, who owned the gardens from 1866. Today, this, the largest of the palatial gardens on Valdštejnská, is being restored and is to be opened to the public.

The Southern Gardens comprise two distinct gardens with stunning views, namely the Paradise Garden (Rajská zahrada) to the west and the Garden on the Ramparts (zahrada Na Valech) to the east. They were laid out during the Renaissance period although their present appearance is largely the work of Slovenian architect Jože Plečnik, who worked here in 1920–24; in 1930 he also created the Garden on the Bastions (zahrada Na Baště) to the left of the castle's main gate (see no. 58). A stone obelisk in the Southern Gardens marks the place where a pair of 'defenestrated' Catholic imperial governors landed in a dung heap in 1618 (see no. 26). The gardens can also be entered by the so-called Bull Staircase from the Castle's Third Courtyard and via a path to the right hand side of the First Courtyard that runs outside the ramparts.

Other places of interest nearby: 18, 19 20, 21, 23

23. The Hidden World of General Wallenstein

Prague 1 (Malá Strana), the Wallenstein Gardens (Valdštejnská zahrada) on Letenská
Metro A to Malostranská; Tram 22, 23 from Národní třída, 12, 20 from náměstí Kinských

A fragment of the oldest known gardens in Prague, the so-called Vojan's Gardens (Vojanovy sady), is still to be found in the city's Lesser Quarter (Malá Strana) on Letenská. Scant documentary evidence tells us that this surprisingly tranquil spot once formed part of a Bishop's mansion built in 1248. The gardens later fell under the auspices of the Order of English Virgins, whose Church of St. Joseph (kostel sv. Josefa) stands nearby (see no. 50). Much more is known about an equally historic garden situated just across Letenská, through a gateway in an innocuous-looking 9-metre high brick wall. This is the celebrated, though well concealed, Wallenstein Garden, restored recently to its former Baroque glory.

Albrecht Wenceslaus Eusebius von Wallenstein (1583–1634) was a Protestant nobleman who converted to Catholicism in 1620, becoming commander of the Imperial Catholic armies of Habsburg Holy Roman Emperor and King of Bohemia Ferdinand II (1619–37). As General Wallenstein (originally Waldstein) he won a series of stunning military victories, conquering much of Germany and defeating the Swedes in 1632, during the Thirty Years War against the Protestant nobility (1618–48). Wallenstein was also a shrewd property developer and used his not inconsiderable income in buying up more than twenty houses and gardens in Lesser Quarter, in order to demolish them and create a plot for his own palace. Following a design by the Milanese architect Andrea Spezza, and using a team of skilled Italian craftsmen, work on the Wallenstein Palace (Valdštejnský palác) commenced in 1624 and took six years to complete.

Although it has some elements of late Renaissance mannerism, the palace is generally regarded as being the first secular Baroque building in Prague. With its double-height ceremonial hall (Rytířský sál), containing a fresco of Wallenstein as the god Mars in his chariot, Flemish tapestries, chandeliers and staffed by 700 servants, the Wallenstein Palace very nearly succeeded in outshining Prague Castle (Pražský hrad) itself.

The secret walled garden behind the palace, conceived on the model of formal secluded Italian gardens *(Giardino secreto)*, provided the perfect finishing touch to Wallenstein's flamboyant dream home, with fountains, a lake, and bronze statues by Adriaen de Vries. An outsize arcaded pavilion *(Sala Terrena)* has a fresco depicting Wallenstein as Achilles during the Trojan War and there is a riding school that once contained a thousand horses (now used by the National Gallery for temporary art exhibitions). Most unusual is the so-called Grotto, or Dripstone Wall, being a man-made representation of a cavern wall smothered with stalactites and stalagmites among which can be spied carved faces, frogs, snakes and monsters. Even an aviary is worked into this extraordinary garden fantasy.

The curious grotto in the Wallenstein Gardens (Valdštejnská zahrada)

Unfortunately for the egotistical Wallenstein, his all too visible desire to outshine the Emperor, together with the uncovering of secret negotiations he had been conducting with the Swedish army, led to the Emperor's Jesuit advisors campaigning for his expulsion. Having rejoined the Protestants Wallenstein was on the verge of having himself proclaimed King of Bohemia in 1634 when he was assassinated by Irish mercenaries following orders from the Emperor. The Thirty Years War eventually petered out in 1648 and Habsburg Catholic rule was reimposed. The bronze statues in Wallenstein's garden were looted by vanquished Swedish troops as they retreated from the city, finding their way eventually to the Royal Gardens of Drottningholm near Stockholm; those seen in the Wallenstein Garden today are early 20th century copies. Today, the Wallenstein Palace serves as the seat of the Senate of the Czech Parliament.

Other places of interest nearby: 1, 2, 4, 5, 22

24. The Müller Villa

Prague 6 (Střešovice), the Villa Müller (Müllerova vila) at Nad Hradním vodojemem 14
Metro A to Hradčanská then Tram 1, 18

With the dawn of the 1920s, the architecture of many major European cities underwent great changes as the ornate organic motifs of Art Nouveau gave way to the pared down cubic and cylindrical forms of Modernism. The use of ornament for ornament's sake was rejected and old-fashioned craftsmanship sidelined in favour of new technological innovations and the introduction of reinforced concrete. It was the age of Walter Gropius and the German Bauhaus movement, of the austere Functionalism of Le Corbusier and Mies van der Rohe, and of the creation of what would eventually be called the International Style. Czechoslovakia's golden age of Modernism was the interwar period, when the movement was linked firmly to the nation's newfound independence and democracy.

Another leading light during this time was the architect Adolf Loos (1870–1933), whose finest work, the Villa Müller, can be found tucked away in Prague's 6th district of Střešovice. Loos was born into the family of a sculptor in Brno, Moravia and went on to study architecture in Dresden. During the following decades he spent time in North America, Paris and London settling eventually in Vienna, where his distinctive villas, shops and other buildings can still be found.

Loos returned frequently to Brno, as well as to Prague, where in 1928–1930 he oversaw the construction of the Villa Müller, which he had designed together with the Prague architect Karel Lhota. The construction magnate Dr. František Müller, co-owner of the building company Kapsa-Müller, commissioned the villa. From the outside, the building is conceived as an austere whitewashed cube, broken only by asymmetrical groupings of window openings. By direct contrast, the interior is constructed with marble, mahogany and walnut, highly polished and cleanly delineated. It was typical of Loos that not only did he design the building but he also had a hand in the choice of fixtures and furnishings. The rooms themselves are set at different levels according to his own *Raumplan* design, whereby rooms of varying heights are wound in an ascending spiral around an imaginary axis. This was a radical departure from the layout of traditional buildings in which floors ran the full width of the structure. The exciting spacial layout of the Villa Müller

The Villa Müller (Müllerova vila) in Střešovice

is crowned by a summer dining room on the top floor that opens onto a terrace with a stunning view of Prague Castle (Pražský hrad). Now completely restored to the way it would have appeared in the 1930s, it is hard to believe that after the Second World War the villa was used as the State Pedagogical Publishing House and later by the Institute of Marxism-Leninism.

25. Bohemia's First Monastery

Prague 6 (Břevnov), the Břevnov Monastery (Břevnovský klášter)
on Patočkova
Metro A to Hradčanská then Bus 108, 174; Tram 22 from Národní
třída

Břevnov is home to Bohemia's first monastery (Břevnovský klášter)

Halfway between Prague Castle (Pražský hrad) and the historic battleground of White Mountain (Bílá hora), in the western district of Břevnov, can be found Břevnov Monastery (Břevnovský klášter) (see no. 26). As Bohemia's first monastery it was co-founded by the Přemyslid Duke Boleslaus II (972–999) and Bishop Vojtěch in AD 993 for the Benedictine order; only the Benedictine convent of St. George in Prague Castle is older (see no. 18). Vojtěch had earlier entered a Benedictine monastery in Rome and was canonised after being murdered in 997 whilst attempting to Christianise the Prussians. During the reign of the subsequent Přemyslid Duke Břetislav I (1035–55) the monastery was damaged by fire and rebuilt, after which it received an early Gothic reworking in c. 1300.

Between the end of the Přemyslid dynasty and the arrival of the House of Luxembourg the monastery was reduced to rubble during the Hussite Wars (1420–36). Not until 1708–45 was the monastery rebuilt once again, this time as an extensive Baroque complex of buildings to a design by the famous father-and-son team of Kryštof and Kilián Ignáz Dientzenhofer (together with Pavel Ignác Bayer).

Entered through an elaborate columned gateway erected in 1740 the individual buildings of the monastery are ranged around a large courtyard, the most impressive of which is undoubtedly the monastery church itself, the so-called Basilica of St. Margaret (bazilika sv. Markéty) built in 1715. Of the original 10th century Romanesque church the atmospheric remains of a vaulted crypt are preserved in the cellars, including the gravestone of the Benedictine hermit Vintíř from the early 14th century. Above stands the nave of the Baroque church, its uncluttered interior, clean white stuccoed pilasters and lofty painted ceilings considered by many to be the Dientzenhofers' greatest commission. The paintings themselves, in a distinctive palette of grey-blue, yellow and rust-red, are the work of Jan Jakub Steifels and depict St. Benedict, St. Vojtěch, St. Margaret and other Czech saints. The paintings found in the side altars are by Petr Brandl. The sculptures in the nave, as well as the organ, pulpit and altar, are the work of the craftsman Matěj Wenceslaus Jäckel and the joiner Josef Dobner, the altar having probably been designed by Kryštof Dientzenhofer.

Other buildings of note in the complex include a cloistered convent with a winter refectory (1709–20) built adjacent to the eastern flank of the church, the prelacy (1720) with its Theresian Hall (marking a visit by Habsburg Empress and Queen of Bohemia Maria Theresa (1740–80) and her husband Franz of Lothringen in 1753), various frescoed salons and the Summer Refectory wing, with its library and billiards room extending out into a Baroque garden. Such splendour makes it hard to imagine that for forty years prior to the Velvet Revolution the Communist Ministry of the Interior used the monastery as a repository for its files on suspicious foreigners.

According to local legend, the name Břevnov comes from the word **břevno**, meaning 'wooden beam'. It is recounted how two brothers were out looking for timber one day and came across a spring with a huge hewn beam lying next to it. So pleased were they that they built a cottage on the spot and named the place Břevnov. Later, when the monastery was built nearby, it took the same name.

26. The Star Palace and the White Mountain

Prague 6 (Liboc), the Star Palace (letohrádek Hvězda) in the Star Game Reserve (obora Hvězda) off Bělohorská
Metro A to Hradčanská then Bus 108, 174; Tram 22 from Národní třída

In 1534 the Holy Roman Emperor and King of Bohemia Ferdinand I (1526–64) founded a royal game reserve on the western side of Prague, in what is today the district of Liboc. It supplemented the much older Royal Game Reserve (Královská obora) in Stromovka Park in Bubeneč and in order to distinguish between them the new one was called the New Game Reserve (Nová obora) (see no. 33). In 1547 the Emperor's second son, Archduke Ferdinand of Austria (1529–95), was made governor of Bohemia and in 1555–56 he created something extraordinary in the New Game Reserve, namely the Star Palace (letohrádek Hvězda). It is said that the Archduke designed this unusual Renaissance summer palace-cum-hunting lodge himself, its curious plan in the form of a six-pointed star satisfying his interest in numerology; it is also claimed that he dug the hole for the foundation stone himself. In time the Star Palace, with its tessellated Banqueting Hall floor and beautiful stucco by Italian artists Giovanni Campione de Bossi and Andrea Avostalis, lent its name to the reserve itself, which was renamed the Star Game Reserve (obora Hvězda).

Archduke Ferdinand's unusual star-shaped hunting lodge (letohrádek Hvězda)

28. Down the British Sewers

Prague 6 (Bubeneč), the Eco-Technical Museum (Ekotechnické muzeum) at Papírenská 6
Metro A to Hradčanská, then Bus 131

Modern subterranean Prague is well represented by the highly unusual Eco-Technical Museum (Ekotechnické muzeum) at Papírenská 6 on the riverbank at Bubeneč (Prague 6). Here can be found an abandoned wastewater treatment plant (stará kanalizační čistírna), now a listed historical monument, which is considered to be one of the most important examples of Czech industrial archaeology. The plant was originally part of a sewerage system built between 1899 and 1906 to a design approved by the engineer Sir William Heerlein Lindley (1853–1917). He was one of three sons of the famous British engineer William Lindley, who between them were responsible for civil engineering projects in more than thirty cities across Central and Eastern Europe. These included the construction of waterworks in Hamburg and other German cities, Warsaw and Lodz in Poland, Budapest, St. Petersburg and Moscow, as well as an ambitious water supply system for the oil city of Baku in Azerbaijan.

Lindley's wastewater plant in Prague remained operational for 61 years, closing down eventually in 1967 when a new one was opened on the nearby river island of Císařský ostrov. In the 1990s a group of enthusiastic amateur industrial archaeologists converted the abandoned Art Nouveau buildings into a museum, which opened in September 1996 to mark the 90th anniversary of the opening of the original plant. As a part of the museum's strictly guided tour, visitors get the chance to visit part of the labyrinth of brick-vaulted tunnels that was constructed *below* the main building on health grounds: it is an experience that will not be quickly forgotten! Here is preserved much of the original water treatment system, including a superbly contructed wastewater inlet, where sewage from across the city arrived by pipeline, and a cavernous vaulted hall containing filtration screens and sand traps. On the ground floor above is a fine pair of Breitfeld, Daněk & Co. steam-powered pumping engines that were kept running 24 hours a day from 1906 until 1926, when the plant was electrified, and which are still in working order; they are put into operation during the museum's annual Steam Weekend (víkend pod parou). The tour finishes outside at the rear of the building, where the remains of the plant's ten sedimentation tanks can

Brick-vaulted tunnels in Prague's abandoned sewage works

be made out; the sludge collected here was sold to farmers as fertiliser and the treated water was piped safely out to the middle of the Vltava.

After leaving the museum a short walk down nearby Mýnská will reveal the monumental remains of Bohemia's oldest mechanised paper factory, recently converted into apartments, close to where Emperor Rudolph II (1576–1611) built a watermill (see no. 33).

Two other industrial museums, both in Prague 4, are the Prague Waterworks Museum (Muzeum pražského vodárenství) at the Podolí Waterworks (Podolská vodárna) at Podolská 17, and the Gas Museum (Plynárenské muzeum) at U Plynárny 500 in Michle. The former is located in a monumental building erected between 1923 and 1928 on the site of the old waterworks of 1885 and chronicles the history of Prague's waterworks from the first private pipeline laid in the 12th century, through the Vltava water installations of the Renaissance era, right up to the present day; a highlight is the original filtration plant of the building's architect, Antonín Engel. The Gas Museum is located in an original building of the Michle Gasworks, built in 1925–27, and illustrates the history and technology of the Czech gas industry from earliest times onwards.

29. Baba's Ideal Housing Estate

Prague 6 (Baba), the Czech Werkbund Housing Estate 'Baba' on
Matějská, Na Ostrohu, Na Babě and Nad Pat'ankou
Metro A to Hradčanská, then Bus 131

With some justification Prague has been called Europe's largest open-air museum, most visitors rarely looking further than the Gothic, Baroque and Art Nouveau splendours of the city centre. However, for the explorer with a broader interest in architecture, a visit should be made deep into Prague 6, where there is an unusual Modernist housing estate called 'Baba'.

The construction of the Baba estate, as with similar ones in Vienna and Budapest, was inspired by the success of the *Weissenhofsiedlung*, a housing exhibition that had been mounted by the *Deutsche Werkbund* (German Work Federation) in Stuttgart in 1927. The Werkbund was a group of enterprising architects and designers founded in Munich in 1907 by Hermann Muthesius. Somewhat similar to the Viennese *Wiener Werkstätte* and the English Arts and Crafts Movement in their production of quality products, they differed in being unopposed to reaping the financial rewards made possible through industrialised mass-production.

In September 1932 the Czech *Werkbund* mounted their own model housing exhibition under the guidance of Modernist architect and town planner Pavel Janák (1882–1956). The location selected was the Baba ridge, with the Vltava running along the east side and the wooded slopes of the Silent Šárka Gorge (Tichá

Czech Modernism at the Baba housing estate

Šárka) on the west. The estate comprised thirty-three houses designed by the likes of Josef Fuchs, Josef Gočár, František Kavalír, Oldřich Starý, and Ladislav Machoň. Set side-by-side, so that their qualities could be judged comparatively, they are strung out across the sloping terrain so as to maximise the view from each building. The houses were individually and specifically designed to provide simple, affordable yet innovative living spaces for ordinary families. It was hoped that they might provide a practical alternative to the dreary tenements and apartment blocks of old.

Meant only to be temporary, the geometric *Bauhaus*-style houses, which still appear modern today, were ultimately bought up by the Czech *avant-garde*, having proved too expensive for the original target market. Although not open to the public many of the houses still contain their original fixtures and fittings, their façades clearly visible from the pavement.

By contrast, on U Matěje at the western end of the Baba ridge, there stands the Baroque hilltop Chapel of St. Matthias (sv. Matěj). It replaced a Gothic shrine dating back at least as far as 1404, founded according to legend by the Přemyslid Duke Boleslaus II (972–999). Whilst out hunting here, Boleslaus was attacked by a bear but saved at the last moment by St. Matthias. The saint explained that the animal was a creature of the devil, sent to places where the unchristened were laid to rest, in this case the troops of the warrior Ctirad, killed during the War of the Czech Amazons (see no. 27). To prevent the same thing happening again the saint instructed the grateful Boleslaus to erect a shrine.

At the opposite end of the ridge can be found an enigmatic ruin (zřícenina na Babě). Known locally as the Wine Press, probably because a vineyard once occupied the area, it is in actual fact the remains of a summerhouse built in 1650 by Servatius Engel, one of the vineyard owners. He selected this spot because of its stunning views over Prague, which can still be enjoyed by visitors today.

30. The Treasure of Bare Hill

Prague 6 (Suchdol), Goats Ridges (Kozí hřbety) and Bare Hill (Holý vrch)
off Kamýcká
Metro A to Dejvická then Bus 147 to its terminus on Kamýcká
in Suchdol

The number 147 bus that departs from bustling Vítězné náměstí in the built-up district of Dejvice reaches its terminus amidst farm land on the edge of peaceful Suchdol, in the far northwestern corner of Prague. From here it is only a short walk to the city boundary, where a way-marked trail on the right-hand side leads through a leafy grove, upwards to a craggy ridge. This remarkably rugged area is known as Goat Ridges (Kozí hřbety), an apt name since the visitor needs to be sure-footed on the rocky terrain. Walking along the ridge through its wind-

Bare Hill (Holý vrch) was the site of a rich prehistoric cemetery

swept stands of Silver Birch and Pine trees is invigorating and there are fine vistas northwards across the countryside.

At the end of the ridge the path drops steeply into the valley of the River Únětický, known locally as Silent Valley (Tiché údolí). Now a nature reserve in which can be found several old watermills, the valley stretches away northwards to the village of Roztoky, outside the Prague boundary – and the scope of this book.

On the opposite side of Silent Valley rises the rocky fastness of Bare Hill (Holý vrch), where in 1928 a very important discovery was made. An amateur archaeologist uncovered a cemetery dating back to the Early Bronze Age of Central Europe, its 70 or so graves containing valuable bronze daggers inlaid with gold and amber. The prehistoric community that created the cemetery is known today as the Únětice Culture (únětická kultura) after a village of the same name a little way upstream. The culture has been dated to 1800–1600 BC and its remains have been found across the Czech Republic, southern and central Germany, and western Poland. Undoubtedly the most characteristic of these remains are the distinctive triangular ornamental daggers, thought to have been status symbols and always made of pure copper (the use of copper alloys to produce bronze did not occur until the Late Bronze Age).

Further information about the Únětice Culture, and the prehistory of the Czech Republic in general, is given in both the National Museum (Národní muzeum) at Wenceslas Square (Václavské náměstí) 68 and the Museum of the City of Prague (Muzeum hlavního města Prahy) at Na Poříčí 52, both in New Town (Nové Město).

31. A Chapel's Moving History

Prague 7 (Letná), the Chapel of St. Mary Magdalene (Kaple sv. Máří Magdaleny) on nábřeží Edvarda Beneše near Čech Bridge (Čechův most)
Metro A to Malostranská then Tram 12 or Metro A to Staroměstská then Tram 17

Seated on the left bank of the River Vltava, below the Letná Gardens (Letenské sady), is one of Prague's smallest and least known religious buildings. It is not marked on many maps and few guidebooks mention it.

Known as the Chapel of St. Mary Magdalene (Kaple sv. Máří Magdaleny) the building started life as a chapel of the Order of Cyriacs

The Chapel of St. Mary Magdalene (Kaple sv. Máří Magdaleny) has not always stood near the Čech Bridge (Čechův most)

(a branch of the more famous hospital Order of the Cross with the Red Star), whose church and cloister once stood on the opposite bank. Set in a monastic vineyard it was built in its present form in 1635, to a design by the Italian architect Giovanni Battista de Barrifis, and takes the form of an early Baroque stuccoed rotunda. As such, it continues a tradition of ecclesiastical rotundas in Prague stretching back to the 12th century (see no. 76). Inside the chapel there can still be seen fragments of the paintings that once adorned its walls.

Like most of Prague's religious buildings the Chapel of St. Mary Magdalene was closed down during the 1780s, as part of the anti-clerical reforms of Habsburg Holy Roman Emperor and King of Bohemia Joseph II (1780–90); soon in ruins it was used as a timber store. Unlike most churches, however, it was not restored until 1908, when the nearby Art Nouveau Čech Bridge (Čechův most) was constructed (see no. 38). During the Second World War the chapel narrowly escaped destruction when it came under fire from German troops attempting to suppress the May uprising in the last week of the conflict.

However, what really sets the building apart is its most recent history. In 1955, the busy junction where the bridge makes landfall and joins nábřeží Edvarda Beneše was re-designed and a planned new intersection threatened the chapel. A bold solution was proposed: to physically move the building to a new location a little further upstream. Thus, in February 1956 the chapel was lifted in one piece and placed onto a custom built railway. At a speed of one metre every eight minutes it was moved 30.75 metres from its original location to its very own bastion jutting out into the Vltava. The Chapel of St. Mary Magdalene entered Czechoslovak history books as the country's first building to be relocated in such a way.

For an impression of how the Chapel looked originally pay a visit to the Museum of the City of Prague (Muzeum hlavního města Prahy), where it is represented in Antonín Langweil's incredible scale model of the city as it appeared in the early 19th century (see no. 55).

Other places of interest nearby: 38, 40, 41

32. All Things Technical

Prague 7 (Holešovice), the National Technical Museum (Národní technické muzeum) at Kostelní 42 (closed for renovation until 2010)
Metro C to Vltavská then Tram 25, 26; Tram 8 from náměstí Republiky; Tram 12 from Malostranské náměstí

Prague's National Technical Museum (Národní technické muzeum) began life in 1908 as the Technical Museum of the Czech Kingdom and was housed in the Renaissance surroundings of the Schwarzenberg Palace (Schwarzenberský palác), just outside Prague Castle. It was one of Europe's first technical museums. As the collection grew and more space was needed so an architectural competition was held to design a new building. The winner was the architect Milan Babuška, whose Functionalist building was erected between 1937 and 1940, immediately east of the Letná Gardens (Letenské sady) in the district of Holešovice. The museum's aim is to illustrate the development of science and technology in Czechoslovakia, which until the Second World War was one of Europe's most innovative and industrially advanced countries. The arrival of Communism changed all that and so today the museum also acts as a reminder to natives and visitors alike of everything the country has achieved.

Directly opposite the museum is a near-identical building erecetd at the same time, which contains the little-known National Museum of Agriculture (Národní zemědělské muzeum): illustrating the development of food production and processing in Czechoslovakia during the 19th and 20th centuries, its collections relating to brewing, baking, butchery, distilling, wine making and canning are far more interesting than they sound.

The Letná Gardens (Letenské sady) themselves, laid out in 1858, contain several interesting technological remains, not least of which is Europe's oldest fairground carousel, constructed in 1892 and standing in front of the Technical Museum; it is said that a herd of twenty one horses was specially slaughtered for their hides in order to cover the life-size model horses. On the riverside beyond is the circular Brussels Pavilion, a relic from the Czechoslovak display at the Expo '58 World's Fair in Brussels (examples of Czech jewellery exhibited at the fair can be found in the Prague Jewellery Collection (Pražský kabinet šperku) in a converted riverside brickyard at Cihelná 28 in Lesser Quarter).

Towards Prague Castle there is a huge metronome erected by David

Car made by the Czech Jawa company displayed in the fascinating National Technical Museum (Národní technické muzeum)

Černý in 1991 on an oversized stone pedestal once occupied by a 15 metre-high statue of Stalin. Made up of 226 granite blocks and weighing 15 000 tons, the statue was one of the largest in Europe until it was destroyed by order of Moscow in 1962; the regular swaying of the metronome is said to signify both the transience of political regimes as well as the permanence of Prague.

Finally, there is the elegant Hanau Pavilion (Hanavský pavilon), a survival from the Centennial Bohemian Exhibition of industry and Culture held nearby in 1891 (see no. 35). Made of cast-iron in the neo-Renaissance style it originally housed an exhibit for the foundries of Prince Frederick William of Hanau (1832–1889); later donated to the City of Prague the pavilion was dismantled and moved to its present location in 1898 and today contains a restaurant.

33. Emperor Rudolph's Incredible Water Tunnel

Prague 7 (Holešovice), Rudolph's Tunnel (Rudolfova štola) in Stromovka Park off U Výstaviště
Metro C to Nádraží Holešovice then Tram 5, 12, 14, 15, 17

In 1583 the Habsburg Holy Roman Emperor and King of Bohemia Rudolph II (1576–1611) moved his imperial court from Vienna to Prague and for the first time in two centuries the city became the capital of an empire. Despite growing dissension from Protestants within Bohemia in the run-up to the Thirty Years War, as well as the threat of Ottoman invasion to the south, Prague experienced a dazzling golden age.

The emperor was a royal eccentric renowned for his generous commissions bringing together artists, scientists, astronomers and alchemists (see nos. 20 & 48). A typical yet little-known Rudolphine project can be found in the former Royal Game Reserve (Královská obora) between Holešovice and Bubeneč. The history of the area, known today as Stromovka Park, goes back to 1268 when the Přemyslid King Otakar II (1253–78) created a hunting ground here. It became royal property in 1320 only to be laid waste during the Hussite Wars (1420–36). During the reign of Rudolph the reserve was re-planted, re-stocked and extended westwards as far as the so-called Emperor's Mill, marked today by the street name Za Císařským mlýnem, meaning 'behind the Emperor's Mill' (see no. 28).

As part of Emperor Rudolph's ambitious restoration of the reserve he also created the so-called Large Pond in order to provide drinking water for wild game. To supply the pond with water he commissioned an extraordinary engineering feat, namely the thousand metre-long Rudolph's Tunnel (Rudolfova štola). Constructed between 1584 and 1593 to a design by Italian court painter Giuseppe Arcimboldo the tunnel is hewn from the solid rock of the Letná massif. Experts from the silver mining town of Kutná Hora undertook the excavation work, which involved simultaneous tunnelling from both ends, as well as five vertical shafts dug from the surface in order to remove waste and provide ventilation. Today, a tiny, red-tiled building on the riverbank upstream from the Štefánik Bridge (Štefánikův most) marks the inlet from the Vltava, from where the tunnel runs downwards towards a monumental outlet, barred by a metal grille, above the lake in Stromovka Park. Rudolph's Tunnel is not open to the public but a sense of how it might feel to

The outlet of Emperor Rudolf's water tunnel (Rudolfova štola) in Stromovka Park

walk through it is offered by the pedestrian-cum-river tunnel under the Prašný most Bridge, at the western end of the Stag Moat (Jelení příkop) north of Prague Castle (the city's only other pedestrian tunnel was excavated below Vítkov Hill in 1951 and connects Tachovské náměstí in Žižkov (Prague 3) with Karlín (Prague 8)).

The sturdy construction of Rudolph's Tunnel has accounted for its survival despite numerous calamities suffered by the surrounding reserve. In 1611 Rudolph was succeeded by Habsburg Holy Roman Emperor and King of Bohemia Matthias (1611–19), and then Ferdinand II (1619–37), and the court was moved back to Vienna. The Royal Game Reserve thus lost much of its importance and it was damaged both during the Thirty Years War (1618–48) and during the reign of Habsburg Empress and Queen of Bohemia Maria Theresa (1740–80), when Saxon and Prussian armies camped here and felled all the trees. In 1792 the reserve was again restored, this time to host the coronation of Habsburg Holy Roman Emperor and King of Bohemia Francis I (1792–1835), although it was never again stocked with game.

Other places of interest nearby: 34, 35, 36

34. Marold's Mighty Panorama

Prague 7 (Holešovice), the Marold Panorama (Maroldovo panoráma) on
U Výstaviště
Metro C to Nádraží Holešovice then Tram 5, 12, 14, 15, 17

On Sunday 30th May 1434 two Czech armies met in fratricidal combat on a hill between the villages of Hřiby and Lipany, 40 kilometres east of Prague. On one side were the allied forces of moderate Hussites and Catholic nobility, together with the citizens of Prague and Plzeň, whilst on the opposite side were the radical Hussites of Tábor and East Bohemia. The radicals were defeated and their military power broken, bringing to an end the revolutionary phase of the period known in Bohemian history as the Hussite Wars.

Exactly five hundred years later, on 30th May 1934, an incredible painting of what became known as the Battle of Lipany was unveiled at the Prague Exhibition Grounds (Výstaviště) in Holešovice (see no. 35). Known as the Marold Panorama (Maroldovo panoráma) it was the brainchild of Bohemian painter Luděk Marold (1865–98) and had been created originally for the Prague Exhibition of Architecture and Engineering in 1898. Measuring 11 metres high and 95 metres wide the mighty painting took the form of a diorama running around the inside wall of a circular wooden pavilion. The painting's execution was a team effort, with Marold drawing on the expertise of landscape painter Wenceslaus Jansa, colourist Theodor Hilšer, equestrian expert Ludvík Vašátko, and most importantly Karel Štapfer, who was responsible for the carefully reconstructed terrain in the foreground that gives the panorama its unforgettably three dimensional feel. Some 82 000 people visited the painting on its first showing and it remained a popular draw until February 1929, when the roof of the pavilion collapsed after a heavy snowfall. Fortunately, the damaged painting could be restored and a public collection generated enough money to erect the sturdy dodecagonal structure that still houses the panorama today.

The Battle of Lipany was a brave subject to depict in such a prominent public work since it represented in the most graphic terms a civil war in which Czech fought against Czech. The roots of the Hussite Wars stretch back to the early 14th century and the end of the Přemyslid dynasty, following the assassination of King Wenceslaus (Václav) III (1305–06) in 1306. An invasion by Rudolph I of Habsburg (1306–1307) supplanted the Přemyslids and kick-started six centuries of almost

A part of the Marold Panorama (Maroldovo panoráma) on U Výstaviště

unbroken Luxembourg and Habsburg dynastic rule. Emigration of German nobles into Czech lands soon followed, the new arrivals quickly gaining influence over church and economy, imposing merciless rule on the peasants and inevitably coming into conflict with their Czech counterparts.

The reign of Holy Roman Emperor Charles IV of Luxembourg (King Charles I of Bohemia) (1346–78) heralded in a new golden age. The emperor spoke out against church corruption and refused to accept papal dictates north of the Alps, yet he still felt obliged to give half his land to the clergy. His son, Wenceslaus (Václav) IV (1378–1419), continued to rail against the church but nowhere near as effectively as Jan Hus, the firebrand rector of Prague's Charles University (Univerzita Karlova) (see no. 54). Hus was deemed a heretic by the church and burned at the stake in 1415, thereby becoming a martyr to the dual Czech cause of church reform and independence from German dominance.

In 1419 an agitated mob of Czech nobles 'defenestrated' seven members of the city council from the window of the New Town Hall (Novoměstská radnice) on Charles Square (Karlovo náměstí) in New Town (Nové Město), angry that they would not release those imprisoned for supporting church reform (see nos. 58 & 68). The action precipitated not only the death of Wenceslaus but also further rioting in an attempt to prevent his brother, Sigismund (1419–20), from taking the throne.

The new king was roundly denounced, as was Rome, by radical preachers such as Jan Želivský, in response to which the Pope called for a holy crusade against Bohemia. Following the burning of nine monks in Prague, Rome's call to arms was taken up across Europe and the Czechs were soon surrounded. However, with a potent moral cause behind them, and a charismatic leader in the shape of the one-eyed commander Jan Žižka in front, Hussite forces not only repelled the Catholic crusaders at the Battle of Vítkov Hill but actually managed to extend their sway as far as the Baltic coast (see no. 56). For the next fifteen years an interregnum was declared as the Hussite Wars proper unfolded.

Žižka died in 1424 heralding a division within the Hussite camp itself, namely between moderate Hussites, known also as Utraquists, and radical Hussites, called Taborites. The moderates were mostly middle class, whose leadership was based at the University. By contrast, the radicals came predominantly from the lower class and occupied a classless fortified stronghold, where property was shared and services were held exclusively in Czech.

Žižka was succeeded as military commander by the Taborite Procopius the Great (Prokop Holý), who continued to repel papal forces and in 1425–26 invaded Silesia and Saxony. Realising his holy war could not be won, the Pope invited the Czechs to attend the Council of Basel in 1433 resulting in the *Compactata*, whereby moderate Hussites were coaxed back into the Catholic church and received considerable religious freedoms, and Sigismund of Luxembourg was recognised as king for the second time (1436–37). Not surprisingly the Taborites rejected the agreement resulting in a bitter civil war between the two factions that led to the destruction of the Taborites at the Battle of Lipany, as depicted in Luděk Marold's painted panorama.

Until his early death in 1898, aged just 33, Marold lived on the top floor of what was once Antonín Chmel's smoked meat factory at U Zvonařky 1 in Vinohrady (Prague 2). Converted into a sumptuous *Belle Époque* hotel during the 1890s, Marold was responsible for the superb neo-Renaissance ceiling frescoes still preserved in what is now the Le Palais Hotel; Marold's own apartment is now occupied by rooms 407–412.

Other places of interest nearby: 33, 35, 36

35. Exhibitions Old and New

Prague 7 (Holešovice), the Exhibition Grounds (Výstaviště)
at U Výstaviště
Metro C to Nádraží Holešovice then Tram 5, 12, 14, 15, 17

In 1791, on the occasion of the coronation of Habsburg Holy Roman Emperor Leopold II (1790–92) as King of Bohemia, a great Industry Exhibition was staged to impress the new ruler with Bohemian craftsmanship. A hundred years later in 1891 a Centennial Bohemian Exhibition of Industry and Culture was planned to celebrate the anniversary of that exhibition, the location for which would be a 40 hectare plot carved out of the eastern part of Stromovka Park, the former Royal Game Reserve (Královská obora) of Rudolph II (1576–1611) (see no. 33). Between May and October some 3.5 million visitors attended the Exhibition Grounds (Výstaviště) as well as its satellite exhibit, the Petřín Observation Tower (see no. 10).

When the exhibition had finished, some of its smaller pavilions were relocated elsewhere, for example the Czech Hikers' Club pavilion (see no. 10) and the Hanau Pavilion (see no. 32). Meanwhile, the main exhibition hall – the so-called Industry Palace (Průmyslový palác) – continued to be used as Prague's premier exhibition space (e.g. the Ethnographic Exhibition (1895), the Exhibition of Architecture and Engineering (1898), the Chef and Waiter Exhibition (1922) and the International Exhibition of Cars (1923)). However, by 1928 the function of the Industry Palace had been replaced by the new Exhibition Palace (Veletržní palác) down the

A detail of the Industry Palace (Průmyslový palác) on U Výstaviště

hill at Dukelských hrdinů 47; large trade fairs eventually moved permanently to Brno.

A visit to the old Exhibition Grounds makes for a fascinating trip, since they contain several architectural oddities. These include one of the world's largest Planetaria (see no. 47), the unexpected Sea World (Mořský svět), with its tropical fish and free-swimming sharks, the incredible Marold Panorama depicting the Battle of Lipany (see no. 34), and the National Gallery's Lapidárium, constructed originally as a pavilion for the 1891 exhibition and then remodelled in Baroque-Art Nouveau style for the architecture exhibition of 1898 (see no. 34). It contains a collection of more than two thousand sculptures dating from the 11th to 19th centuries, removed from their original locations in order to preserve them, including many original statues from Charles Bridge (Karlův most).

The Industry Palace itself is still standing, its curvilinear wrought iron and glass structure, ornate stucco decoration and one million panes of stained glass making it the first expression of Art Nouveau in Prague. In 1948 it was the venue for a Communist congress that approved the expropriation of all factories employing more that fifty people. The palace was renamed Congress Palace and the grounds became the Julius Fučík Park of Culture and Relaxation, named after a Communist journalist murdered by the Nazis. Now called the Exhibition Grounds once more, the Industry Palace is used today to host medium-sized trade fairs.

To the rear of the Industry Palace lies Lunapark, an old-fashioned fairground with its antiquated ghost train and rifle ranges, as well as the illuminated dancing Křižík Fountain (Křižíkova Fontána). The latter was created originally by the renowned Czech engineer and inventor František Křižík, responsible for illuminating the Exhibition Grounds and for designing Prague's first electric tramway that brought visitors from a funicular railway at Letná to the Exhibition Grounds at Stromovka (see no. 36).

Other places of interest nearby: 33, 34, 36

36. Prague By Tram

Prague 7 (Holešovice), Historic Tram 91 (historická tramvaj 91) from
U Výstaviště
Metro C to Nádraží Holešovice then Tram 5, 12, 14, 15, 17

A 40-minute ride on Prague's so-called Historic Tram 91 (historická tramvaj 91) makes for an unusual way of seeing the city centre. The wooden-framed vintage tramcar runs in a circle from the old Prague Exhibition Grounds (Výstaviště) in Holešovice (Prague 7) (see no. 35) and down along the lefthand bank of the Vltava into Lesser Quarter (Malá Strana) in Prague 1. After travelling through Lesser Quarter Square (Malostranské náměstí) the tram crosses the river by means of the Legions' Bridge (most Legií). Passing the National Theatre (Národní divadlo) on Národní třída it then skirts New Town (Nové Město) to the south before trundling northwards through Wenceslas Square (Václavské náměstí), around the eastern edge of Old Town (Staré Město), and back up to Výstaviště via Republic Square (náměstí Republiky) and the Štefánik Bridge (Štefánikův most).

By contrast, Tram 22 is a standard service that offers a much longer but no less fascinating ride across almost the full width of the city. It starts on Průmyslová in the eastern suburb of Hostivař (Prague 15) and traverses Prague 10 and Prague 2 (Nové Město) by way of Charles Square (Karlovo náměstí). Like the Historic Tram, it too crosses Legions' Bridge (most Legií), except on this occasion in the opposite direction, *from* Národní třída *into* Lesser Quarter (Malá Strana). After passing through Lesser Quarter Square (Malostranské náměstí) the tram winds its way up Chotkova to Prague Castle (Pražský hrad), then ascends even further to the Strahov Monastery (Strahovský klášter) in Hradčany (see no. 11). From here a fast downhill stretch takes the tram past the Břevnov Monastery (Břevnovský klášter) in Prague 6 (see no. 25) out towards its eventual terminus at the historic White Mountain (Bílá hora) (see no. 26).

For the full history of Prague's public transport system, from horse-drawn trams to trolleybuses and the Prague Metro, a visit to the Prague Public Transport Museum (Muzeum městské hromadné dopravy v Praze) at Patočkova 4 in Střešovice (Prague 6) is highly recommended. The museum is suitably located in an old tram depot built in 1909, which provides the perfect backdrop for its collection of historic vehicles, photographs, models and other ephemera. It is from a hall on one side of the museum that the Historic Tram 91 is dispatched during the summer months.

The idea of a public transport museum in Prague was first mooted in 1929, when a vintage 1886 horse-drawn tram was set aside for preservation. However, the collection really came about during the early 1960s in connection with a massive renewal of rolling stock. Many historic vehicles were thus saved and the collection today includes 41 rail vehicles *(tramvaje)*, three trolleybuses *(trolejbusy)* and five buses *(autobusy)*.

Historic Tram 91 (historická tramvaj 91) prepares to depart from U Výstaviště

Although horse-drawn omnibuses had operated in Prague since 1829 it was the introduction of horse-drawn trams in 1875 that marked the arrival of regular public transport in the city. In 1891 the Czech inventor and electrical engineer František Křižík (1847–1941), a renowned pioneer of electric transport, unveiled the country's first electric tramway at Letná (see no. 10). Křižík followed this on 19th March 1896 with the opening of the city's first *public* tramway, the Praha-Libeň-Vysočany line. In 1897 the Mayor of Košíře opened the Smíchov-Košíře tramway and shortly afterwards the Královské Vinohrady line went into business. On 1st September the Electric Company of the Royal Capital City of Prague was established, quickly taking over most of the previously privately owned tramways, as well as the entire horse tram network. In 1905 the new company even built a tramway across the Charles Bridge (Karlův most) with specially concealed electrical contacts to preserve the bridge's ancient appearance! By 1907 the tram network exceeded 50 kilometres and boasted 255 motorised cars and 102 trailers.

Despite the dislocation of the First World War, when many tram lines were reserved for freight and funeral cars, the First Czechoslovak Republic witnessed a golden age for Prague's trams, with the network increasing to 100 kilometres in length by 1927, along which 647 motorised cars and 748 trailers ran. From 1922 onwards, as adjacent municipalities were incorporated into Prague, a bus network was developed to service the outskirts of the city and in 1936 a trolleybus service was inaugurated too. In 1938 some 282 million journeys were made on the tram system alone.

With the nationalisation of the energy industry in 1946, the old

Electric Company was broken up and its Transport Unit transformed into today's Prague Public Transit Company. By 1965 Prague had 28 tramlines used by a fleet of 973 motorised cars, including a new, larger-sized 4-axle model, and 542 trailers. At the same time a radical change in public transport policy saw the decision to transfer the city centre's tram system underground, to increase bus services using cheap Soviet oil, and to scrap trolleybus services. By 1971 a fleet of 571 buses was servicing Prague's burgeoning suburban residential developments as well as further municipalities incorporated in 1968 and 1974.

Meanwhile, work had begun in 1967 on the excavation of the new underground railway, the first part of which (Line C) opened in 1974, with Lines A and B following in 1978 and 1985 respectively. This scaled-down version of Moscow's sprawling Metro now runs for 50 kilometres and includes 51 stations but pales in comparison next to the 136 kilometres still covered by Prague's venerable old tram system.

There are three other ways of touring Prague by historic means, namely horse-drawn carriage, vintage car and riverboat. Carriage and car rides begin near the clock tower on Old Town Square (Staroměstské náměstí) during the tourist season and boats set sail throughout the year from the embankment below Palackého náměstí, on the right bank of the Vltava. Although the Prague Steamship Company (Pražská paroplavební společnost) no longer enjoys the monopoly on river traffic it had in 1865, its boats can still be seen taking tourists on sightseeing cruises, despite the river having been dammed in 1937 and 1943, rendering it effectively useless for freight and passenger traffic.

Other places of interest nearby: 33, 34, 35

37. The Horses of Modern Troy

Prague 7 (Troja), the Troja Château (zámek Troja) and Prague Zoo (Zoo Praha) on U Trojského zámku
Metro C to Nádraží Holešovice then Bus 112

During the second half of the 17th century, following the Thirty Years War (1618–48) in which Habsburg forces eventually crushed those of the Protestant nobility, Catholic aristocrats were rewarded with large tracts of land on which to erect palaces (see nos. 6 & 23). One such recipient was Count Václav Vojtěch Baltazar of Šternberk, a Czech nobleman eager to prove his allegiance to the Habsburg throne. The result was the Troja Château (zámek Troja), a huge Italianate Baroque villa built in 1679–1705 and surrounded by formal French gardens; it was designed by French architect Jean-Baptiste Mathey and worked on by Italian craftsmen. The château's Main Hall is decorated with a riot of *trompe l'oeil* murals depicting the Habsburgs vanquishing the Turks, whilst outside there is a double staircase adorned with sculptures of the Olympian gods battling the Titans. The name 'Troja' has been used since the end of the 17th century, when the nearby ruins of an old summerhouse, built by Alžběta of Lobkovice, reminded visitors of the ruins of ancient Troy, as described by classical writers.

On the terraced hillside behind the château can be found the St. Clara Vineyard, one of the few remaining vineyards in Prague. Count Šternberk's former wine cellar is located nearby at U Trojského zámku 35, a natural cave sixteen metres below the ground that today provides the atmospheric location for the Svatá Klára Restaurant. Beyond the vineyard lie the Prague Botanical Gardens (Botanická zahrada Praha) founded in 1968 to augment the University's increasingly cramped garden at Na Slupi in New Town (see no. 72).

To the west of the château's gardens lies Prague Zoo (Zoo Praha), established in 1926–31 and considered one of the most beautiful in Europe. The zoo is world renowned for its breeding programme of threatened species, including the Siberian Tiger, Clouded Leopard, Komodo Dragon, and Cuban Ground Iguana; in 1942 the first polar bear cub bred in captivity was born here.

The zoo's greatest success, however, has been the breeding of more than 200 Przewalski's Horses (kůň Převalského), known also as the Asiatic or Mongolian Wild Horse (the first foal was born in Prague in 1928 giving the city the world's longest breeding line). Pronounced '(p)she-

A rare Przewalski's Horse at Prague Zoo (Zoo Praha)

vahl-skee' the horse is named after General Nikolai Przhevalsky (1839–88), an explorer and naturalist employed by the Russian Tsar. In 1881, after hearing rumours of the existence of a stocky wild horse with erect mane and a black stripe on its back, the general was sent to Central Asia to look for it. Later on, in 1889–91, Russian and German hunters returned with some foals and by 1900 some fifty-four foals had been captured for aristocratic and zoo collections in Europe (it is from twelve of these original animals that today's global population of c. 1980 is descended).

Unfortunately, during the 20th century the native population of the horse declined rapidly due to hunting by Kazakh and Kyrgyz hunters, lack of water, harsh winters, and grazing competition from domestic goats and sheep. The last wild herd was seen in Mongolia in 1967, with a final solitary horse recorded there in 1969. So it was in 1977 that the Foundation for the Preservation and Protection of the Przewalski Horse (FPPPH) was established in the Netherlands, and by 1992 two small herds had been re-introduced back into Mongolia; other herds were established in West China (Xinjiang Province), Uzbekistan, Kazakhstan, Hungary, Ukraine, and even on the hills of North Wales. It is thought that about 300 horses are now roaming freely in reserves in Mongolia and West China alone. Instrumental in this success was a programme of exchange to prevent inbreeding, based on the international studbook held by Dr. Evžen Kůs at Prague Zoo: the most detailed in the world it contains the records of 4900 Przewalski's Horses held captive between 1899 and the present day.

38. Along the Paris Boulevard

Prague 1 (Josefov), Pařížská
Metro A to Staroměstská; Tram 17, 18 along eastern riverbank

In the wake of the revolutionary activity for reform that swept Europe in 1848, in which the Jews of Prague had played a significant part, the city's ancient Old Town Jewish Quarter was incorporated into the city proper; it was named Josefov after Habsburg Holy Roman Emperor and King of Bohemia Joseph II (1780–90), who had instigated the first move towards freeing the Jews from their ghetto in 1781 (see no. 40). The walls around the quarter, which had been standing since the 13th century, were torn down and the inhabitants permitted to live anywhere in the city. Before long the wealthy moved out and Prague's poor flooded in, transforming the area into an unhealthy slum. In 1893 the authorities took the decision to clear the area completely, leaving only the Old Jewish Cemetery (Starý židovský hřbitov) and the handful of synagogues seen today (see no. 41).

It was decided to replace Prague's lost Jewish Quarter with much-needed housing, as part of an urban building project known as the Prague Renewal. To achieve this an entirely new thoroughfare was carved out, running northwards from Old Town Square (Staroměstské náměstí) and cutting Josefov practically in two. The broad street was named Pařížská třída (Paris Boulevard) by Prague's city planners, who were impressed by similar large-scale rebuilding projects in Paris (plans to continue the boulevard south of Old Town Square to Wenceslas Square (Václavské náměstí) came to nought).

Throughout the late 1890s and early 1900s new housing blocks were thrown up along Pařížská, as well as in the smaller surrounding streets, such as Široká, Maiselova and Břehová. Although it is often maintained that the style chosen for these buildings was Art Nouveau – the so-called *Le Style Moderne* pioneered in the city after whom Pařížská was named – this is not generally the case (see no. 63). Whilst Art Nouveau elements will be found here, usually in combination with Historicist Neo-Gothic, Neo-Renaissance and Neo-Baroque façades, the prevailing style is Eclecticism, popular in most cities of the Habsburg Empire during the late 19th century. As its name suggests, Eclecticism involves a combination of elements from all the major European architectural styles used on the same façade. With such a vast pattern book to draw from, it is thus quite normal to find Gothic oriels, Renaissance arcades

An Art Nouveau façade on Pařížská

and Baroque domes intermingled on the same frontage; indeed, some of the buildings on and around Pařížská are veritable textbooks of bygone architectural styles.

Although many commentators have criticised Eclecticism for being a stale and backwards-looking style, it had the advantage that no two buildings ever seemed the same. In order to expedite the building boom of the late 19th century, apartment blocks in cities such as Prague, Vienna and Budapest had to be constructed quickly, being in effect little more than huge brick-built boxes disguised cleverly with ornately plastered façades. Expensive carved stone was rarely used, other than for door lintels and stairs, whereas the scope for cheap plasterwork was almost limitless – and Eclecticism provided endless inspiration. For the unitiated visitor walking along Pařížská today, the truth about the construction of the boulevard's grand buildings is only revealed where the plaster has come away through neglect, bright red bricks revealing themselves once more!

Although the area along the banks of the Vltava was not included in the late 19th century renewal of Josefov, the Paris Boulevard was laid right to the water's edge, where it crosses to the opposite bank by means of the Čech Bridge (Čechův most). Named after the Czech poet and writer Svatopluk Čech, the bridge is superlative amongst Prague's ten or so river crossings in that it is both the shortest (169 metres) and the only one to be undertaken in the Art Nouveau style. It was designed by Jan Koula and Jiří Soukup and was constructed in 1905–08 using an arching steel framework supported on two stone piers; its original surface was made of Australian hardwood. At either end there are pairs of columns supporting bronze Goddesses of Victory created by the sculptor Antonín Popp, at the base of which are booths once occupied by toll collectors. The piers supporting the bridge are sculpted like the prow of a ship, their figureheads formed by female torchbearers upstream and dragons downstream, guarding the city's crest. The Austrian Emperor and King of Bohemia, Francis Joseph I (1848–1916) was present at the official ceremony to lay the bridge's keystone in 1907.

Other places of interest nearby: 31, 40, 41

39. A Quiet Gothic Corner

Prague 1 (Staré Město), the Convent of St. Agnes of Bohemia (klášter
sv. Anežky České) at U Milosrdných 17
Metro B to náměstí Republiky then Tram 5, 8, 14

A quiet corner of the Convent of St. Agnes of Bohemia (klášter sv. Anežky České)

St. Agnes of Bohemia (sv. Anežka Česká) (1211–82) is a patron saint of the Czech Republic and was canonised by Pope John Paul II shortly before the Velvet Revolution in 1989. Despite being the daughter of the Přemyslid Duke Otakar I (1197–1230), first King of Bohemia, Agnes did not wish to become the wife of a European monarch. Instead she became a nun, accepting the rule of St. Claire of Assisi (1194–1253), one of the first followers of St. Francis of Assisi (1182–1226) and founder of the Order of Poor Claires, the female branch of the Franciscan Order (see no. 45). In 1231, together with her brother King Wenceslaus (Václav) I (1230–53), Agnes founded a convent of Claire nuns in Old Town (Staré Město) and appointed herself abbess. In the convent grounds there was also established a Hospital of St. Francis run by lay brothers (see no. 49).

Despite their convent being converted into an armoury and mint by the Hussites during the Hussite Wars (1420–36), the Poor Claires returned to the convent in 1626, only to see the building damaged during the great fire of 1689. Despite being closed down in 1782 by order of Habsburg Holy Roman Emperor and King of Bohemia Joseph II (1780–90), being converted into a poor house and workshops, and only narrowly avoiding demolition, St. Agnes's convent is still standing today, tucked away off the busy tourist routes at U Milosrdných 17, in the northern reaches of Old Town.

Now called the Convent of St. Agnes of Bohemia (klášter sv. Anežky

České) it was the first Gothic building to be constructed in Prague, the style having arrived from France in 1230. The complex still retains its plain Gothic atmosphere, thanks in part to an authentic restoration following extensive flood damage in 2003; the cloister, Lady Chapel, Church of St. Francis, and Church of the Holy Saviour, now stripped of later additions, provide a wonderful contrast to Prague's cluttered Baroque churches. The Convent also provides the perfect backdrop for the National Gallery of Prague's Collection of Medieval Art in Bohemia and Central Europe from the period 1200–1550; included are paintings in the so-called 'Beautiful Style' from the reign of Přemyslid King Wenceslaus (Václav) II (1278–1305). After leaving the Convent it is worth exploring the surrounding alleyways, especially Řásnovka and Haštalská, which are equally atmospheric.

Prague has many extant Gothic structures, including several that are justifiably well-known. These include the Basilica of St. George (see no. 18), the twin-towered Cathedral of the Virgin Mary before Týn (chrám Panny Marie před Týnem) on Old Town Square (Staroměstské náměstí), with its Gothic side portal and arcaded school next door, and several churches re-worked in the Baroque period (e.g. St. James's and St. Thomas's (see nos. 44 & 50); there are also fine Burgher houses (e.g. the House at the Stone Bell (see no. 43)), and numerous towers (e.g. the Old Town and Lesser Quarter Towers on Charles Bridge (see no. 2), the Powder Gate (Prašná brána) (see no. 9), and the New Town Hall (see no. 66)). However, for each of these categories there are examples that are less well-known, including the haunted Church of St. Anne (see no. 52), the Laundry Church of St. John (see no. 3), the fortress-like St. Giles (kostel sv. Jiljí) on Husova, and the charming St. Vojtěch (kostel sv. Vojtěcha) on Vojtěšská; there are also little-known Gothic houses, concealed as the ground level was raised to avoid flooding, including the Maltese Knight's tavern (see no. 5) and the House of the Lords of Kunštát and Poděbrady (see no. 51); and there are easily missed Gothic towers including the Judith and Henry Towers (see no. 2). One of the last Gothic buildings constructed in Prague was the Vladislav Hall (Vladislavský sál) in the Old Royal Palace (Starý královský palác) at Prague Castle (Pražský hrad). Completed in 1502 and notable for being the largest Gothic vaulted space in Central Europe, the hall is where the first Bohemian kings were elected, its Riders' Steps enabling knights to enter without dismounting. The 5-metre high rectangular windows of 1493 mark the very first appearance of the Renaissance style in Bohemia (see no. 21).

40. The Oldest Working Synagogue in Europe

Prague 1 (Josefov), the Old-New Synagogue (Staronová synagóga) at Červená 2
Metro A to Staroměstská; Tram 17, 18 along eastern riverbank

"In us all it still lives – the dark corners, the secret alleys, shuttered windows, squalid courtyards, rowdy pubs, sinister inns...the unhealthy old Jewish Town within us is far more real than the hygienic town around us" (Franz Kafka).

Prague's earliest Jewish community is recorded on the left bank of the Vltava during the 10th century. In 1096, during the First German Crusade, Prague witnessed its first pogrom – called by some historians the 'First Holocaust' – followed by another in 1142, which prompted the Jews to relocate to a new settlement around what is now Pařížká on the east bank. The reigning Přemyslid rulers of Bohemia tolerated the Jews because of their valuable commercial acumen and allowed them to erect a protective wall around their settlement. Despite this the Pope decreed in the 13th century that Jews should wear distinctive clothing and be segregated from Christians. Any further expansion of their settlement was forbidden and their walls were henceforth to be gated giving the impression of a ghetto.

With the end of the Přemyslid dynasty in the early 14th century and the accession of the Catholic Luxembourg and Habsburg dynasties, German immigration flourished, the new arrivals dividing Prague into three autonomous areas: the castle district (Hradčany), Lesser Quarter (Malá Strana) and Old Town (Staré Město). Orthodox Jews trading in Lesser Quarter were relocated to the ghetto, where they soon established their own synagogues and burial ground. During the Hussite Wars (1420–36) the Jews sided with the Hussites against the German Catholics as a result of which their persecution continued.

The Habsburgs had a love-hate relationship with the Jews based on expediency, resulting in the community being banished temporarily in 1543–45, 1557 and 1745–48. Despite this the Jews continued to play an important part in Prague's culture and economy and in 1781 Habsburg Holy Roman Emperor and King of Bohemia Joseph II (1780–90) gave them their first real rights with his Edict of Tolerance, allowing them to live just outside the ghetto, although insisting they agreed to being 'Germanised'.

tweezers stand for a doctor, a crown for a scholar, scissors for a tailor and a mortar for an apothecary. Incidentally, the black headstones are the oldest, cut in the 15th century from sandstone, whilst the white ones, of marble, date from the 16th and 17th centuries. Today, the cemetery, together with its Former Ceremonial Hall (bývalá Obřadní síň) erected in 1908 and the nearby Baroque Klausen Synagogue (Klausova synagóga), forms the centrepiece of Prague's Jewish Museum (Židovské muzeum).

Gravestones in Josefov's Old Jewish Cemetery (Starý židovský hřbitov)

It is possible, however, to escape the tourists and experience more intimately Prague's Jewish past by visiting its relatively unknown suburban cemeteries. Now in various states of abandonment, having been vandalised and encroached on by building developments after the Second World War, their headstones are inscribed variously in Hebrew, German and Czech. Typical are the remains of the Old Jewish Cemetery at Žižkov (Prague 3) in Mahler Park (Mahlerovy sady) on Fibichova. Founded originally in 1679–80 as a plague cemetery it was later chosen as Prague's main Jewish burial ground following the closure of the Old Jewish Cemetery in Josefov in 1787. Eventually, pressure from the burgeoning suburbs of Žižkov and Vinohrady saw the cemetery closed in 1891 and replaced with Žižkov's New Jewish Cemetery (Nový židovský hřbitov) (see no. 57). Despite there being an estimated 37 800 bodies still in the ground at the old Žižkov cemetery, including respected rabbis and important scholars, physicians, artists and noblemen, only relatively few headstones are visible. The reason for this is that post-war development of the area under the Communists went entirely unchecked, reducing the once important cemetery from 3.3 hectares to a mere 0.5 hectares. When the Mahler Park was established many of the headstones were buried with full rites but unfortunately with the erection of the 216 metre-high Žižkov television transmitter in 1989, many of them were dug up again and destroyed and the cemetery's ceremonial hall sold off. It remains something of a scandal that this was ever allowed to happen.

Rather more complete is the Old Jewish Cemetery of Smíchov (Prague 5), on a hilltop off U Starého židovského hřbitova (1788–1921), as well as Smíchov's New Jewish Cemetery on Peroutkova (1903–73). Notable tombs at the latter include that of the Porges von Portheim family, founders of the Smíchov textile industry. Most famously the Smíchov Jewish community was home to Albert Einstein in 1910–11, when he taught theoretical physics in the city (a wall plaque marks his former house at Lesnická 7).

Finally, there is the lost Old Jewish Cemetery of Libeň and Karlín (Prague 8), at the eastern end of the Libeňský Bridge (Libeňský most) (16th century–1892), whose function was taken over by the still atmospheric New Jewish Cemetery of Libeň and Ďáblice (1892–1975) further north on Na Malém klínu.

Other places of interest nearby: 38, 40, 42

42. In Franz Jackdaw Square

Prague 1 (Staré Město), Franz Kafka's birthplace at náměstí Franze
Kafky 5
Metro A to Staroměstská; Tram 17, 18 along eastern riverbank

"It was late in the evening when K. arrived. The village was deep in snow. The Castle hill was hidden, veiled in mist and darkness, nor was there even a glimmer of light to show that a castle was there. On the wooden bridge leading from the main road to the village, K. stood for a long time gazing into the illusory emptiness above him".

Few writers have imprinted so strong a personality on a city without actually mentioning it by name than Franz Kafka (1883–1924). To this day, Prague remains haunted by the spirit of characters such as Gregor Samsa and Joseph K., and the darkly bizarre plotlines played out in novels such as *Die Verwandlung (Metamorphosis)* (1915), *Der Prozeß (The Trial)* (1925) and *Das Schloß (The Castle)* (1926); a large part of the Franz Kafka Museum, opened in 2005 at Cihelná 2b in Lesser Quarter (Malá Strana), is devoted to the way in which Kafka (meaning 'jackdaw' in Czech) gives his stories such a strong sense of place and peculiar sense of reality without using real placenames.

Kafka's father was a kosher butcher in Southern Bohemia, who gravitated towards the German-speaking upper classes upon arriving in Prague, a necessity for advancement in the city's Jewish society. Kafka himself was born in Prague's Old Town (Staré Město), on July 3rd 1883. Although the actual tenement block at what is now náměstí Franze Kafky 5 was demolished in 1897, its doorway was retained and in 1902 incorporated into the building seen here today. At the corner is a bust of Kafka and inside is a small but fascinating Kafka exhibition (Expozice Franze Kafky).

As a young boy Kafka lived with his family in the black and white *sgraffitoed* House at the Minute (Dům U minuty) on the southwest corner of the nearby Old Town Hall (Staroměstská radnice); still visible is the balcony to which young Franz was sometimes banished by his father. From 1887 to 1893 Kafka attended the German grammar school *(Volksschule)* a couple of roads away on Masná and in 1901 he took his Matura exam at the German Gymnasium on the third floor of the Baroque Golz-Kinsky Palace (palác Golz-Kinských), back on the eastern side of Old Town Square; number 12 in the same building was once his father's fancy goods store, now home to the Franz Kafka Bookshop.

A bust marks Franz Kafka's birthplace at náměstí Franze Kafky 5

Whilst studying for a law degree at the Charles University (Univerzita Karlova) Kafka became acquainted with many of the future leaders of Prague's Jewish-German cultural scene, and together they formed the so-called Prague Circle. After graduating in 1906 he worked briefly, and unhappily, for the Italian insurance company Assicurazioni Generali, escaping in 1908 to a more rewarding job at the Workers' Accident Insurance Institute (Dělnická úrazová pojišt'ovna). It is a little-known fact that whilst here Kafka is credited with the invention of the first civilian hard hat, receiving a medal in 1912 because of its effect in reducing fatalities in Bohemian steel mills. Meanwhile, the Kafka family moved from the Three Kings' House (dům U Tří králů) at Celetná 3 to Pařížská 36, where Kafka wrote the short story *Das Urteil (The Judgement)* (1912) in just eight hours. They then moved to the Oppelthaus on the corner of Old Town Square with Pařížská, where Kafka wrote his disturbing *Metamorphosis*.

Between 1915 and 1917 Kafka lived in lodgings at Dlouhá 16 (where he commenced work on *The Trial*), then in his sister's house at Golden Lane 22 (Zlatá ulička) in Prague Castle (Pražský hrad), and in the Schönborn Palace (Schönbornský palác) at Tržiště 15 in Lesser Quarter, now the American Embassy; ill health would eventually force him back to the family home. In 1920 he began a relationship with the radical journalist Milena Jesenská, although the real love of his life was Dora Diamant, with whom he considered settling down. Unfortunately, Kafka died from tuberculosis-induced starvation on June 3rd, 1924, not helped by a lifetime of depression and anxiety, and was buried in the New Jewish Cemetery at Žižkov (see no. 57). Thankfully, Kafka's best friend Max Brod disobeyed the author's wishes to have his papers burned and much of his work was published posthumously, although it would be banned during the Nazi period.

Always an outsider on account of his Jewish ancestry and use of German in a time of fervent Czech nationalism, Kafka captured perfectly the sense of alienation and persecution felt by so many during the early 20th century: so perfectly perhaps that the authorities have only in the last few years acknowledged him with a statue, outside the Spanish

Synagogue on Vězeňská. It is a typically surreal work, by Jaroslav Rona, depicting a Golem-like headless figure carrying a diminutive Kafka on its shoulders.

Numerous other Czech writers have been deeply inspired by Prague, including Rainer Maria Rilke, Milan Kundera, former President Václav Havel, and Jaroslav Hašek, whose unfinished novel *The Good Soldier Švejk* (*Osudy dobrého vojáka Švejka*) (1923) provides a comic ripost to Kafka's work. Another, sometimes-overlooked writer is Gustav Meyrink (1868–1932), born the illegitimate son of an actress in Vienna. His mother moved to Prague in 1883, where he completed his schooling and remained for the next 23 years. Meyrink's early short stories combine fantasy and humour, together with satire over what he saw as the complacency of the *bourgeoisie*. However, in 1891 after suffering a nervous breakdown he contemplated suicide, only to be deterred by an occultist leaflet placed fortuitously under his door. As a result, his later works were shaped by a growing interest in the occult. He also experimented with hallucinogenic drugs, practised yoga, studied Eastern philosophy and became a Buddhist. Meyrink's first and best-known novel was *Der Golem* (*The Golem*) published in 1915, for which Prague's old Jewish Ghetto provided the background. This was followed by *Das grüne Gesicht* (*The Green Face*) in 1916, *Walpurgisnacht* in 1917, and *Der Weiße Dominikaner* (*The White Dominican*) in 1921. His final novel, *Der Engel vom westlichen Fenster* (*The Angel of the West Window*) was published in 1927 and is built around the colourful lives of the 16th century alchemists, John Dee and Edmund Kelley (see no. 20). Between them Kafka and Meyrink created a mysterious and 'other worldly' image of Prague in which everything differs from its outward appearance. This multi-layered approach would play a pivotal role in early 20th century German literature and cinema.)

Other places of interest nearby: 43, 47

43. The House at the Stone Bell

Prague 1 (Staré Město), the House at the Stone Bell (dům U Kamenného zvonu) at Staroměstské náměstí 13
Metro A to Staroměstská; Tram 17, 18 along eastern riverbank

Jutting out from the southern side of the Golz-Kinský Palace (palác Golz-Kinských), on the east side of Old Town Square (Staroměstské náměstí), stands a building whose true identity was only 're-discovered' during routine renovation work in the 1960s. Known as the House at the Stone Bell this Gothic burgher house was erected in the early 14th century but then 'lost' in 1685 beneath a great Baroque reconstruction, a fate suffered more commonly by Gothic churches. To add insult to injury, the whole lot was encased in a neo-Baroque plaster shell in 1899.

What was revealed once the layers were carefully peeled away was a house façade without match east of the Rhine. The dominant feature of the building is its 3-storey tower with pointed windows on the first and second floors between which are niches for statues. Unfortunately, during the Baroque makeover, the fine sandstone ashlar walls were shorn of their original Gothic detailing, the 12 000 or so fragments of window tracery, door frames, vaulting and other decorative elements being unceremoniously dumped in the building's cellars. The fortuitous discovery of these remains permitted a painstaking restoration of the building to be made between 1980 and 1987, using a combination of original fragments and newly cut pieces. The stone bell that gives the house its name was also re-hung on the street corner, local legend claiming that it fell from the tower of the nearby Cathedral of the Virgin Mary before Týn (chrám Panny Marie před Týnem).

Inside the building, original Gothic paintings were uncovered on the walls and the timbered ceilings, and these have also been carefully reconstructed. Historians are now of the opinion that the building dates back to the late 13th century and that in the early 14th century it was rebuilt as a Gothic palace for Queen Eliška Přemyslovna. It was inside these very walls that her son, Crown Prince Charles of Luxembourg, later Holy Roman Emperor Charles IV (King Charles I of Bohemia) (1346–78), is thought to have stayed after coming to Bohemia in 1333. At that time Prague Castle (Pražský hrad) had been damaged by fire and so the prince, who was caretaker ruler while his father John of Luxembourg (1310–46) was away, had to find lodgings in the town.

The House at the Stone Bell (dům U Kamenného zvonu) in a corner of Old Town Square (Staroměstské náměstí)

During the Baroque reconstruction of the palace in 1685 a beautiful courtyard was created, between the side wings beyond the tower, which is still extant today. Since being restored the House at the Stone Bell has been used by the Prague City Gallery for exhibitions – especially retrospectives of Czech artists – as well as concerts.

Other places of interest nearby: 42, 44, 47

44. The Minorites and the Mummified Hand

Prague 1 (Staré Město), the Church of St. James (kostel sv. Jakuba) on the corner of Malá Štupartská and Jakubská
Metro B to Náměstí Republiky; Tram 14 from Václavské náměstí

The Gothic Church of St. James, lying to the east of Old Town Square (Staroměstské náměstí), was built by the Order of Friars Minor for their monastery founded here in 1232; King John of Luxembourg (1310–1346) and Queen Eliška Přemyslovna held their wedding feast here in 1311. Known also as the Minorites, or more commonly the Franciscans, the friars were a male Mendicant (or Begging) Order following in the footsteps of St. Francis of Assisi (1182–1226). Their official Latin name is the *Ordo Fratrum Minorum* – literally Order of Little Brothers – although Francis himself referred to them as *Fratricelli*, meaning Little Brothers (Franciscan brothers are informally called Grey Friars).

With its 30 metre-high presbytery (1291–1308) and impressive triple nave (added in the late 14th century) the Church of St. James remains the city's second longest church after the Cathedral of St. Vitus (chrám sv. Víta). During the great fire of 1689 the church was gutted, as a result of which its façade, windows, doorways and interior were completely remodelled in the prevailing Baroque style of the late 17th century. This accounts for its exuberantly stuccoed entrance portals, barrel-vaulted ceiling, magnificent organ and no less than 20 or so side chapels, decorated by master painters such as Petr Brandl and Václav Vavřinec Reiner. Also noteworthy is the pyramidal tomb of Bohemian Chancellor Count Jan Wenceslaus Vratislav of Mitrovice, created by Ferdinand Maximilian Brokoff in 1714–16; its decoration is considered by many to be the finest example of Czech Baroque sculpture. A ghoulish legend relates how muffled sounds were heard emanating from the tomb *after* the count had been interred. Several years later, when the tomb was opened for another family member to be buried, it was discovered that the count had been buried alive, his face permanently contorted from fruitless attempts to raise the stone lid imprisoning him.

Another gruesome tale associated with the church concerns the mummified human forearm hanging from a chain on the righthand side as one enters the building. It is said to have belonged to a thief who in 1400 attempted to steal pearls from a statue of the *Pieta* (the Virgin Mary cradling the dead body of Christ) in a niche on the High

Altar. The Virgin grasped the man's arm and refused to let go despite prayers from the friars and the congregation. Eventually there was no choice but to summon the executioner and to amputate the arm, which was later displayed in the church as a warning.

Mummified remains also exist in the crypt beneath the Church of the Virgin Mary Victorious (kostel Panny Marie Vítězné) in Lesser Quarter (Malá Strana) (see no. 7). They are the bodies of White Friars, that is Catholic monks of the Carmelite order, interred here during the 17th and 18th centuries and have been preserved by the dry environment and circulating air (the crypt can be visited by request only).

A Baroque portal leads into the Church of St. James (kostel sv. Jakuba) on Jakubská

A curious Baroque church custom was the clothing of saintly skeletons as objects of veneration. An example is the skeleton of St. Boniface displayed in a glass sarcophagus in the nave of the Church of St. Thomas (kostel sv. Tomáše), at Josefská 8 in Lesser Quarter. His skeletal hand clutches a flaming heart, symbol of the Order of Augustinian Hermits for whom the church was originally built. St. Boniface (c.672–c.754) was an Anglo-Saxon missionary sent from England to Germany in order to spread Christianity and was martyred in Frisia. In accordance with Catholic tradition his corpse was dismembered and various parts sent as relics to churches across Europe, including Louvain, Mechlin, Bruges, Fulda and Erfurt. The rich burghers of Lesser Quarter purchased the bones for the Church of St. Thomas when they financed a Baroque remodelling of the original Gothic church following a fire in 1723. Further Baroque dressed skeletons can be found in the Loreto Chapel in Hradčany (see no. 13).

Other places of interest nearby: 43, 45, 46

45. The Pre-Revolutionary Canteen

Prague 1 (Nové Město), the U Rozvařilů canteen at Na Poříčí 26
Metro B to Náměstí Republiky; Tram 24 from Václavské náměstí

With the Velvet Revolution and the collapse of Communism in 1989, Prague was quick to sweep away most of the trappings of the Communist state, restoring the city's hitherto dilapidated public buildings to their former glory and adapting Communist-built edifices to different usages (see nos. 4, 60 & 64). However, for a taste (quite literally!) of the old days there still remain a couple of traditional pre-revolutionary workers' canteens carrying on their business as if it were still the 1950s. Now an endangered species they are important examples of living social history.

The U Rozvařilů at Na Poříčí 26 is a case in point named after a medieval house and brewery that stood here until 1937. It is a perfect example of what is known in Czech as an *automat*, that is a fast food canteen serving cheap traditional Czech standards by the plateful, together with beer. Favourites include hearty onion and potato soups *(polévka)*, goulash *(guláš)*, dumplings *(knedlíky)*, fried cheese *(smažený*

The U Rozvařilů canteen on Na Poříčí offers pre-Revolutionary dishes

sýr), and open-faced sandwiches of meat, smoked fish or cream cheese *(chlebíčky)*. Customers select their dish at the counter, where the menu and service is defiantly Czech, pay the cashier and then move to a high table and sit on a stool. This is something of a concession to modern times as food was originally eaten whilst standing. The white-aproned staff and the chrome and mirrored backdrop complete the experience.

Another canteen offering pre-revolutionary fare, albeit in rather more decorous surroundings, is U Bakaláře, surprisingly well hidden at Celetná 13 in Old Town. Meaning 'At the Bachelor', it too offers soup and goulash, as well as more substantial favourites, such as roast knuckle of pork, sauerkraut and sliced bread dumplings *(vepřo, knedlo, zelo)*, beef in cream sauce *(svíčková)*, and sweet fruit dumplings *(ovocné knedlíky)*, the latter a meal in themselves! It has traditionally been popular with the students of nearby Charles University (Univerzita Karlova).

A further example of a Communist-style eatery is the Nedělní cukrárna at Vítězné náměstí 3 (Prague 6). Translated as 'Sunday Patisserie' this canteen-cum-general store with its stand-up tables and chrome shelves piled high with confectionery has not changed since Communist times; it is renowned for its cakes and Russian fish salad *(rybí salát)*. Vítězné náměstí itself, once home to a statue of Lenin, leads onto Jugoslávských partyzánů (Avenue of Yugoslav Partisans) at the end of which is the Crowne Plaza Hotel at Koulova 15. Formerly the Hotel International, it is one of the city's last bastions of the Communist art style known as Socialist Realism (see no. 60).

Other places of interest nearby: 44, 46

46. Cubism at the House of the Black Madonna

Prague 1 (Staré Město), the House of the Black Madonna (dům U Černé Matky Boží) at Celetná 34
Metro B to Náměstí Republiky; Tram 14 from Václavské náměstí

The highly influential *avant-garde* artistic style known as Cubism was developed in Paris between 1907 and 1914 by the Spanish artist Pablo Picasso (1881–1973) and the French artist Georges Braque (1882–1963). It should be noted, however, that whilst these painter-sculptors sought inspiration from the likes of Paul Cézanne and Georges-Pierre Seurat, cubist forms had been used much earlier in the sculpture of Africa, Oceania and Alaska.

Cubism in early 20th century Paris saw artists breaking down the natural form of their subject matter into simplified geometric fragments, analyzing them, and then re-assembling them into a new kind of abstract aesthetic space. In contrast to traditional artistic styles, where the perspective of the subject is viewed from a single fixed viewpoint, cubist work portrays the subject from a range of perspectives, depicting multiple views simultaneously. The result is an interwoven surface of flattened yet shifting planes emphasised by the use of a neutral colour palette.

In Prague, the thrilling artistic endeavours of Picasso and Braque, as well as the architectural efforts of the Slovenian-born Jože Plečnik (1872–1957), made a deep impression on a group of radical sculptors

The Cubist House of the Black Madonna (dům U Černé Matky Boží) on Celetná

and architects, who got together in 1911 as the Group of Fine Artists (Skupina výtvarných umělců) (see no. 58). The SVU group was unique in the architectural world in rejecting the methodical logic of impending Modernism and adapting instead the techniques of Cubist painting to architecture. By embracing the Baroque legacy of rippling, rhythmic surfaces the repeated geometrical shapes of Cubist façades merged remarkably well with the city's existing urban fabric. The best known example of Czech Cubist architecture is the House of the Black Madonna (dům U Černé Matky Boží) at Celetná 34 in Old Town (Staré Město), built in 1911–1912 as a department store to a design by Josef Gočár (1880–1945). The architect extended the Cubist technique inside the building, not only to the stairs but also the brass chandeliers to be found in the recently restored Café Grand Orient on the first floor (incidentally, the building is so-called because of the ebony statue displayed outside, which was taken from one of the buildings that stood previously on the site). Like all Czech Cubist architecture, it is the play of light and shadow on the various geometric and prismatic elements of the building that create ever-shifting visual forms, as well as three-dimensional volume not always possible in Cubist painting.

A Cubist apartment block by Otokar Novotný (1880–1959) can be found in Josefov, at the corner of Bílkova and Elišky Krásnohorské, and at Spálená 4 in New Town (Nové Město) there is Emil Králíček (1877–1930) and Matěj Blecha's (1861–1919) aptly-named Diamant building (1912–1913), with its Cubist steps, floor design and light fittings. Meanwhile, far to the north on Ďáblická (Prague 8), there is a largely unrealised Cubist cemetery (Ďáblické hřbitovy), only its entrance pavilions and surrounding wall having been completed in 1913 to a design by Vlastislav Hofman. However, for the purest expression of Czech Cubist architecture one must travel south to the district of Vyšehrad. Here can be found a row of three Cubist houses on the riverbank at Rašínovo nábřeží 6–10, as well as a perfect Cubist apartment block, called House Hodek, erected in 1913–14 at Neklanova 30; both are the work of Cubist architect Josef Chochol (1880–1956). Another Cubist building can be found along the street at number 2, designed by Antonín Belada, whilst just around the corner at Libušina 3 is the stunning Kovařovicova Vila (1912–1913), again by Chochol; even the garden has a Cubist gate and railings set at a jaunty angle.

Until the First World War brought a halt to most artistic endeavours, Czech Cubism manifested itself in other ways too, not only in paintings but also sculpture, furniture and glasswork, samples of which are on display in the National Gallery of Prague's Museum of Cubism within the House of the Black Madonna (the museum shop, Kubista, specialises in original and reproduction Cubist art). Prague can even boast the world's only example of a Cubist street lamp, again the work of Králíček and Blecha, erected in 1912 in the northern corner of Jungmannovo náměstí. The southern side of the square is dominated by the Adria Palace at Národní třída 40, completed in 1925 for an insurance company and representative of the so-called Rondo-Cubist style. Pioneered by the palace's architects Pavel Janák and Josef Zasche, Rondo-Cubism, with its use of circular forms and folk symbols grafted onto a Cubist base, was a deliberate post-war attempt at creating a national style of architecture representative of the First Czechoslovak Republic; another example is Gočár's Bank of the Czechoslovak Legions (1921–1923) at Na Poříčí 24. Sometimes held up as the last gasp of pre-Modernism, Rondo-Cubism proved a dead end and the architects of Prague soon turned to the austere, flat-fronted style of Functionalism (see no. 24).

Other places of interest nearby: 42, 43, 44, 45, 47

47. Prague's Unique Astronomical Clock

Prague 1 (Staré Město), the Prague Astronomical Clock (pražský orloj)
on Staroměstské náměstí
Metro A to Staroměstská; Tram 17, 18 along eastern riverbank

Most of Prague's 8 million annual visitors will at some point or another find themselves standing in front of the medieval astronomical clock on the southern wall of the Old Town Hall (Staroměstská radnice). Pronounced 'prash-skee or-loi' this famous landmark at the foot of a 69.5 metre-high tower can hardly be considered hidden or little-known – but it is certainly unusual.

The oldest part is the mechanical clock and astronomical dial, dating back to 1410 and made by clockmaker Mikuláš of Kadaň and Jan Šindel, the latter a professor of astronomy and mathematics at Charles University (Univerzita Karlova). The clock was only the third of its kind, the first having been constructed in Padua in 1344. Around 1490 the calendar dial below was added and the façade decorated with intricate Gothic sculptures. In 1552 the clock was repaired by Jan Táborský, who wrote erroneously that one Master Hanuš had created the clock. This error was not corrected until the 20th century by which time a tenacious myth had been born. To account for the clock's breakdown local legend recounted how Hanuš sabotaged his work by thrusting his arms into the mechanism, either because he hadn't been paid or else because the town councillors had blinded him in order to prevent him from creating such a beautiful clock for anyone else. The clockmaker died as a result and his timepiece died with him until its eventual repair.

Despite the Old Town Hall being seriously damaged during the Second World War Prague's astronomical clock is today in full working order and huge crowds gather on the hour between 8am and 8pm to watch it chime. Not much in reality actually happens though, other than a skeletal figure of Death on the righthand side turning over an hourglass, a clockwork parade of twelve wooden apostles led by St. Peter walking across the two windows above (added in 1865–66), and a tiny golden cockerel crowing from its perch at the top.

Once the show is over and the audience has dispersed, however, the rest of the clock's iconography, as well as its actual timekeeping elements, can be scrutinised more closely. First of all, three other sculpted figures can be identified at the same level as that of Death, reminding the onlooker that it is a lesson in medieval morality being given each

Prague's unique Astronomical Clock (pražský orloj) on Old Town Square (Staroměstské náměstí)

hour. Standing next to the skeleton is a Turk, a euphemistic symbol for Lust, as well as cruelty and treachery (though really it should be renamed). On the other side of the clock appears Vanity gazing into his mirror, as well as Greed in the form of a miser clutching his moneybag. Each time Death pulls on his rope in order to strike the hour, onlookers should reflect on their own behaviour. Directly below are two further pairs of figures, namely a philosopher and an angel on the left and an astronomer and a chronicler on the right, representing fair rule over the city and all it has achieved. Between them is a beautiful, gold-painted calendarium with twelve medallions, symbolising the months, and twelve smaller ones depicting the signs of the Zodiac; in the centre is the city's coat of arms and around the edge are the various Saints' days. It is the most recent addition to the clock, the original having been painted by Josef Mánes in 1866 and now displayed in the Museum of the City of Prague (Muzeum hlavního města Prahy) (see no. 55).

Above the calendarium is the astronomical clock proper, a confusing mass of dials and symbols quite alien to the untrained eye. It helps to view the clock more as a mechanical astrolabe – a device used in medieval astronomy to represent the position of the Sun and Moon in the sky (in other words a primitive planetarium). The stationary painted background depicts the Earth as a blue circle in the centre, reflecting the old view that it was located at the centre of the Universe. The blue area above is that part of the sky above the horizon, the red/black areas representing the portion below. Thus, during the daytime an armature carrying a flaming Sun sits over the blue part, at dawn and dusk over the red part, and at night over the black. The eastern (lefthand) horizon

tronomia nova, published in 1609 under Emperor Rudolph's patronage, based on the raw observational data he had inherited from Brahe. In this and his *Harmonice Mundi* Kepler laid out his three laws of planetary motion, namely that the planets moved in ellipses rather than circles, that they did not travel at a uniform speed, and that the time they took to orbit increased in proportion to their average distance from the sun. Thus, Kepler translated Nicolaus Copernicus's radical heliocentric view of the heavens into a precise mathematical formula and legitimised the telescopic discoveries of his contemporary Galileo. With the death of Rudolph in 1612 Kepler left Prague to take up a post in Linz and died in Regensburg.

Those interested in modern astronomy might like to visit the Planetarium at Královská obora 233 on the edge of Stromovka Park (Prague 7), its 15 metre-high **Cosmorama** dome and three projectors making it one of the largest planetaria in the world; for a look at the real cosmos visit the Štefánik Observatory (Štefánikova hvězdárna) on Petřín Hill, built in 1927–28, and the Ďáblice Observatory (Hvězdárna Ďáblice) at Pod Hvězdárnou 768 (Prague 8).)

Other places of interest nearby: 42, 47, 49, 50, 51

49. The Secret World of the Knights of the Cross

Prague 1 (Staré Město), the Charles Bridge Museum (Muzeum Karlova Mostu) at Křižovnické náměstí 3
Metro A to Staroměstská; Tram 17, 18 along eastern riverbank

In 1212 the Holy Roman Emperor Frederick II (1194–1250) issued a formal edict, known as a Golden Bull (the latin *bulla* being the monarch's personal seal), bestowing the hereditary crown of Bohemia upon the Přemyslid Duke Otakar I (1197–1230). Despite such an historic accolade, the first King of Bohemia's daughter Agnes (1211–82) chose not to become the wife of a European monarch but instead to become a nun. She accepted the rule of St. Claire of Assisi (1194–1253), an early follower of St. Francis (1182–1226), and in 1231 founded a convent of Poor Claires with herself as abbess at U Milosrdných 17 in Prague's Old Town (Staré Město) (see no. 39).

In the grounds of what is now known as the Convent of St. Agnes of Bohemia (klášter sv. Anežky České) a Hospital of St. Francis was also

founded. The hospital was not only a place where the ill were catered for but also *hospes* (Latin for guests and travellers). Lay brothers ran the hospital, inspired by other hospital orders such as the Knights of St. John. In 1237, at Agnes's own instigation, Pope Gregory IX promoted the brothers to a distinct order – the so-called Order of the Cross with the Red Star; they remain the only holy order of Czech origin and the only male order to be founded by a woman.

In 1252 the Order of the Cross with the Red Star, from whose ranks would later come many of Prague's bishops, built themselves a new church and hospital near the end of what is now

The ruins of the Judith Bridge (Juditin most) lie directly beneath the Charles Bridge Museum (Muzeum Karlova Mostu)

Charles Bridge (Karlův most). At that time the Romanesque predecessor to the bridge, the Judith Bridge (Juditin most), stood here and the brothers acted as gatekeepers with the right to collect tolls (see no. 2). Today, nothing of this older bridge, nor of the Order's original church and hospital, can be seen above ground. However, first impressions can be deceiving and there is a surprise in store for those visiting the Charles Bridge Museum (Muzeum Karlova Mostu) at Křižovnické náměstí 3. In a small room at the far end of the museum there is a metal staircase leading down to where excavated fragments of the Judith Bridge can still be seen. From the late 13th century the ground level hereabouts had been raised artificially in an attempt to avoid repeated flood damage by the Vltava (the bridge itself was destroyed by a flood in 1342). As a result, many 12th century Romanesque structures, including the remains of the Judith Bridge, now lie hidden below today's pavement level (see no. 51). Fragments of the Judith Bridge are also visible on the west bank in the foyer of the Hotel Rezidence Lundborg at U Lužického semináře 3.

A curious grotto is hidden beneath the Church of St. Francis (kostel sv. Františka)

Off the entrance hall to the museum can be found a doorway that leads to the cellar of the adjacent green-domed Baroque Church of St. Francis (kostel sv. Františka), built for the Order in 1679–85 to a design by French architect Jean-Baptiste Mathey. Here lie the walls of the Order's original church, now concealed deep underground, which were re-used as the foundations for the Baroque church directly overhead. Around the time the new church was constructed the remains of the old church were converted into a curious subterranean chapel-cum-grotto, bristling with artificial stalactites and stalagmites made from a mixture of crushed eggshells and dust.

Other places of interest nearby: 42, 47, 48, 50, 51

50. Triumphalism in Stucco and Stone

Prague 1 (Staré Město), the House at the Golden Well (U Zlaté studny)
at Karlova 3
Metro A to Staroměstská; Tram 17, 18 along eastern riverbank

Following the death of the Polish Jagiellon King Louis II (1516–26) at the Battle of Mohács ,against the Ottoman Turks in 1526, the Austrian ruler Ferdinand I inherited the crown of Bohemia through his marriage to the daughter of the previous Bohemian ruler, the Jagiellon King Ladislaus II (1471–1516). Ferdinand's reign (1526–64) heralded almost four centuries of Habsburg rule during which the elected crowns of both Bohemia and Hungary would be converted into Habsburg hereditary possessions.

As ruler of Austria, Bohemia and Hungary – and eventually Holy Roman Emperor – Ferdinand created an absolute and centralised monarchy. However, the reign of this staunchly Roman Catholic monarch was inevitably coloured by the religious and ethnic tensions that had surfaced during the Hussite Wars (1420–36) (see nos. 34 & 54). In 1547, for example, the Bohemian Estates rebelled against Ferdinand after he ordered the Bohemian army against German Protestants. With the help of Spanish forces, Ferdinand regained Prague by force and restricted the privileges of Bohemian towns.

In order to counteract Czech Protestantism and reimpose Catholicism Ferdinand invited Jesuit missionaries to Prague in 1556, as part of the Counter-Reformation. When Ferdinand's namesake and successor Ferdinand II (1619–37) also failed to deliver religious tolerance to the Protestants of Bohemia, the Czech nobility took matters into their own hands, expelling the Jesuits and electing their own king. Such independence was to be shortlived and Catholic imperial forces crushed the Protestants at the Battle of White Mountain (Bílá hora) in 1620 (see no. 26). The ensuing Peace of Westphalia saw Protestantism outlawed in Bohemia and for the next three centuries the province of Bohemia would be 'Germanized' and ruled from Vienna.

The Jesuits returned and for the rest of the 17th century they dominated political and cultural life in Prague, bringing with them the exuberant, Italian-influenced architecture of the Counter-Reformation known as Baroque. Said to derive from the Portuguese word for 'rough pearl', Baroque architecture is a predominantly ecclesiastical style found in Catholic countries during the late 16th and 17th centuries. The dramatic and seemingly unrestrained use of dynamic sweeping curves and overscaled ornament on the outside, and the characteristic riot of stucco, gilt, frescoes and statuary within, represented a tangible manifestation of the triumph of the Catholic faith not only over Protestantism but also over the Ottomans and the plague; its deliberate function was to provoke an emotional response in the onlooker. Whatever one may think of the reasons behind such architecture, the Baroque style is undeniably responsible for much of Prague's iconic status as the 'city of a hundred spires'.

A Baroque relief on the House at the Golden Well (U Zlaté studny) on Karlova

Prague's very first Baroque edifice began life as the Church of St. Trinity at Karmelitská 9, at the foot of Petřín Hill in Lesser Quarter (Malá Strana) (see no. 7). Built in 1611–13 by German Lutherans it was commandeered by the Catholics after the Battle of White Mountain and assigned to the Order of White Friars (see no. 26). The church was then remodelled in the Baroque style, with the addition of its typical 'onion dome' tower, and re-dedicated to the Virgin Mary Victorious (kostel Panny Marie Vítězné) in honour of the battle. Inside can be found a copy of a miraculous painting of the Virgin Mary carried into battle by the Catholic armies.

For each of Prague's many well-known Baroque churches there are less well-known ones equally worthy of exploration. A good example is *another* Church of the Virgin Mary Victorious (kostel Panny Marie Vítězné), alongside Karlovarská below White Mountain itself, in the district of Řepy (Prague 17). The most prominent feature of this almost Mediterranean-looking cloistered church is its high, lantern-topped dome by Italian architect John Santini.

Most visitors will want to see the Cathedral of St. Nicholas (chrám sv. Mikuláše) in Lesser Quarter Square (Malostranské náměstí), Prague's finest Baroque church. It was commissioned by the Jesuits and built between 1703 and 1761 to a design by the renowned father and son team of architects, Kryštof and Kilián Ignáz Dientzenhofer; the latter created the 80 metre-high frescoed cupola whilst his son-in-law, Anselmo Lurago, was responsible for the adjacent late Baroque (Rococo) belfry, in reality a municipal lookout tower, hence the absence of Jesuit statuary, last used by Communist-era secret police! The church's flamboyantly decorated nave contains the largest fresco in Europe, namely Jan Lukáš Kracker's *Life of St. Nicholas* painted in 1761–62, and Mozart played the organ here in 1787.

With such statistics in mind it is easy to overlook the Church of St. Thomas (kostel sv. Tomáše), almost concealed by houses at nearby Josefská 8 (see no. 44). It is a successful example of the conversion of existing structures (in this case a Gothic church finished in 1379, with a later Renaissance portal) into triumphantly Baroque ones. Again the work of Kilián Ignáz Dientzenhofer, a Baroque façade and dome were fused onto the old structure in 1723–31, whilst the interior ceilings were covered with *trompe l'oeil* frescoes by renowned Baroque artist Václav Vavřinec Reiner.

Other lesser known Baroque gems nearby include the tiny Church of St. Joseph (kostel sv. Josefa) on the corner of Josefská and Letenská, designed by Frenchman Jean-Baptiste Mathey, and further south, along Karmelitská, the early Baroque Church of Mary Magdalene, now deconsecrated and home to the Czech Museum of Music (České muzeum hudby).

On the other side of the river, at the eastern end of Charles Bridge (Karlův most), stands the Clementinum (Klementinum), a former Jesuit college and the largest Baroque ensemble in Prague (see no. 48). It is dominated by both the unmistakeable red dome of the Church of St. Francis (kostel sv. Františka) and the ornate façade of the early Baroque Church of St. Saviour (kostel sv. Salvátora), standing at right angles to each other (the latter, completed in 1653, is the most important Jesuit church in Bohemia). Confronted by such imposing structures it is easy for those crossing the bridge from the Lesser Quarter to miss the Eastern Orthodox Church of St Clement (kostel sv. Klimenta), a little further along Karlova, another Dientzenhofer church, built in 1711–15 and with some superb frescoes.

Similarly, the exaggerated façades of the Church of St. Nicholas (kostel sv. Mikuláše) in Old Town Square (Staroměstské náměstí), built by Dientzenhofer junior for the Benedictines in the 1723–35, and the Church of St. Ignatius (kostel sv. Ignáce), erected in Charles Square (Karlovo náměstí) in 1665–70, with its attached Jesuit College (Jezuitská kolej) converted into a hospital after the Jesuits were expelled in 1773, should not deter the explorer from venturing farther afield in search of more obscure Baroque edifices. The unusually-shaped Church of St. John of Nepomuk on the Rock (kostel sv. Jana Nepomuckého na Skalce) a little farther south is a good case in point (see no. 71).

Catholic triumphalism also manifested itself in non-ecclesiastical architecture, most notably in overtly Baroque palaces such as the Kaiserstein Palace (Kaiserštejnský palác) at Lesser Quarter Square (Malostranské náměstí) 23, its four rooftop statues representing the seasons, the frothy Rococo Archbishops' Palace (Arcibiskupský palác) directly in front of Prague Castle (Pražský hrad), and Lurago's Late Baroque (Rococo) Golz-Kinsky Palace (palác Golz-Kinských) in the northeast corner of Old Town Square, used today as an exhibition space by the National Gallery of Prague (Národní galerie v Praze).

More intimate by comparison are those palaces erected by Catholic aristocrats on land that once belonged to Czech nobles, expelled after the Battle of White Mountain. Often adorned with Italianate gardens they give Lesser Quarter its definitively Baroque feel, unchanged since the 18th century (see nos. 6 & 22). The back streets of Old Town contain interesting secular Baroque remains too, in the shape of burgher houses, whose emphatically Baroque façades often conceal earlier Romanesque and Renaissance cores. A fine example is the allegedly haunted House at the Golden Well (U Zlaté studny) at Karlova 3, a Renaissance building with a superb Baroque stuccoed façade added in 1701 and depicting Sts. Roch and Sebastian, protectors against the plague (see no. 52).

Other places of interest nearby: 47, 48, 49, 51, 52

51. Subterranean Prague

Prague 1 (Staré Město), the House of the Lords of Kunštát and
Poděbrady (dům pánů z Kunštátu a Poděbrad) at Řetězová 3 (currently
closed for restoration)
Metro A to Staroměstská; Tram 17, 18 along eastern riverbank

The streets of Prague's Old Town (Staré Město) were laid out during the 12th and early 13th centuries, after the Přemyslid Duke Otakar I (1197–1230) had been made hereditary King of Bohemia by Holy Roman Emperor Frederick II (1194–1250). One of the functions of Old Town was to house the influx of German merchants arriving during this period. The area's main thoroughfare was Charles Street (Karlova ulice), part of the Royal Route (Královská cesta) used by coronation processions. The most important buildings in and around the street were constructed in the prevailing Romanesque style, their solidly built ground floor reception

rooms containing distinctive chunky columns supporting round arches and barrel vaults inspired by Roman architecture. However, during the late 13th century the Vltava flooded many times and the low-lying streets of Old Town, as well as Lesser Quarter (Malá Strana) on the opposite riverbank, were repeatedly submerged. Since the river itself could not be lowered, the city fathers took it upon themselves to *raise* the level of the streets by one storey. In doing so these grand rooms became cellars, above which further storeys were added later, in Gothic, Renaissance and Baroque style, thus creating a unique and hidden underworld that will surprise many visitors today (see no. 5).

The Romanesque House of the Lords of Kunštát and Poděbrady (dům pánů z Kunštátu a Poděbrad) is hidden underground on Řetězová

The most impressive of these sunken Romanesque rooms is undoubtedly the House of the Lords of Kunštát and Poděbrady (dům pánů z Kunštátu a Poděbrad) at Řetězová 3, not properly identified as such until the early 1950s. It was first built as a walled farmstead in c. 1150 and then partially buried as part of the flood-protection scheme. Work on the building's upper storeys continued and between 1406 and 1438 it was the property of the senior regional scribe Boček of Kunštát. Then in 1451 it became the palatial home of the Czech Hussite nobleman George of Poděbrady (Jiří z Poděbrad) (1458–71), from where he set out on his mission to become a non-dynastic 'People's King' in the wake of the Hussite Wars (1420–36) (see no. 34). This he achieved in 1458 following the death of the Habsburg Ladislaus I (1453–57), although by 1465 he faced growing opposition from Czech Catholics. The Pope excommunicated him and in 1468 a crusade was sent out under the leadership of the Hungarian King Matthias Corvinus. George of Poděbrady died in 1471 and was succeeded by the Polish Jagiellon dynasty under Ladislaus II (1471–1516), which ruled somewhat ineffectually until the arrival of the Habsburgs proper under Emperor Ferdinand I (1526–64). George of Poděbrady is remembered today for his attempt to seek a system of collective security by offering a message of peace to all European sovereigns in 1464, an act now seen as a forerunner to the League of Nations. Since 1920 his slogan, "God´s Truth Prevails" (Pravda Páně vítězí), has featured on the Presidential Flag, with the word "God" omitted.

Other subterranean Romanesque rooms in Old Town include those below a row of Renaissance houses at Husova 19–21, now used as an exhibition space by the Czech Museum of Fine Arts (České muzeum výtvarných umění), and several partly-subterranean rooms along Štupartská and Celetná, today occupied by shops. Notable examples also exist across the river in Lesser Quarter (Malá Strana), for example below the house at Lesser Quarter Square (Malostranské náměstí) 7 and in the Knights of Malta Restaurant at Prokopská 10 (see no. 5). On both riverbanks can be found fragments of Prague's first stone bridge, the Romanesque Judith Bridge (Juditin most), these too lying deep below the surface (see nos. 2 & 49).

Prague also has many 14th century Gothic cellars, constructed originally as underground storerooms and wine cellars and reused in recent times as atmospheric restaurants. Examples in Old Town include the Flambée Restaurant at Husova 5, Le Terroir Restaurant at Vejvodova 1, the Restaurace U Rotta at Little Square (Malé náměstí) 3, and the U Černé lišky ('At the Black Fox') Restaurant at Mikulášská 2, best seen at night through a pair of tiny street level windows. In New Town (Nové

Město) the restaurant U Modré růže ('At the Blue Rose') occupies a cellar below a former Gothic tower house at Rytířská 16 (see no. 2).

Two historic subterranean locations that are neither wine cellars nor the result of anti-flood measures can be found at Prague Castle (Pražský hrad), namely the former residence of the Přemyslid Prince Soběslav I (1125–40) in the basement of the Old Royal Palace (Starý královský palác), now obscured by subsequent building projects, and the Royal Crypt opened in 1928 beneath the Cathedral of St. Vitus (Cchrám sv. Víta), containing the remains of Emperors Charles IV and Rudolph II, and King George of Poděbrady.)

Other places of interest nearby: 48, 49, 50, 52

52. The Headless Knight of St. Anne's

Prague 1 (Staré Město), the Church of St. Anne (kostel sv. Anny) on Liliová
Metro B to Národní třída; Tram 9 from Václavské náměstí, 17, 18 along eastern riverbank

"Most of all Prague is a breeding ground for phantoms, an arena for sorcery ... she never ceases to enchant with her magic spells ... the old she-devil Prague". Thus wrote Arnošt Procházka (1882–1945), joint-editor in the early 1900s of the influential literary journal *Moderní revue*. Procházka was referring to a now illusory Prague, one that lies behind the cosy image of the golden city of a hundred spires. Welcome, instead, to macabre and mysterious Prague, whose shadowy legacy today provides the backbone for numerous organised twilight tours along the city's haunted streets.

Prague can certainly provide plenty of raw materials in this respect, from alchemists' laboratories, religious fanatics and over zealous executioners to grisly legends, miraculous occurrences and the Frankenstein-like Golem (see nos. 7, 13, 20, 27, 41 & 44). The city has its fair share of ghost stories too, several of which involve spectral medieval knights. A typical example is the headless Swedish knight and his lady said to walk the rooms of the Golden Well House at Karlova 3 (see no. 50). Legend states that the owner of the house murdered them for their money. Two bakers later purchased the house and they soon encountered the ghosts, who offered them gold in return for a decent burial on condition that the gold never left the house. When one of the bakers disobeyed this instruction he was found in the cellar well with golden coins still in his pocket, apparently drowned by the ghosts. An alternative telling of the tale involves the ghost of a young housemaid, drowned in the well whilst trying to locate the source of a mysterious light. When her body was retrieved a treasure was revealed!

Another ghostly knight appears every Friday at midnight just around the corner on Liliová. There was once a Dominican convent here from which the Gothic Church of St. Anne (kostel sv. Anny) remains, surrounded by gloomy cobbled alleyways. The ghost is that of a Knight Templar from the old buildings, who roams the streets on horseback with his head under his arm. It is said that he was executed for a crime to which he has still not confessed. Again the story has an alternate version, this time in the form of a young nun also carrying her head in her hands, having been beheaded by her own father after refusing

Even by day the Church of St. Anne (kostel sv. Anny) on Liliová has a special atmosphere

to marry the husband he had selected.

An equally unlucky knight once lived on nearby Platnéřská. He murdered his mistress but was cursed by her before she died so that he turned into iron. His statue by Ladislav Šaloun, the sculptor of the statue of Jan Hus in Old Town Square (Staroměstské náměstí), can be seen on the wall of the New Town Hall (Nová radnice) on Mariánské náměstí.

And then there is the ghost of a Turkish merchant in Týn Courtyard (Ungelt), forever carrying a jewel box containing the head of the young woman he murdered because she married another man whilst he was away ... Prague, it seems, is indeed a breeding ground for phantoms!

Other places of interest nearby: 50, 51, 53, 54

July 6th. Meanwhile, any visitor to Prague will be reminded of the fire-brand prophet and martyr by Ladislav Šaloun's Art Nouveau statue in Old Town Square (Staroměstské náměstí), showing Hus surrounded by his Hussite supporters. Erected in 1915 to mark the 500th anniversary of Hus's death, the Habsburg authorities refused it an official unveiling. The Nazis later draped the statue in swastikas and during the Prague Spring of 1968 it was shrouded in black as a protest against the Soviet invasion (see no. 4). Around the base of the statue are inscribed the words of Hus himself: "Milujte se, pravdy každému přejte" (Love each other, wish truth to everyone).

An often forgotten fact about Hus is that he was responsible for introducing the use of accents (known as diacritics) into Czech spelling, in order to represent each sound by a single symbol. His work was continued by philosopher Jan Comenius (1592–1670), whose most important contribution was the *háček* used over the letter 'č', as illustrated in the Pedagogical Museum of J. A. Comenius (Pedagogické muzeum J. A. Komenského) at Valdštejnská 20 in Lesser Quarter (Malá Strana).)

Other places of interest nearby: 51, 52, 63

55. A Miniature Prague in Paper

Prague 1 (Nové Město), the Museum of the City of Prague (Muzeum hlavního města Prahy) at Na Poříčí 52
Metro B/C to Florenc; Tram 8 from náměstí Republiky, 3, 24 from Václavské náměstí

Ceramic models for sale in Prague are similar to Antonín Langweil's paper model of the city itself

Most European cities have changed enormously over the last two centuries, their historians turning to old maps and engravings in order to gain an impression of how their surroundings once looked. In Prague, however, the task is made easier by virtue of a unique paper model to be found in the Museum of the City of Prague (Muzeum hlavního města Prahy) on Na Poříčí, itself a neo-Renaissance building constructed in the late 1890s.

Built at a scale of 1:480 and covering almost 20 square metres the model was the brainchild of Antonín Langweil (1791–1837), the son of a peasant from the hop-growing town of Žatec in north-western Bohemia. Always interested in drawing, Langweil studied at the Academy of Fine Art in Vienna, returning to Prague in 1819 to found a printing workshop. By 1822 a lack of money had forced Langweil to sell up and take a servant's post at the library of the Charles University (Universita Karlova), where he used his spare time to indulge his interest in the miniature rendering of portraits and vistas.

A turning point came in 1826 when a three-dimensional model of Paris was exhibited in Prague: Langweil was totally enthralled with it. Taking this as his cue, he commenced work on a scale model of Prague, a task that would consume him for eleven years until his early death in 1837. The model is based on a city plan by Josef Jüttner dated 1811–15 and published by the National Museum in 1820. Within three years Langweil had built some 600 models of the houses of Old Town and exhibited them. The public were impressed giving Langweil the impetus to continue in his work, adding the churches of Old Town, as well as Lesser Quarter (Malá Strana), the castle district (Hradčany) and Josefov. The model was again exhibited in 1834 but by this time Langweil's health was poor, not helped by the prospect of having to support his wife and five daughters. Plans to tour the model around Bohemia came to nothing and Langweil even approached Emperor Francis I (1792–1835) for funding but received only 150 guldens, and that after a wait of three years. Eventually, after an abortive attempt to sell the model to Count Rudolph Chotek, supreme governor of Bohemia, Langweil succumbed to tuberculosis aged just 46. In 1840 Emperor Ferdinand V (1835–48) purchased the model from Langweil's widow and it was presented to the Museum of the Kingdom of Bohemia, now the National Museum, where it remained until being moved to its present location in the 1950s.

Today, Langweil would be comforted in the knowledge that not only historians but also citizens and visitors alike gain knowledge and enjoyment from his paper model. Thanks to Langweil's painstaking attention to detail we are able once more to glimpse at the irrevocably altered façades and long lost thoroughfares of old Prague, right down to the house signs, drains and even broken windowpanes! It is especially useful when attempting to reconstruct the district of Josefov, whose Jewish Quarter was cleared *after* the model was made.

By way of a supplement to Langweil's model, the museum's semi-circular staircase provides the backdrop for Venetian theatre artist Antonio Sacchetti's *Panorama of Prague*, a splendid painted vista looking across Charles Bridge from Lesser Quarter.

Tucked away in the northern part of New Town (Nové Město), not far from the Museum of the City of Prague, is the little-visited Postal Museum (Poštovní muzeum) on Nové Mlýny, dedicated to the design and printing of Czech stamps, some of which were the work of Art Nouveau artist Alfons Mucha (1860–1939). Outside the building, which is a former mill whose owner commissioned the painted interiors in 1847, stands the 16th century New Mill water tower. Philatelists might also be interested in the Postcards Family Museum (Muzeum pohledů) at Liliová 4 in Old Town (Staré Město), containing a collection of postcards and other ephemera from 1890 to 1930.)

56. The Biggest Horse in the World

Prague 3 (Žižkov), the equestrian statue of Jan Žižka and the National Monument (Národní památník) on Vítkov Hill off U Památníku
Metro B/C to Florenc then Bus 133, 207

Prague's 3rd district of Žižkov is named after a colourful hero of the Hussite Wars (1420–36), the one-eyed commander Jan Žižka, whose huge bronze equestrian statue on Vítkov Hill can be seen for miles around. The hill itself is named after Vítek of Hora, the owner of one of several long-vanished vineyards established here by Holy Roman Emperor Charles IV of Luxembourg (King Charles I of Bohemia) (1346–78). It was here on Vítkov Hill, on 14th July 1420 that Hussite peasant forces led by commander Žižka successfully repelled the superior imperial army of Emperor Sigismund (1419–20) sent by the Pope to crush heretical Bohemia: in so doing a Czech patriotic legend was born. So successful a general was Žižka that Hussite forces extended their sway as far as the Baltic coast, necessitating an interregnum that lasted for the next fifteen years. However, with Žižka's death in 1424 Hussite unity became more strained resulting eventually in bitter civil strife and the fratricidal destruction of radical Hussites at the Battle of Lipany (see no. 34).

The statue of Jan Žižka was erected on July 14th 1950, on the 230th anniversary of the Battle of Vítkov. Modelled by the sculptor Bohumil Kafka it remains the largest equestrian statue in the world. The 9 metre high statue weighs 16,764 kg – the sword alone weighing 110 kg – and the whole, including the stone pedestal, soars to 22 metres. To the Communist authorities at the time Žižka was something of an anti-Western hero and so they hoped the statue's presence would endear them to the local populace.

Rearing up behind the statue is the seemingly contemporaneous National Monument (Národní památník), an enormous concrete cenotaph 142 metres long, 28 metres wide, and 31.5 metres high. Designed by Jan Zázvorka it was actually erected between 1929 and 1933, as a memorial to those who died fighting the Austro-Hungarian Empire during the First World War. The monument was opened officially on October 28th 1938, twenty years after the founding of the First Czechoslovak Republic, and almost immediately closed by the Nazis.

In 1953 the National Monument was commandeered by the Communists and converted into a monument to the Heroes of the Working Class. For a time the embalmed body of Czechoslovakia's first Com-

The colossal equestrian statue of Jan Žižka on Vítkov Hill

munist President, Klement Gottwald (1896–1953), was displayed here after the style of Lenin's preserved remains in Moscow's Red Square. Poor preservation techniques and rising maintenance costs, however, led to Gottwald's corpse being eventually cremated; in 1990 the ashes returned to his family for burial in the nearby Olšany Cemetery (see no. 57). With Vítkov Hill now peaceful and free from propaganda once more, the Žižka statue and the National Monument can slowly shake off their Soviet associations and reminding onlookers once again of their pre-Communist origins.

57. The Day of All Souls

Prague 3 (Žižkov), the Olšany Cemetery (Olšanské hřbitovy)
on Vinohradská
Metro A to Flora or Želivského

Some time around the 11ᵗʰ century a pilgrim returning from the Holy Land was cast by a storm onto a desolate island. There he encountered a hermit who told him that amongst some rocks there was a chasm that communicated directly with purgatory and from which could be heard the voices of tortured departed souls. The hermit also said that demons complained about the efficacy of prayers of the faithful – especially those of the monks of Cluny in France – in rescuing these souls. Upon his eventual return the pilgrim hastened to Cluny and told the Abbot there of his experiences; the Abbot promptly set aside November 2ⁿᵈ as a day of intercession for all souls in purgatory. Before long the custom had spread to other Cluniac establishments – and eventually throughout the Western Church.

All Souls' Day is still set-aside by the Roman Catholic Church for the commemoration of the faithful departed, based on the doctrine that their souls, which at death have not been cleansed of venial sin, can attain the beatific vision through the prayers of others. To witness All Saints' Day first hand a trip to Prague's Olšany Cemetery (Olšanské hřbitovy) in Žižkov is highly recommended. By the end of the day the cemetery is aglow with flickering candles, many of the graves are decorated with flowers, and countless prayers have been uttered.

The overgrown yet beautiful Olšany Cemetery is Prague's largest, containing the remains of more than a million people. It occupies the former site of the village of Wolšany, the first bodies being buried here during the bubonic plague epidemic of 1679–80, when small parochial graveyards inside the city walls were unable to cater for the resultant 30 000 corpses. Further visitations of the plague in 1713–14 and 1772 saw a fully-fledged cemetery emerge and in 1787 Olšany became Prague's central cemetery by decree of Habsburg Emperor Joseph II (1780–90), whose Funeral Edict forbade further burials within the city limits. It was during this period that many of the city's crypts and graveyards were emptied and the remains re-located to Olšany, as well as to the Lesser Quarter Cemetery of Smíchov on the west bank (see no. 79).

Olšany Cemetery is divided into ten parts, each numbered according to their age. Cemetery I is the oldest, being the site of the original plague cemetery marked to-day by a chapel of St. Rochus, patron saint against plagues. Cemetery II dates from 1787 and Emperor Joseph's Funeral Edict; the others were opened up during the following century. The most elaborate monuments can be found in Cemetery V, laid out in 1861, its incumbents being mostly members of wealthy families, artists and other celebrities of the day. Most atmospheric are the lines of abandoned, bricked-up mausoleums now crumbling and heavy with ivy.

Mausolea in Žižkov's Olšany Cemetery (Olšanské hřbitovy)

There are two some-what controversial graves at Olšany. The first is that of Czechoslovakia's first Com-munist president, Klement Gottwald (1896–1953), who died after catching a cold at Stalin's funeral. His embalmed remains were at first kept in the National Monument on Vítkov Hill but were returned to his family in 1990 for re-burial in an anonymous-looking mass grave of former party members in Cemetery V (see no. 56). The other is that of the student Jan Palach (1948–69), who committed sui-cide by self-immolation in protest against the Soviet-led invasion of Czechoslovakia in 1968, designed to crush the liberalising reforms of Alexander Dubček's government during the Prague Spring. His grave soon became the focus of dissent and in 1973 the authorities removed the body; it was returned in 1990 and can be found in Cemetery IX to the right of the main entrance.

Along the eastern flank of the Olšany Cemetery, on Izraelská be-yond Jana Želivského, lies Žižkov's New Jewish Cemetery (Nový židovský hřbitov), used from 1890–91 onwards after Žižkov's Old Jew-ish Cemetery on Fibichova had been abandoned (see no. 42). Still in use today, although only a fraction of it has been occupied since the Sec-ond World War, its most famous occupant is Franz Kafka. His simple

The Grave of Jan Palach in the Olšany Cemetery (Olšanské hřbitovy)

grave lies just inside the entrance from the Želivského Metro, at the southern end of row 21, by the wall. The cemetery also contains important monuments to victims of the Holocaust, ashes from those who perished in the Nazi prison camp at Terezín (Theresienstadt), and a memorial to the 200 Jewish victims lost when the ship *Patria* sank in Haifa harbour in November 1940, during a bungled attempt to prevent them being deported. There is also a military graveyard here (čestná vojenská pohřebiště) honouring the Czech war dead of the First World War, as well as the 436 Red Army troops who died liberating Prague in May 1945, and soldiers of the British Empire who died on Czechoslovak territory during the Second World War. A third cemetery, to the south of the Jewish Cemetery and a short way along Vinohradská, is the Vinohrady Cemetery (Vinohradský hřbitov), noteworthy for containing the family tomb of former President Václav Havel (1989–2003).

Other places of interest nearby: 58

58. A Modernist Noah's Ark

Prague 3 (Žižkov), the Church of the Sacred Heart of Our Lord (kostel Nejsvětějšího Srdce Páně) on náměstí Jiřího z Poděbrad off Vinohradská
Metro A to Jiřího z Poděbrad; Tram 11 from near Václavské náměstí

Between 1753 and 1775, the previously disparate wings of Prague Castle (Pražský hrad) were amalgamated into the homogeneous neo-Classical ensemble seen today. The architect was Nicolo Pacassi, personal architect of Habsburg Empress and Queen of Bohemia Maria Theresa (1740–80). Not until the 1920s would another architect be afforded the privilege of leaving such a distinctive mark upon this predominantly medieval structure.

This time the architect was the Slovenian-born Jože Plečnik (1872–1957), his home town of Ljubljana being at that time a part of the Austro-Hungarian Empire. In 1894–97 Plečnik studied alongside the renowned Viennese architect, Otto Wagner, as a result of which he was immersed in the so-called Viennese Secession, a movement that rejected the backward-looking decorative elements and staid construction techniques of the 19th century in favour of the organic motifs and new materials of the Art Nouveau.

In 1911 Plečnik moved to Prague in order to teach at the Academy of Applied Arts, where he stressed both the principles of Classical architecture as well as the value of folk-art traditions. In 1920 he came to the attention of Tomáš Garrigue Masaryk (1850–1937), President of the First Czechoslovak Republic, whose office was Prague Castle (his bronze statue stands in Hradčanské náměstí). Keen to imbue the castle with a more contemporary appearance befitting to a modern seat of government Masaryk appointed Plečnik Chief Architect. Consequently, between 1920 and 1934 he undertook numerous diverse projects at the castle, including the renovation of the Southern Gardens (see no. 22), the installation of various monuments (e.g. the 17 metre-high granite obelisk to the dead of the First World War in the Third Courtyard and the nearby Bull Staircase, based on the Palace of Knossos on Crete), and the creation of new internal spaces, such as the Plečnik Hall with its three tiers of abstract Doric columns.

For all he achieved at Prague Castle, Plečnik's undoubted triumph in the city can be found farther east, in the district of Vinohrady. Built between 1922 and 1933 the Church of the Sacred Heart of Our Lord (kostel Nejsvětějšího Srdce Páně) was inspired by Noah's Ark, hence

The Modernist Church of the Sacred Heart of Our Lord (kostel Nejsvětějšího Srdce Páně) in Žižkov

the strong resemblance of the church to a ship. Its windows are strung out like portholes along the top of the external, glazed-brick walls and there is a broad tower symbolising a mast in full sale. At the top of the tower is a huge transparent clockface mimicking somewhat the rose windows of Gothic cathedrals. The interior is no less unusual, with a coffered wooden ceiling giving the impression of being below deck and an altar made of marble from the Bohemian Forest (Šumava) highlands of southwestern Bohemia. Like his equally innovative Church of the Holy Ghost in Vienna (1910–13), the church comprises one large nave without columns, creating a bright and lofty space for worship much in the tradition of early Christian basilicas. Not surprisingly, Plečnik's bold and idiosyncratic mix of stylistic elements, from neo-Gothic to Functionalist, won plaudits from many architects and the church remains one of Prague's most inspirational pieces of modern architecture.

Two further examples of ecclesiastical Modernism can be found in the surrounding streets. Pavel Janák's Functionalist Huss Oratory (Husův sbor) was erected in 1931–33 on the corner of Dykova and U Vodárny and is noteworthy for the copper chalice on its slender belfry – a symbol of the Hussite movement and Czech Reformation – as well as one of Central Europe's largest *columbaria*, or urn repositories, in its basement. Also a modern Czech Hussite structure is Josef Gočár's 1930s-styled Church of St. Wenceslaus (kostel sv. Václava) on náměstí Svatopluka Čecha, identified by its lighthouse-like tower, again topped off with a chalice.

Other places of interest nearby: 57

59. The Art Nouveau Railway Station

Prague 1 (Nové Město), the Main Station (Hlavní nádraží) at
Wilsonova 8
Metro C to Hlavní nádraží; Tram 5 from náměstí Republiky, 9 from
Národní třída

One of the largest but least appreciated buildings in central Prague is its Main Station (Hlavní nádraží). Part of the reason for this is that most people take railway stations for granted, eager to escape them upon arrival and frustrated at them when departure is delayed. Another reason is that Hlavní nádraží, like so many other city stations, is decidedly unkempt and tends to be the haunt of the homeless and other lost souls, especially at nighttime. However, it would be a pity to dismiss this grand building as being unworthy of exploration, since behind its unkempt appearance there lurks an Art Nouveau masterpiece (see no. 63).

Standing just north of the neo-Renaissance State Opera (Státní opera), and almost opposite the less well-known

A detail of Prague's Art Nouveau Main Station (Hlavní nádraží) on Wilsonova

Jubilee Synagogue (Jubilejní synagoga) (see no. 40) and Henry Tower (Jindřišská věž) (see no. 2), the Main Station was first constructed in the neo-Renaissance style in 1870–71. Part of the building project involved the digging of a railway tunnel through the Vinohrady Hill to the south. Within just two decades it was decided that the station building was no longer adequate as Prague's gateway to Europe and so a competition was launched in 1899 to design a suitable replacement: the winning entry was by architect Josef Fanta (1856–1954). The old building was demolished and the new one erected between 1901 and 1909, to be called the Franz Joseph Station after the reigning Austrian Emperor and King of Bohemia, Francis Joseph I (1848–1916). The entrance building alone is 214 metres in length and has an entrance hall decorated with statuary, plastered pilasters and graceful wrought iron balustrades. The crowning glory is a painted, domed rotunda, around the balcony of which can be found Fanta's Café (Fantova kavárna). Beyond the entrance hall lie the platforms themselves, covered in typical *fin de siècle* style by a steel and glass canopy, 76 metres wide and 18 metres high. As such, the building is well within the great tradition of monumental railway stations from the age of steam.

For a while the station was known as Wilson Station (Wilsonovo nádraží) after the American President Woodrow Wilson (1856–1924), who had supported the notion of an independent state of Czechoslovakia (see no. 69). Also named after the President is the busy Wilsonova road directly in front of the station, which effectively isolates it together with the nearby State Opera (Státní opera) from the rest of central Prague. During the 1970s a huge new subterranean departures and arrivals hall was added to the station, which gives no clue whatsoever as to the Art Nouveau glories that lie above. Occupying three levels and supporting the busy Wilsonova road above, it is a classic example of ultra functional, late Communist design.

Not quite as grand as Main Station is Masarykovo nádraží a couple of roads away on Havlíčkova, its elegant glazed arrivals hall finished off with green-painted palmettes and lions' heads. Built in the neo-Classical style it is the oldest station in Prague, the first train arriving here in 1845.

Other places of interest nearby: 60

60. Re-Using Prague's Communist Legacy

Prague 1 (Nové Město), the Gallery Art Factory at Wenceslas Square
(Václavské náměstí) 15
Metro A/B to Můstek; Tram 9 from Národní třída, 3, 14, 24 from Karlovo
náměstí

Much of the architectural legacy of Prague's Communist era (1948–89)
is uniformly concrete, grey and grim (see no. 4). Some structures continue to fulfil their original functions, albeit in a different guise, for example the Žižkov television mast – at 216 metres high the tallest structure in Prague – built insensitively on top of an ancient Jewish cemetery
(see no. 41); whilst it continues to transmit television and radio signals
it now also functions as a café and tourist attraction and is adorned with
David Černý's bizarre climbing baby sculptures *(Miminka)*. Similarly,
the over-sized Česká typografie building between Na Poříčí and Na
Florenci in New Town (Nové Město), formerly the office of the Communist newspaper *Rudé Právo* ('Red Right'), is still a newspaper office
although it now produces the respectable left-of-centre paper called
simply *Právo*. Another example is the Máj ('May') department store,
opened in 1975 at Národní třída 26 and once the pride of Communist
Czechoslovakia's retail industry. Having been snapped up by the American K-Mart company after the Velvet Revolution it is now a branch of
Tesco.

Other Communist-era structures have been cleverly adapted to entirely new uses. A good example is the Gallery Art Factory at Wenceslas
Square (Václavské náměstí) 15, occupying what was once a newspaper
printing works. The industrial feel of the 500-square-metre former
manufacturing hall has been retained, despite being refurbished in Pop
Art style, and the gallery now acts as one of Prague's largest exhibition
spaces for contemporary modern art. Other examples of adaptive reuse
of old factory spaces in Prague include the Matrix Club inside a former
frozen meat plant at Koněvova 13 in Žižkov (Prague 3), the Abaton Club
inside the old Interplast factory on Na Košince, off Povltavská in Libeň
(Prague 8), and the Mecca Club at U Průhonu 3 in Holešovice (Prague
7), also in a reused factory.

Other Communist-era institutions still carry on almost as if the
events of 1989 had never occurred, for example the city's handful of remaining pre-revolutionary canteens (see no. 45) and shops (see no. 67),
the latter including the ubiquitous neighbourhood grocery stores called

The Gallery Art Factory on Václavské náměstí was once a Communist-era printing press

potraviny (meaning 'provisions'). Unmistakeable too are the monotonous prefabricated tower blocks *(paneláky)*, thrown up across the city's outer suburbs during the 1960s and 70s as an affordable answer to the post-war housing crisis. They are generally clustered around metro stations such as Zličín (Prague 17) on Metro B, and Budějovická (Prague 4) and Háje (Prague 11) on Metro C, the latter called Kosmonautů during the Communist era accounting for the pair of Soviet cosmonauts standing near the entrance.

Unsullied reminders of Prague's Socialist experiment are also manifested at two other locations in the city. The first is the hulking glass extension to the National Theatre (Národní divadlo) on Národní třída, known as the Nová scéna (New Scene). Designed by Karel Prager in 1983 it is still home to the Magic Lantern (Laterna Magika) 'black light' theatre company, which in its day was a Communist showpiece. The second is the Plavecký stadion Podolí at Podolská 74 in Podolí (Prague 4), Prague's biggest swimming centre and a good example of the Communist ethos of 'sport for the masses'.

There are still other Communist-era installations that have been simply abandoned, for example the warren of nuclear bunkers carved out around Vítkov Hill in Žižkov. They were excavated as an emergency communications centre and were accessed through various inconspicuous steel doors on Jeseniova and Prokopova. A bombproof tunnel system also exists below Prague Castle. It was constructed at great expense in order to connect the presidential residence, which from 1948–89 was in the Baroque Dientzenhofer Summer Palace in the Royal Garden (Královská zahrada) to the north, with the rest of the Castle. However, fearing the tunnels might be used by counter-revolutionaries, they were sealed off with concrete slabs. Probably most indicative of the era is an anonymous-looking doorway opposite the British Embassy at Thunovská 14 in Lesser Quarter (Malá Strana), behind which is a tiny room once occupied by a member of the Communist secret police charged with keeping a permanent watch on comings and goings: until recently the spyhole for his camera was still visible!

This odyssey of Communist architecture concludes with several unusual hotels, the first of which, the towering Crowne Plaza Hotel at Koulova 15 in Dejvice (Prague 6), was built by the Communists as the Hotel International and is a striking example of the style known as Socialist Realism; its intact Marxist-Leninist décor includes a scene above the main entrance of Russian war heroes being greeted enthusiastically by Czech peasants. Several other hotels, built well *before* the Communist era, were nationalised in 1948 and then re-used again *after* the Velvet Revolution. The Carlo IV, for example, at Senovážné náměstí 13 in New Town (Nové Město), was built originally as a bank, then converted into a Communist post office, and eventually transformed into a hotel. Similarly, the Arcotel Hotel Teatrino at Bořivojova 53 in Žižkov (Prague 3) began life as an Art Deco theatre, was then allowed to rot as a Communist cultural centre, and has recently been re-born as a stylish hotel; its cavernous dining room occupies the former auditorium. Also of interest is the Bohemia Plaza at Žitná 50, which still contains a small Catholic chapel on its second floor once deemed illegal under Communism.

Other places of interest nearby: 59, 61

61. The Concrete Picture Palace

Prague 1 (Nové Město), the Lucerna Cinema in the pasáž Lucerna at
Vodičkova 36
Metro A/B to Můstek; Tram 9 from Národní třída, 3, 14, 24 from Karlovo
náměstí

Czech cinema has a long and fascinating history, from silent classics
in the 1920s through the New Wave of the 1960s to the renaissance of
Prague's legendary Barrandov Film Studios during the 1990s (see no.
82). It is therefore not surprising that Prague has its fair share of avid
filmgoers with a dozen modern multiplexes to cater for them. However,
hidden amongst the city's hundred or so silver screens are a couple of
historic picture palaces that retain something of the glamour and ex-
citement from the golden age of cinema.

The most exuberant of Prague's old cinemas is undoubtedly the Lucerna at Vodičkova 36. An interesting way of approaching it is via a series
of covered shopping passages (*pasáže*) built during the 1920s as a forerunner to department stores (see nos. 66 & 68). The first is reached by
walking down Krakovská from Wenceslas Square (Václavské náměstí)
and then turning right into the so-called *pasáž* Blaník, an old arcade
with faded brass fittings and a cinema mosaic depicting the muses. At
the end turn left into Ve Smečkách, where a right turn leads into another *pasáž*. Here, after turning right along Štepánská, can be found
the *pasáž* Lucerna on the left. It is actually part of the Lucerna Palace, a
huge complex of shopping arcades and entertainment centres that was
the first building in Prague to have a concrete superstructure. The Palace comprises two wings, one facing Vodičkova opened in 1910 and a
second facing Štěpánská completed in 1921, and was built by a consor-
tium that included the grandfather of former president Václav Havel.

Elevated above the shops in the *pasáž* Lucerna is the wonderful,
Moorish-tinged Art Nouveau lobby of the Lucerna Cinema. Now serving as a bar with the added attraction of the occasional piano player, its
broad windows open out onto the shopping arcade below. The cinema
itself retains other period features such as a traditional cloakroom, a
balcony and a cloth curtain in front of the screen. In the cellars under-
neath are the popular Lucerna Music Bar, where the likes of Louis Arm-
strong and Josephine Baker once played, and the Lucerna Great Hall,
its columned ballroom and marbled balconies now used for popular
music concerts.

A quite different cinema is the Kino Aero at Biskupcova 31 in Žižkov (Prague 3). Opened in 1932 in the courtyard of a sprawling, down-at-heel apartment block it offers the sort of traditional experience that a cinema audience between the wars might still recognise. The programming, however, is the most progressive in the country with films being sourced from all over the world. A typically Bohemian addition is the three-holed drinks holder attached to the seat backs to hold a beer mug, juice cup and shot glass – only in Prague!

One further cinema of interest is the tiny MAT Studio at Karlovo náměstí 19 in New Town (Nové Město), specialising in Czech classics and featuring a bar decorated with old film posters and props.

David Černý's controversial sculpture of Saint Wenceslaus hangs outside the Lucerna Cinema on Vodičkova

Other places of interest nearby: 60, 62, 65

62. The Unfinished Cathedral of the Virgin Mary

Prague 1 (Nové Město), the Church of the Virgin Mary of the Snows
(kostel Panny Marie Sněžné) on Jungmannovo náměstí
Metro A/B to Můstek; Tram 9 from Národní třída, 3, 14, 24 from Karlovo
náměstí

On August 6th, 366AD the Virgin Mary appeared in a dream to a wealthy Italian called John of Rome. Being childless, John together with his wife had earlier decided to dedicate their considerable wealth to the memory of the Virgin and had prayed for just such divine inspiration. In the course of the dream Mary instructed the couple to build a church in her name on the Esquiline, one of Rome's famous seven hills. Upon approaching the hill they found it covered with a layer of snow in which the clear outline of a church miraculously appeared. So it was that Rome's Church of the Virgin Mary of the Snows, the city's first church bearing the Virgin's name (hence its alternate name of St. Mary Major), came into being.

Subsequently, numerous other churches bearing this name were built across Europe, an unusual example of which can be found on Prague's Jungmannovo náměstí. Here, towering over the surrounding streets is the curiously truncated torso of a church once intended to be a cathedral. The building was founded by Holy Roman Emperor Charles IV of Luxembourg (King Charles I of Bohemia) (1346–78) to commemorate his own coronation and it was his intention that it should provide the venue for the coronation of future Bohemian kings (the coronation of the Emperor is depicted above a Gothic doorway in the north wall). As such its magnificence was intended to be equal if not superior to that of the Cathedral of St. Vitus (chrám sv. Víta) in Prague Castle (Pražský hrad), accounting for the incredible 34 metre-high cupola of the buttressed presbytery seen today. It contains the main altar and would have formed the eastern arm of the completed church. Unfortunately, little more of the building was ever finished due to the onset of the Hussite Wars (1420–36) and the lack of funds thereafter. During this period hundreds of poor citizens congregated in the building to listen to the sermons of the Hussite firebrand, Jan Želivský. In time, half-built walls were dismantled by the White Friars (a Mendicant Carmelite Order), to whom the church had been given by Charles IV, and the marooned presbytery became their church proper; a rose window today looks over the site where a vaulted chancel had originally been planned (now occupied by a Classicist-style courtyard). In 1603 the church was taken over by the Franciscans, who renewed the presbytery ceiling with Renaissance vaulting. To this day the building remains the tallest church in Prague, although it is worth noting that the planned nave would have stood another six metres higher. Superlative too is the black-and-gold main altar dating from 1650 that lays claim to being the tallest Baroque columned altar in the country.

The unfinished Church of the Virgin Mary of the Snows (kostel Panny Marie Sněžné) on Jungmannovo náměstí

Just south of the Church of the Virgin Mary of the Snows (kostel Panny Marie Sněžné), squeezed in between the bustle of Wenceslas Square (Václavské náměstí) and Jungmannova, can be found the Franciscan Garden (Františkánská zahrada), a wholly unexpected oasis of calm in the heart of the city. One of the few remaining medieval monastery gardens in Prague, they were laid out by the White Friars mentioned above, whose former monastery, rebuilt in the 17th century, stands alongside the southern wall of the church. The gardens were used for the cultivation of altar flowers and medicinal herbs and there is still a herb garden here today, adjacent to a charming early 18th century Baroque pavilion added after the gardens had been taken over by the Franciscans in 1603.

Other places of interest nearby: 54, 61, 64, 65

63. Some Gems of *Le Style Moderne*

Prague 1 (Nové Město), the Topič House at Národní třída 9
Metro B to Národní třída; Tram 9 from Václavské náměstí, 17, 18 along
eastern riverbank

Art Nouveau, known also as *Le Style Moderne*, was a style in art, architecture and design that came about during the 1880s and peaked in popularity in the early 1900s. Typified by highly stylized realism and elaborate decoration based on flowing floral motifs, the style pioneered not only the novel use of materials (e.g. exposed iron and irregular pieces of glass) but also of new industrial processes for mass production. Its name was derived from a shop in Paris called Maison de l'Art Nouveau, which showcased objects that followed this new design approach. However, the French capital was not the only city in which the demand for radically self-conscious design was being fuelled by a growth in population and production; by the early 20th century Art Nouveau had left its mark as far away as Chicago, Vladivostok, Riga and Barcelona.

Viewed by art historians today as the prelude to the pared-down ergonomics of 20th century Modernism, Art Nouveau represented different things in different places and gave rise to several distinct regional variations. In Germany and the Netherlands, for example, where it was known as *Jugendstil* after the *avant-garde* journal *Jugend* ('Youth'), the result was a hard-edged academic style with its own typography drawn from German printmaking. In Vienna it was termed the *Secession* and was spearheaded by the artist Gustav Klimt, who together with Josef Hoffmann and Koloman Moser seceded from the staid and mainstream school of Historicism favoured by the Habsburg court. In Budapest, the architect Ödön Lechner went one step further and used the new style to attempt a Hungarian national form of architecture, suffused with potent symbolism from Hungary's mythical past. As for Prague, during the late 19th and early 20th centuries the city was in the throes of the so-called Czech National Revival, with rapid industrialisation creating both working-class political movements as well as a renaissance in the Czech arts (see no. 76). The city's artists and architects embraced wholeheartedly the ideals of Art Nouveau, using it both decoratively and politically, until the First World War brought a violent halt to further artistic experimentation.

Tucked away on Národní třída in New Town (Nové Město) two gems of pure Czech Art Nouveau can be found, namely the insurance building at number 7, whose uppermost windows spell out patriotically the word 'PRA-HA', and the Topič Publishing House at number 9, with its gilded floral swags and coloured Bohemian glass. Both buildings were designed by the architect Osvald Polívka (1859–1931) and erected in 1907–08. Not to be missed too is the row of once grand apartment houses on the nearby Masaryk Embankment (Masarykovo nábřeží), especially the dilapidated Hlahol House at number 16 as well as the Hilbert House at number 26, with its stunning Art Nouveau vestibule.

By contrast, Prague's renowned Grand Hotel Europa, not far away at Wenceslas Square (Václavské náměstí)

The Art Nouveau Topič House on Národní třída once belonged to a publisher

25, is usually thronged with tourists. Constructed in flamboyant Art Nouveau style in 1903–05 to a design by the architects Bedřich Bendelmayer and Alois Dryák it has lavish interiors by the likes of Bohumil Hübschman, Jan Letzel and Ladislav Šaloun. Far more modest is the Peterkův dům, just across the road at number 12. Designed by Jan Kotěra (1871–1923) in the 1890s this building with its restrained use of Art Nouveau ornamentation is cited as one of Prague's very first Art Nouveau buildings. It stands in stark contrast to the stucco peacocks, frogs and floral motifs smothering the overblown U Nováků building just around the corner at Vodičkova 30, again by Osvald Polívka.

Probably the most famous expression of Art Nouveau architecture in Prague is the Municipal House (Obecní dům, or more officially Representační dům hlavního města Prahy) at Republic Square (náměstí Republiky) 5. Completed in 1912 as an arts and cultural centre, it was designed by Antonín Balšánek and Osvald Polívka. The fact that it was built on the former site of the Royal Court of King Wenceslaus (Václav) IV (1378–1419) only added potency to a building that was already hailed as a patriotic celebration of Czech nationhood (see no. 9). Thus, the domed façade with its riot of stucco and swirling ironwork carries a large mosaic entitled *Tribute to Prague* by Karel Špilar, and the Smetana Hall inside, the city's largest concert venue, has ceiling mosaics depicting Czech myths. The decoration of the interior was undertaken by prominent Czech artists of the day, including murals by Alfons Mucha (Mayor's Hall), Max Švabinský (Rieger Hall), Jan Preisler (Palacký Hall), and Mikoláš Aleš (basements), as well as sculptures by Josef Václav Myslbek, Ladislav Šaloun and Čeněk Vosmík. On October 28th 1918 the building provided the perfect backdrop for the declaration of the First Czechoslovak Republic (the anniversary of the birth of Czechoslovakia is still marked by a public holiday, known variously as Independence Day or Czech Founding Day, despite the country no longer existing); likewise, during the Velvet Revolution in 1989, it was here that the first meeting took place between the defeated Communist government and the newly organised Civic Forum (Občanské fórum) of democratic president-in-waiting, Václav Havel (see no. 64).

Located behind the Municipal House, at U Obecního domu 1, is the less well known and wholly apolitical Hotel Paris. The architect Jan Vejrych constructed it in Art Nouveau style in 1904 and its sumptuous public rooms are still adorned with their original light fittings and ceramic mosaics. The hotel played prominent in Bohumil Hrabal's novel *I Served the King of England* and its visitors' book contains signatures from patrons as disparate as film director Oliver Stone, supermodel Eva Herzigová, Belgian action hero Jean Claude Van Damme, and former Czech President Václav Havel.

It should not be forgotten that Art Nouveau manifested itself in other ways too, such as glass, jewellery, textiles, furniture and graphic arts. One of Prague's greatest practitioners was Alfons Mucha (1860–1939), who won international recognition for his Sarah Bernhardt posters and went on to design postage stamps and banknotes for the state and a stained-glass window in the Archbishop's Chapel of St. Vitus's Cathedral (chrám sv. Víta) (see no. 71). His work can be seen today in the Mucha Museum (Muchovo muzeum) in the Kaunický palác at Panská 7 in New Town (Nové Město), as well as in the Museum of Decorative Arts (Uměleckoprůmyslové muzeum) at 17. listopadu 2 in Old Town (Staré Město).

Other places of interest nearby: 53, 54, 62, 64

64. Where the Velvet Revolution Began

Prague 1 (Nové Město), the Schirding Palace (Schirdingovský pálac) at Národní třída 16
Metro B to Národní třída; Tram 9 from Václavské náměstí, 17, 18 along eastern riverbank

When Mikhail Gorbachev visited Prague in 1988 his spokesman was asked what he thought the difference was between Alexander Dubček's abortive attempts at democratization of Czech Communism in 1968, known as the Prague Spring, and *glasnost*, the Russian premier's own policy of political liberation: the answer was "twenty years".

Those twenty years since Warsaw Pact troops had reinstated Communist orthodoxy on the streets of Prague had been marked by a sense of political apathy, demoralisation and totalitarian consumerism. Protests against the regime tended to be intellectual ones, centred on dissident groups such as Václav Havel's Charter 77 and its monitoring of human rights abuses. Havel was born in Prague in 1936 and worked as a stagehand at the Divadlo Na zábradlí (Theatre on the Balustrade) at Anenské náměstí 5 in Old Town (Staré Město). This is where he first began penning his parodies of life under Communism, such as *The Garden Party* and *The Memorandum*, writings that led to his arrest by the StB Secret Police (Státní bezpečnost) in 1978 and subsequent four-and-a-half-year imprisonment. Havel's prison cell was in the Convent of St. Bartholomew at Bartolomějská 9 in Old Town, which had been confiscated from the Order of Grey Sisters by the Communists for use as an interrogation and prison facility. Later restituted back to the nuns, the premises are now the much-storied Unitas Hotel.

After his release, Havel lived in an apartment on Rašínovo nábřeží in New Town (Nové Město), designed by his grandfather and now standing alongside the postmodernist 'Fred and Ginger' building, erected in the 1990s. The Secret Police kept him under constant surveillance and took up almost permanent residence in a house nearby. One of Havel's favourite haunts during his years as a dissident was the Kavárna Slavia at Smetanovo nábřeží 2, the city's most renowned literary café (see no. 65). In 1989 he was sent to prison again, for nine months.

On November 17th 1989, the grave of the Romantic poet Karel Hynek Mácha (1810–36) in Vyšehrad Cemetery was used as the assembly point for a peaceful student demonstration, marking the 50th anniversary of

A modest memorial at Národní třída 16 is where the Velvet Revolution began

the closing of Czech universities by the Nazis (see no. 76). Renewed optimism arising from the recent fall of the Berlin Wall led to more than 50 000 people attempting to march on Wenceslas Square (Václavské náměstí). The procession got as far as a modern arcade built inside the Baroque Schirnding Palace (Schirndingovský pálac) at Národní třída 16 (known also as the Kaňkův dům after its architect, F. M. Kaňka), where police forcibly broke it up. The action would herald the start of what became known as the Velvet Revolution and is today marked by a public holiday, called Struggle for Freedom and Democracy Day. Each year people gather at this otherwise ordinary spot to quietly remember the beginning of the end of Czech Communism.

With talk of police brutality in the air, another demonstration was called and on November 20th 200 000 people congregated to demand the resignation of the government. Although the police were restrained this time the government could do little to suppress the public groundswell. A committee of opposition groups became the Civic Forum (Občanské fórum) fronted by Václav Havel and on November 24th, together with Alexander Dubček, he addressed 300 000 supporters in Wenceslas Square. As the government lost control of the media, so the scenes were broadcast around the world. Workers across the land were galvanised into supporting a general strike on November 27th and a further mass meeting was staged in front of the huge Sparta Stadium (Stadion Sparta) north of the Letná Gardens (Letenské sady), ironically where enforced Communist May Day parades had previously been held.

Despite promising free elections and admitting that the Soviet invasion of 1968 had been wrong, the writing was on the wall for the government of Communist Prime Minister Ladislav Adamec. On December

27th, barely more than a month since the revolution had started, a coalition of strongly reformist Communists and a majority of Civic Forum non-Communists took control, with Václav Havel as president. With not a single life lost, Havel's co-revolutionary Rita Klímová dubbed the whole episode the Velvet Revolution.

The serious business of the economic transformation of Czechoslovakia took rather longer to bring about. In 1992 the right-of-centre Civic Democratic Party (ODS) under Václav Klaus was voted into power and it set in motion a rapid programme of decentralisation and privatisation. On January 1st 1993 Klaus backed Slovak independence and the two countries parted peaceably without need of a referendum (the so-called Velvet Divorce). Václav Havel thus served as the last president of Czechoslovakia (1989–92) and the first president of the Czech Republic (1993–2003), albeit now sidelined into a predominantly ceremonial role.

The first four years of the new Czech Republic witnessed huge economic changes as foreign investors moved in to capitalise on Prague's vast untapped potential for profit and development. Needless to say, not everyone benefitted and the shift to capitalism brought its fair share of corruption; on the other hand Prague has become one of the most popular tourist cities in Europe with six million visitors in 2005. Havel himself stood down as President in 2002 and in 2004 the Czech Republic's accession to the European Union was formalised.

Other places of interest nearby: 53, 54, 62, 63, 65

65. Coffee, Absinth and Opium

Prague 1 (Nové Město), the Kavárna Divadla komedie in the pasáž
Vlasty Buriana at Jungmannova 1
Metro B to Národní třída; Tram 9 from Národní třída, 3, 14, 24 from
Karlovo náměstí

*The minimalist interior of the Kavárna
Divadla komedie on Jungmannova*

Bohemia's first coffee house *(kavárna)* was established in a house on Dražického náměstí in Prague, at the Lesser Quarter (Malá Strana) end of the Charles Bridge (Karlův most). It was here during the late 17th century that Greek merchant Deodatus Damascenus sold and brewed coffee beans. The building is known as the House at the Three Ostriches (U Tří pštrosů) after a supplier of ostrich feathers called Jan Fuchs, who rebuilt the house as a result of damage inflicted during the Hussite Wars (1420–36). It was Fuchs who had the beautiful ostrich frescoes painted on the building's façade, which were only re-discovered when the building was renovated in 1938.

For a complete contrast in premises, visit the Kavárna Divadla komedie, a theatre café well hidden inside the Vlasty Buriana shopping passage, connecting Jungmannova with Vladislavova in New Town (Nové Město). Such covered passages *(pasáže)* were built in Prague during the 1920s as a precursor to department stores, other examples of which connect Spálená 15 and Opatovická, Jungmannova and Vodičkova, and Jungmannova and Vodičkova via the Franciscan Garden (Františkánská zahrada) (part of the latter – the Světozor *pasáž* – includes a magnificent stained glass advertisement for Czech electronics company Tesla).

The Functionalist architect Josef Karel Říha designed the building containing the Vlasty Buriana *pasáž* in 1928–29, as the headquarters for a mining and metallurgical company. The café itself has a striking vaulted skylight of glass blocks, echoed discreetly in the curves of its marble staircase as well as its 1920s-style bent-tube chairs (a similar skylight adorns Oldřich Tyl's Černá růže (Black Rose) *pasáž*, built in 1930 between Na Příkopě 12 and Panská). The café resembles Mies van der Rohe's experimental interior in the so-called International Style at his Villa Tugendhat in Brno, wherein Modernist spatial aesthetics were expounded using new industrial production techniques.

Prior to this, during the first two decades of the 20th century, Prague boasted a café society to match that of Vienna and Paris and a handful of these *Belle Époque* coffee houses are still in business. In New Town there is the Café Imperial at Na Poříčí 15, notable not only for once being the very epitome of decadence during the inter-war years of the First Czechoslovak Republic but also for its incredible sculpted Art Nouveau wall tiles. Even more grand is the Kavárna Obecní dům at Republic Square (náměstí Republiky), an outstanding example of a Czech Art Nouveau coffee house. Completely renovated in 1997 it opened originally on November 22nd 1912 as part of the arts and cultural centre known as the Municipal House (Obecní dům) (see no. 63).

More modest is the Café Montmartre at Řetězová 7 in Old Town (Staré Město), another legendary First Republic meeting place, where Czech literary characters such as Gustav Meyrink *(The Golem)* and Jaroslav Hašek *(The Good Soldier Švejk)* once met (see no. 42). It is said that during the 1930s the café's heady mix of absinth, opium and jazz music led to black masses and orgies! Other Old Town coffee houses are the first floor Café Louvre and billiard hall at Národní třída 20, which opened originally in 1902, the Grand Café Orient in the Cubist House of the Black Madonna (dům U Černé Matky Boží) at Ovocný trh 19, and the Kavárna Slavia opposite the National Theatre (Národní divadlo) at Smetanovo nábřeží 2, long popular with writers, actors and artists (it was immortalised in Jaroslav Seifert's poem *Café Slavia*). Bedřich Smetana lived in the house above and composed his operas *The Bartered Bride* and *Dalibor* here. More recently dissident and former President Václav Havel (1989–2003) used the café to plot the downfall of Communism. On the wall hangs Viktor Oliva's painting *The Absinth Drunkard*. Absinth is often cited as being the ultimate Bohemian tipple – it is 70 per cent proof – and is made from bitter distilled Wormwood sweetened with anise and then coloured green. Needless to say, the potentially hallucinogenic drink was banned under Communism as being a bourgeois drink!

Tea houses are also to be found in Prague and it is said that the one in the Art Nouveau Grand Hotel Europa at Wenceslas Square (Václavské náměstí) 25, now a restaurant, is an exact replica of the tea salon on board the legendary White Star liner, *Titanic*.

Other places of interest nearby: 61, 62, 64, 66

66. The Tailors' *Ell* and the Prague Meridian

Prague 2 (Nové Město), the New Town Hall (Novoměstská radnice) on
Charles Square (Karlovo náměstí)
Metro B to Karlovo náměstí; Tram 6, 18, 22, 23 from Národní třída

Prague's numerous town halls, once the administrative centres of the
city's four distinct quarters, have witnessed many of the city's tumultu-
ous historical events, including fire (see no. 16), execution (see no. 26)
and 'defenestration' (see no. 34). A little-known function of these public
buildings, however, has been to provide readily accessible, government-
approved measuring gauges for use by tradesmen and passers-by in the
days before reliable tape measures. They take the form of an exactly-
measured steel bar, known as an *Ell*, attached firmly to the outside of
the building. Once popular with the cloth trade, but now obsolete, the
length of an *Ell* was derived from the distance between an adult man's
elbow and the tip of his middle finger. The accepted length of an *Ell* var-
ied across Europe between 50 and 70 centimetres, with a Czech *Ell* being 59.3 centimetres. One can be found on the door of Hradčany Town
Hall (Hradčanská radnice). Worked into the late Renaissance *sgraffitoed* façade of the building can also be seen the emblem of Hradčany, as
well as the double eagle of the Austrian monarchy, leaving onlookers in
no doubt as to the official function of the building – and thus the reli-
ability of the gauge (see no. 16).

A second example of an *Ell* was attached to the tower of the New
Town Hall (Novoměstská radnice) on Charles Square (Karlovo náměstí)
in New Town (Nové Město) during the 18th century. It is actually set
about two metres above pavement level, it is said to avoid vandalism;
during market time an official would measure tradesmens' cloth here
for a small fee by mounting a wooden box. Attached to the same wall
can be seen the end of a chain, once used to close off the street for security reasons.

The New Town hall itself is an interesting building with a cheq-
uered past. The oldest part is the east wing overlooking Vodičkova
and dating from 1377, to which the distinctive Gothic corner tower was
added in 1452–56. Even before the tower was added the building had
played a significant part in Czech history since it was here on 30th July
1419 that an angry mob of Czech nobles 'defenestrated' seven members
of the city council in the wake of the execution of Hussite preacher Jan

Hus. The action precipitated the death of King Wenceslaus (Václav) IV (1378–1419) of the Luxembourg dynasty and eventually caused the Pope to launch a Catholic crusade against Hussite Bohemia; a sixteen-year interregnum and the Hussite Wars (1420–36) resulted. Following a fire in 1559 the southern wing of the New Town Hall, first built in the early 15th century, was given the Renaissance appearance it has today. Eventually, with the merging of the 'four towns' of Prague in the late 18th century the New Town Hall became a prison and torture chamber, known locally as the Bastille, where Czech dissidents from the 1848 uprising against the Habsburgs were imprisoned. Today the building serves the more peaceful role of cultural and social centre.

A tailor's ell on the New Town Hall (Novo-městská radnice) on Karlovo náměstí

Like the Prague *Ell*, another of the city's oft-ignored little details can be seen set into the cobblestones of Old Town Square (Staroměstské náměstí), close to the statue of Jan Hus. It is a metal strip known as the Prague Meridian (pražský poledník) denoting Prague's geographical position on the 50° line of latitude, one of the imaginary lines drawn across the surface of the Earth parallel to the Equator. Although the meridian strip is today only used as a zero marker from which to measure distances inside the city, it was once used by Praguers to set their clocks at high noon, when the sun cast the shadow of a nearby Column of Our Lady across the meridian. The column was destroyed in 1918.

Other places of interest nearby: 67, 69, 70

67. For Book Lovers Only

Prague 1 (Nové Město), the Globe Bookstore & Café at Pštrossova 6
Metro B to Národní třída or Karlovo náměstí; Tram 14 from Václavské
náměstí, 17, 21 along eastern riverbank, 6, 9, 18, 22, 23 from Národní
třída

Looking inside the Globe Bookstore & Café on Pštrossova in New Town

Prague can be a delight for book lovers, the city's myriad bookshops sometimes tucked away along atmospheric back streets making the task of locating them an adventure in itself. That is certainly the case with the Globe Bookstore & Café, Prague's first English language bookshop just around the corner from the renowned U Fleků beer hall in New Town (Nové Město). Aimed squarely at the city's sizable ex-patriate community, it remains the literary heart of post-revolutionary Prague, where browsers, scribblers and writers alike are encouraged to use the cosy reading room and café. It is particularly strong on used fiction, as is Shakespeare & Sons at Krymská 12 in Vršovice (Prague 10), another popular literary destination offering books, coffee and beer.

Catering for a similar audience is the U Knihomola (Bookworm) International Bookstore at Mánesova 79 in neighbouring Vinohrady (Prague 2). The forte here is art and literature in English, French, German and Czech. However, the most eclectic stock for the ex-patriate is probably held at the Big Ben Bookshop at Malá Štupartská 5 in Old Town (Staré Město), where just about everything from dictionaries to bestsellers can be found. (Directly opposite is the Church of St. James (kostel sv. Jakuba), with its grisly mummified arm hanging just inside the doorway (see no. 44).)

One of Old Town's best kept literary secrets is Týnská literární kavárna, a little-known literary café and bookshop at Týnská 6, where local writers and students congregate in a series of cosy arched rooms, as well as a quiet courtyard in summer: it is difficult to imagine that the bustle of Old Town Square (Staroměstské náměstí) lies just beyond its walls.

Another aspect of the Prague book world is its secondhand bookshops, called *antikvariáty* in Czech. Even if you do not read Czech it is a rare pleasure to look around these shops, brimming not just with antiquarian books but also old prints, postcards, maps and posters. Around the corner from the Globe Bookstore, for example, stands Antikvariát Kant at Opatovická 26, whilst a couple of roads north, at Národní třída 40, there is the Antikvariát Galerie Můstek, at the entrance to a splendid old shopping arcade. Good examples in Old Town include Antikvariát Pařížská at Pařížká 8 and Antikvariát Karel Křenek at U Obecního domu 2.

For those who enjoy hunting down unusual shopping locations Prague can offer several. In New Town there is the clerical supplier Charita Florentinum at Ječná 4, the bee-keeping specialist Včelařské potřeby ('Beekeeping Supplies') at Křemencova 8, the Harampádí Antik Bazar at Pštrossova 22, a haven for nostalgia enthusiasts, Jan Pazdera's photography and optical equipment emporium at Vodičkova 28, and Maso Tomáš Turek at Jindřišská 23, a pre-revolutionary butchers' shop (*řezník*), its chrome shelves stacked with all manner of meat products. In Old Town there is Art Deco at Michalská 21, specialising in clothes and jewellery from the 1920s, the French bakery Au Gourmand in a beautifully tiled former butcher's shop at Dlouhá 10, and Eduard Čapek's old-fashioned hardware store a little further along at number 32.

Other places of interest nearby: 67, 69, 70

68. The Island of *My Homeland*

Prague 1 (Nové Město), Slavic Island (Slovanský ostrov) opposite Masarykovo nábřeží
Metro B to Národní třída or Karlovo náměstí; Tram 14 from Václavské náměstí, 17, 21 along eastern riverbank, 6, 9, 18, 22, 23 from Národní třída

The Vltava is the longest river in the Czech Republic, stretching 430 kilometres from its source in the Bohemian Forest highlands on the Czech-German-Austrian border, northwards through Český Krumlov, České Budějovice and Prague, to its confluence with the Labe (Elbe in German) at Mělník. Having drained 280 000 square kilometres of land its waters are carried onwards from this point to the North Sea and eventually out into the Atlantic. On its journey through Prague, the Vltava is often described as a silvery thread, winding its way through the 'golden city of a hundred spires'. What should not be forgotten, however, is that woven into this watery thread are several jewels, namely the Vltava's nine river islands (*ostrovy*), each with its own story to tell.

The most northerly island is called Císařský ostrov (Emperor's Island) and with a length of 3 kilometres it is also the largest. It gained its royal name from the time when Habsburg Holy Roman Emperor and King of Bohemia Rudolph II (1576–1611) extended the Royal Game Reserve (Královská obora) this far and built a watermill and pleasure palace (see no. 33). Unrecognisable today, the island's western half is taken up by Prague's main wastewater treatment plant (see no. 28).

Moving upstream we pass the Karlín district, its riverbank once a cluster of islands connected by footbridges now lost to river straightening projects. Shortly thereafter is ostrov Štvanice (Hunting Island), another large Vltava island, 1250 metres long and 190 metres wide. It was first documented in 1118 as simply the Large Island but gained its present name during the late 18th century, when wild animal hunting nd baiting was a popular pastime here. Baiting was outlawed in 1816 after which in 1914 the island became the site of a small hydroelectric power station built and then in 1932 the site of Prague's first ice rink.

Following the river around the elbow between Josefov and Letná, the next island is Prague's most famous, namely Kampa Island (see nos. 3 & 77). Known as Little Venice because of its solitary canal and medieval watermills, its buildings suffered considerable damage during the city's once-in-a-thousand year flood in 2002. The western end of

71. 'The Marks that Speak'

Prague 2 (Nové Město), the Slavonic Monastery (klášter Na Slovanech)
on Na Slovanech
Metro B to Karlovo náměstí; Tram 17, 21 along eastern riverbank,
18 from Národní třída

In 846AD the grandson of Charlemagne, Louis the German (804–876), King of the Eastern Frankish Empire, appointed Prince Rastislav (846–870) as head of the Great Moravian Empire (occupying what is today the central and eastern parts of the Czech Republic together with Slovakia). Louis hoped that Rastislav would be a co-operative border ruler but the prince soon sought to restrict Frankish influence, which was being spread through priests preaching in German. In 862 Rastislav asked the Byzantine Emperor Michael III (839–867) to send missionaries to Great Moravia to evangelise the Slavs in their own language (see no. 84). The Emperor sent Saints Cyril and Methodius, who are usually credited with devising the so-called Glagolitic alphabet in order to translate the Bible and church liturgies for Slavic audiences. In doing so they laid the foundation not only for the creation of modern Slavic script but also of Slavic literature in general (this explains why one of four lunettes painted on the ceiling of the National Museum's so-called Pantheon of great Czechs is entitled *Methodius Completing the Translation of the Bible in a Slavic Language*, as well as the inclusion of the saints in a stained glass window by Alfons Mucha in St. Vitus's Cathedral (chrám sv. Víta), and why the saints have their own public holiday on July 5th).

The Glagolitic alphabet (*glagolitsa*) is the oldest known Slavic alphabet, the name being derived from the word *glagola*, meaning 'word'. Since *glagolati* also means 'to speak', Glagolitsa is poetically referred to as 'the marks that speak'. Glagolitsa has 41 letters stemming from Greek, Hebrew and Samaritan, as well as possible ancient Slavic runes used in sacred texts of the pre-Christian Slavic religion.

In 864 Louis the German attacked Rastislav and forced him to acknowledge the supremacy of the Franks; in 886 a Frankish bishop banned *Glagolitsa* and dispersed the followers of Cyril and Methodius. Some wound up in Bulgaria, where the Slavic alphabet was used to preserve national identity in the face of growing Byzantine influence from the east. It was here that the Cyrillic alphabet was first created, which would largely replace Glagolitic in the Middle Ages.

Other disciples of Cyril and Methodius found themselves expelled

Modern twin spires identify the Slavonic Monastery (klášter Na Slovanech)

to Bohemia and Croatia, where during the 10th and 11th centuries close linguistic and cultural bonds were forged that still exist today. A unique example of this synthesis is Prague's Slavonic Monastery (klášter Na Slovanech), close to Charles Square (Karlovo náměstí) in New Town. It was founded in 1347 by Holy Roman Emperor Charles IV of Luxembourg (King Charles I of Bohemia) (1346–78), who was keen to lessen the divide between the Western and Eastern Churches. To do this he invited an order of Croatian Benedictines to inhabit the monastery, stipulating that the liturgical language used should be Slavic (or Slavonic) and not Latin. The monastery was consecrated in the presence of the Emperor on Easter Monday March 29th 1372, the anniversary of the day on which Christ appeared to his disciples on the road to Emmaus in Palestine; the building is thus popularly known as the Emmaus Monastery (V Emauzích).

As the only Slavonic monastery in the Holy Roman Empire it soon became a renowned centre of Slavic scholarship and the arts, including a magnificent cycle of 73 Gothic wall paintings around its cloister. In 1395 the monks produced a Glagolitic version of the Gospel, being a copy of an older text written on the Croatian island of Krk. It was bound together with a 12th century Cyrillic book written in Kiev and the whole ornamented with jewels and sacred relics. Known today as the *Évangéliaire de Reims* it was acquired by French Kings in 1546 and used to take their oaths on until 1782.

In 1455 Bohemia's first and only Hussite monastery was established here, the Benedictines being in agreement with Hussite doctrine; later, in the 17th century, the buildings were given a Baroque makeover. In February 1945 the monastery was badly damaged in an allied bombing raid during which the two Baroque towers on its Church of Our Lady and the Slavic Saints were destroyed. These were replaced in 1969 by a pair of ultra modern concrete spires, which compliment nicely the equally unusual, obliquely placed Baroque towers of Kilián Ignáz Dientzenhofer's Church of St. John of Nepomuk on the Rock (kostel sv. Jana Nepomuckého na Skalce), on the other side of the road. On its high altar can be seen a wooden replica of Josef Brokof's famous statue of St. John of Nepomuk carved in 1682 and used as the model for the famous statue on Charles Bridge (see no. 1).

Other places of interest nearby: 70, 72, 77

72. The Giant Water Lilies of Na Slupi

Prague 2 (Nové Město), the Botanical Garden (Botanická zahrada) at Na Slupi 8
Metro B to Karlovo náměstí; Tram 17, 21 along eastern riverbank, 18 from Národní třída

Water lilies in the Botanical Garden (Botanická zahrada) on Na Slupi

South of busy Charles Square (Karlovo náměstí) lie Prague's surprisingly little-visited Na Slupi Botanical Garden (Botanická zahrada), a truly magical realm of plants from around the globe. Although the present-day garden is relatively modern, there have been gardens in New Town (Nové Město) since Holy Roman Emperor Charles IV of Luxembourg (King Charles I of Bohemia) (1346–78) established the area in the 14th century. In 1358 he issued an edict requiring the establishment of vineyards and orchards "on all hills within three miles of the city". During the same period numerous monastery gardens were founded (see no. 62), as well as the city's first apothecary garden at Jindřišská 14, where the main Post Office now stands. It was named the Angel Garden after the Emperor's favourite apothecary, a man called Angelo.

From 1600 onwards the Jesuits tended a botanical garden in Lesser Quarter (Malá Strana) and then, following the Order's dissolution in 1773, new gardens were established in Smíchov on the initiative of the Habsburg Empress and Queen of Bohemia Maria Theresa (1740–80). Opened in 1778 they were soon deemed the most beautiful in Bohemia and were graced with a pavilion by the Baroque architect Dientzenhofer. However, regular flooding of the Vltava, combined with the encroachment of housing, saw the eventual closure of the great garden in 1902. Only a tiny fragment, the Dientzenhoferovy sady, remains today, adjacent to the Jirásek Bridge (Jiráskův most).

Meanwhile, back in New Town in 1845, the Czech Society for the Cultivation of Gardening had established a so-called Social Garden amongst the sloping orchards of Na Slupi. Capacious greenhouses were added in 1882 and in 1897 the garden was donated by the state to Charles University (Univerzita Karlova). Extensive rockeries, ponds and an arboretum were created and numerous plants from the old Smíchov gardens were brought here following their closure. In 1939 the Nazis closed all Czech universities and for the duration of the Second World War the garden lay dormant. In February 1945 several glasshouses were badly damaged during a wartime air raid but by 1949 these had been replaced.

Today, the Na Slupi Botanical Garden is open to visitors once more, offering an eclectic mix of plants and habitats. Of particular interest are its renowned collection of 1500 different cacti and succulents, its towering tropical plants including antler-shaped epiphytes suspended from the roof, and the charming Karlštejn rockery with its display of Czech native plants. Most dramatic of all is the huge Amazonian *Victoria cruziana* water lily growing in a pool inside one of the glasshouses. The species was discovered in 1801 by the German-speaking botanist from Bohemia Tadeáš Haenke, who had been sent to Bolivia by the Spanish government to investigate the flora there. He first saw the lily on the Mamoré River, a tributary of the Amazon, but died before making a full report of his discovery. Eventually named after Queen Victoria, the lily is famous for its night-blooming flowers that last only 24 hours and for being able to support a baby on its leaves, which can grow up to three metres in diameter. Planted from seed each year the lilies at Na Slupi generally flower in May or June.

Plant lovers may also be interested to know that the first potatoes ever grown in Prague were planted in the gardens of a 17th century Irish Franciscan monastery that once stood on the site of the Hibernian Palace (palác U Hybernů), a neo-Classical structure in high Empire style opposite the Municipal House (Obecní dům) at Na Poříčí 3. The monks were called Hibernians after the Latin word for Ireland – Hibernia. Referred to originally as 'ground apples', potatoes soon became one of the most important crops in Bohemia. Rather more glamourous is the story of how Habsburg Holy Roman Emperor and King of Bohemia Ferdinand I laid out splendid Renaissance-style Royal Garden (Královská zahrada) to the north of Prague Castle (Pražský hrad) in the 1530s (see no. 21). Ferdinand's personal doctor was the botanist Pietro Mattioli and it was he who planted Europe's first tulip bulbs here, having been acquired in Turkey at the Emperor's special request. From Prague the tulip later spread westwards, becoming especially popular in Holland.

Other places of interest nearby: 70, 71, 73, 74

73. *Slavonic Dances* and *Moravian Duets*

Prague 2 (Nové Město), the Antonín Dvořák Museum
(Muzeum Antonína Dvořáka) in the Villa Amerika at
Ke Karlovu 20
Metro C to I. P. Pavlova; Tram 4, 6, 10, 16, 22, 23 from Karlovo
náměstí

The charming Antonín Dvořák Museum (Muzeum Antonína Dvořáka) on Ke Karlovu

Antonín Dvořák (1841–1904) followed Bedřich Smetana as the leading exponent of modern Czech classical music, itself a sonic manifestation of the conscious 19th century renaissance of Bohemian culture known as the Czech National Revival (see no. 76). In February 1897 Dvořák told *Harpers* Magazine, "National Music is not created out of nothing. It is discovered and clothed in new beauty, just as the myths and legends of a people are brought to light and crystallised by the master poets. All that is needed is a dedicated ear, a retentive memory, and the power to weld the fragments of former ages together in one harmonious whole ... the music of the people, sooner or later, will command attention and creep into the books of composers".

Antonín Leopold Dvořák was born in the Bohemian village of Nelahozeves, where his father was an innkeeper and butcher, trades he was fully expected to follow. As a child he played in his father's village band and the local schoolmaster undertook his early training as a violinist. At the age of twelve he was sent to school in Zlonice where he was taught the rudiments of music; showing great early promise, his father was persuaded in 1857 to let him go to study seriously at the Prague

Organ School. From 1863 to 1873 Dvořák played violin for the Bohemian Provisional Theatre Orchestra in Prague, for a time under Smetana himself, and then, with encouragement from Johannes Brahms, he took up a life devoted primarily to composition.

In 1891 Dvořák was appointed Professor of Composition at the Prague Conservatory and whilst receiving only grudging acceptance in Vienna, he soon garnered a considerable reputation in Germany and England. Consequently, in 1892 he was invited to America as Director of the National Conservatory of Music in New York. His compositions during this period combined both American and Bohemian influences, most notably his *Symphony No. 9 (From the New World)*, written and first performed in New York in 1893. He eventually returned to Prague in 1895, having resisted invitations from Brahms to go to Vienna, and in 1901 became Director at the Prague Conservatory. Dvořák preferred the relatively simple life in his homeland, where he was now held in great esteem and it was here that he could indulge his other abiding passions, namely railway locomotives and pigeon breeding!

Dvořák's many compositions, which include nine symphonies, operas such as *Rusalka*, cello, violin and piano concertos, string quartets, songs and symphonic poems, often feature a Czech 'national style' drawn from elements of Bohemian and Slavic folk music (for example, the Slavic *dumka* folk song, the slow country waltz of the *sousedská*, the hopping step of the *skočná*, and various Serbian dances). However, unlike Brahms, who in his *Hungarian Dances* offered arrangements of traditional melodies, Dvořák created wholly original works that were characteristic of existing folk music without actually quoting it. Fine examples of such work include his popular sets of songs entitled *Moravian Duets* and *Gypsy Songs*, his *Slavonic Rhapsodies (Op. 45)* and two sets of *Slavonic Dances (Op. 46 & 72)*, and his piano pieces *Legends* and *From the Bohemian Forest*, all of which are characteristic of Slavic folk music yet completely Czech in spirit. Not surprisingly, such works did much to endear the composer to his countrymen.

Dvořák died shortly after the first performance of his last opera *Armida* in a house at Ječná 14 in Prague's New Town (Nové Město) and was buried in Vyšehrad Cemetery (see no. 76). Just around the corner from the house, and partially concealed behind elegant wrought iron gates, is the Villa Amerika at Ke Karlovu 20, which is now home to the Antonín Dvořák Museum (Muzeum Antonína Dvořáka). Well off the beaten track, the renowned architect Kilián Ignáz Dientzenhofer built the villa in 1720 as a Baroque summer palace for Count Jan Václav Michna. Surrounded today by modern buildings, its eyecatching combination of ochre and red plasterwork is unmistakeable. The museum was established by the Dvořák Society and includes scores, photographs and other memorabilia on the ground floor, and a frescoed recital hall upstairs. Outdoor concerts here are especially evocative of the times when the composer would use the villa as a retreat and it is almost impossible to imagine that the building and grounds had been all but abandoned and used as a cattle market before Dvořák arrived. The garden statues and vases are from the workshop of the sculptor Matyáš Bernard Braun.

One of the concert halls in Prague's Rudolfinum is named the Dvořák Hall in memory of the composer; used today for orchestral works it was home to the Lower House of the National Assembly of the First Czechoslovak Republic in 1918–1939 (see no. 76). The Czech composer Josef Suk (1874–1935) also has a hall in the Rudolfinum named after him, which is used for chamber, instrumental and solo vocal performances. The son of a village schoolmaster, Suk entered the Prague Conservatory at the age of eleven. Following his graduation in 1891 he studied composition with Dvořák and soon became his favourite pupil. In 1898 Suk married Dvořák's daughter Otilie, whose death in 1905 brought Suk much sadness resulting in the composition of his *Asrael* symphony. From 1922 he taught composition at the Prague Conservatory, later becoming its director, and as a teacher he exercised a strong influence over a generation of Czech composers. Although he made little use of Czech folk music, he nevertheless enjoyed a long career composing chamber music, orchestral works and a series of symphonic tone poems, including *A Summer's Tale*, *The Ripening* and *Epilog*.)

Other places of interest nearby: 66, 70, 72, 74

74. Curiosities in the Church of Charlemagne

Prague 2 (Nové Město), the Karlov Church (kostel Na Karlově) on Ke Karlovu
Metro C to I. P. Pavlova then Bus 291

Charles the Great (c. 742–814), known commonly as Charlemagne, was King of the Franks from 768 until his death and waged many wars in Europe against the Saxons, Lombards and Magyars. His revival of the Western Empire led to him being crowned first Holy Roman Emperor by the Pope in Rome on Christmas Day 800. Not without reason, therefore, has it often been said that, geographically and politically, Charlemagne 'made' Europe.

More than five centuries later, in 1355, Bohemia's own King Charles I (Charles IV of the House of Luxembourg) (1346–1378) was crowned Holy Roman Emperor. In many ways it could be said that Charles 'made' Bohemia since he concentrated all his energies on the economic and intellectual development of his kingdom. Indeed, he is still referred to as the 'Father of the Nation' *(Otec vlasti)*. High amongst his achievements are the establishment of the Charles University (Univerzita Karlova) (the first university in Central Europe, with the Gothic Carolinum on Ovocný trh at its heart), the construction of both Charles Bridge (Karlův most) and Prague Castle (Pražský hrad), the founding of St. Vitus's Cathedral (chrám sv. Víta), and the establishment in 1348 of New Town (Nové Město).

Perhaps it is no surprise that in the southern part of New Town, on a ridge overlooking the valley of the little Botič river, there is a church dedicated by Charles IV to his rôle model Charlemagne. Known officially as the Church of the Virgin Mary and St. Charles the Great (kostel Panny Marie a sv. Karla Velikého), but abbreviated to Karlov Church (kostel Na Karlově), it was founded by Charles I in 1350, together with an adjacent monastery for the Order of Augustinian Friars. Consecrated in 1377 and based on the burial chapel of Charlemagne at Aachen, Karlov Church is quite unlike Prague's other churches. Most noticeably, it has three cupolas rising mosque-like into the air, the largest of which stands above a magnificent, gilt-frescoed, octagonal nave decorated in the 1730s. It is hard to think that these same walls were badly damaged during the Prussian siege of 1757 in the Seven Years War but a closer look will reveal bullets still lodged in the plaster. The ceiling takes the

The Karlov Church (kostel Na Karlově) on Ke Karlovu with the walls of New Town in the foreground

form of a Renaissance stellar (star-shaped) vault that is 24 metres in diameter and 19 metres high. Created in 1575 to a design by Bonifác Wohlmut, its daring width gave rise to a legend that the architect made a pact with the devil so as to prevent its collapse: for several years afterwards superstitious locals feared entering the building.

Against the southern wall of the church there is the so-called Holy Staircase made of red marble and completed in 1711. The brass crosses attached to its surface mark the location of saintly relics embedded in the stone. Below the staircase lies the Bethlehem Chapel containing life-sized representations of the Holy family. Other objects arousing the visitor's curiosity include a fresco below the organ loft depicting, somewhat surprisingly, the one-eyed Hussite commander, Jan Žižka, against whom the Pope once ordered a crusade, and a painting over one of the side altars giving a rare depiction of the Virgin Mary pregnant. The original painting from which this copy was made was removed by order of the Archbishop of Prague, Jan Breuner.

Like most religious buildings in Prague the monastery next door was also damaged during the Thirty Years War (1618–48), as well as during the Hussite Wars (1420–36) beforehand, and was eventually closed down by order of Habsburg Holy Roman Emperor and King of Bohemia Joseph II (1780–90). From 1789 until the 1920s it was used as a sanatorium for the chronically ill and then in 1975 it became a museum. Under the Communists it was the Museum of the National Security Corps but today it goes under the somewhat friendlier name of the Museum of the Police of the Czech Republic – or the Police Museum. Its display of homemade weapons including swordsticks and pen guns is most unusual.

Other places of interest nearby: 72, 75, 76

75. Mythical Vyšehrad

Prague 2 (Vyšehrad), the Rotunda of St. Martin (rotunda sv. Martina)
on V Pevnosti
Metro C to Vyšehrad then Tram 7, 18, 24; Tram 17, 21 along eastern
riverbank

Although the ancient rock of Vyšehrad (meaning 'castle on the heights')
is home to many legends regarding the founding of Prague it is *not*
where the castle of the first ruling dynasty, the Přemyslid Dukes of
Bohemia, was located. That honour must go to Prague Castle (Pražský
hrad), founded in c. 870 AD by the first historical Přemyslid, Duke
Bořivoj I (c. 870–889). St. Methodius baptised the Duke in 874 and in
1212 his successor Duke Otakar I (1197–1230) gained the hereditary title
King of Bohemia from Holy Roman Emperor Frederick II (1194–1250),
a title held until the royal line ended with the assassination of King
Wenceslaus (Václav) III (1305–06) in 1306.

Vyšehrad's own castle was not erected until the first half of the 10th
century, as a defensive gateway into Prague. During the reign of Vratislav II (1061–92) the rock did actually become the permanent seat of
the Přemyslid dynasty, after they had vacated Prague Castle following
disputes with the Bishop of Prague, who at that time also resided at the
castle in the Old Provost's House (Staré probošství). However, despite
Vratislav building himself a splendid Romanesque palace and founding
the Church of Sts. Peter and Paul (kostel sv. Petra a Pavla) – a basilica
based on St. Peter's in Rome – the dynasty did not remain here long
and returned to Prague Castle during the reign of Soběslav I (1125–40).
Despite this, a visit to Vyšehrad is still highly recommended, not only to
escape the bustling crowds of Prague Castle but also to immerse oneself
in the mythical origins of modern Prague.

History relates how Germanic tribes had filtered into Bohemia in
the 1st century AD, gradually diluting the Celtic tribes they encountered
before being themselves diminished by the incursions of Attila the Hun
in 451AD. Slavic tribes then settled the banks of the Vltava during the
6th and 7th centuries from whom would come the Přemyslids, the first
historic rulers of Bohemia (see no. 84).

Legend, on the other hand, tells how the Vyšehrad rock was the seat
of the first mythical rulers of Bohemia, namely Čech (Bohemus) and
Krok. In the absence of a male heir, Krok's soothsaying daughter Libuše
succeeded him (see no. 27). Worried about the effect of matriarchal rule,

the men of the tribe told Libuše to seek a husband, whereupon she entered a trance: she instructed her white horse to go over the hills and find a ploughman working a pair of spotted oxen. The man was found in the village of Stadice, in the northern part of what is now the Czech Republic, and his name was Přemysl. The two were soon married and the ensuing dynasty took his name (one of four painted lunettes in the National Museum's so-called Pantheon of great Czechs is titled *Přemysl Being Summoned to Rule*).

Another legend relates how Libuše stood on the rock at Vyšehrad and foretold the birth of "a great city whose splendour will reach to the stars". Adding that "mighty lords bend before a low door", she sent out her servants who promptly found two men carving a doorsill (*práh* in Czech) at which spot Prague (Czech *Praha*) was founded (other commentators believe that the name 'Prague' is derived from the flat stones, or sills, found on the Vltava riverbed, which created a natural ford that first attracted settlers to the area).

In order to explore Vyšehrad it is best to access it from the south via an unmarked tunnel at the junction of Lumírova and Krokova. The surrounding brickwork is just a tiny part of the mighty ramparts erected by the Habsburgs in the second half of the 17th century, when they transformed the rock into a military stronghold. A flight of steps leads up to the main entrance into the Habsburg fortress, with the Tábor Gate to the left and the Leopold Gate to the right. Between the two are the remains of the Špička Gate, dating to the 14th century when Emperor Charles IV of Luxembourg (King Charles I of Bohemia) (1346–78) revived the fortunes of Vyšehrad by re-fortifying it and building himself a Gothic palace; he even commenced his coronation procession from here (note the deep incisions in the stonework of the gate, made by soldiers repeatedly sharpening their weapons here). Also dating from this period is a ruined medieval watch house best viewed from the southernmost bastion and known fancifully as the Baths of Libuše.

Upon entering the fortress proper its oldest and most unusual extant structure is encountered, namely the Rotunda of St. Martin (rotunda sv. Martina) on V Pevnosti. The only significant remnant of the original medieval fortress it was erected in the second half of the 11th century and is the oldest extant Romanesque structure in Prague. Together with the Basilica of St. George (bazilika sv. Jiří) at Prague Castle and Romanesque fragments of the former parish church of the village of Zderaz, now incorporated into the Gothic Church of St. Wenceslaus (kostel sv. Václava na Zderaz) on the corner of Dittrichova and Resslova in New Town (Nové Město), the rotunda is one of Prague's few extant

The Rotunda of
St. Martin (rotunda
sv. Martina) inside
the stronghold at
Vyšehrad

Romanesque buildings, most having been concealed when ground levels were raised in the late 13th century as a precaution against flooding (see nos. 18 & 51). Restored in 1878 by the local clergy the building is one of three Romanesque rotundas in Prague, said to have been built in the round so as not to afford the devil a corner to hide in. The others are the Rotunda of Longinus (rotunda sv. Longina) on Na Rybníčku in New Town and the Rotunda of the Holy Cross (rotunda sv. Kříže) on the corner of Konviktská and Karolíny Světlé in Old Town (Staré Město).

After the eventual abandonment of the fortress in 1866 the historic rock was 'reinvented' as a symbol of Czech heritage during the period known as the Czech National Revival (see no. 76). As a result, the Church of Sts. Peter and Paul was reconstructed in 1885–87 by architect Josef Mocker in neo-Gothic style, the pair of spires being added a decade later. Vyšehrad also became a potent resting place for Czech worthies, one of them being the sculptor Josef Václav Myslbek (1848–1922) (see no. 76). A copy of his statue of the legendary Přemysl and Libuše that once adorned the Palacký Bridge (Palackého most) – the original was damaged in an air raid during the Second World War – can be found alongside the church in the Vyšehrad Gardens (Vyšehradské sady). Nearby is the neo-Gothic New Deanery (Nové děkanství), erected in 1877, outside which is a curious trio of granite slabs known as the Devil's Column (Čertův sloup), thought to be the remains of a pillory or lost Romanesque building.

> Vyšehrad's full history, both archaeological and legendary, is illustrated in a recently restored Gothic casemate in the southwest corner of the fortress. Included is the legend of Horymír, a Czech nobleman, and his loyal horse Šemík. Having been sentenced to death, Horymír's life was saved by leaping from the ramparts on horseback. Šemík died in the process and was given his own grave at Neumětely near his master's home. Vyšehrad's Habsburg history is most graphically illustrated by the kilometre-long casemate wall leading off the Brick Gate (cihelná Brána) in the northern ramparts.)

Other places of interest nearby: 74, 76

76. The Last Resting Place of the Czech Patriots

Prague 2 (Vyšehrad), the Vyšehrad Cemetery on Štulcova
Metro C to Vyšehrad then Tram 7, 18, 24; Tram 17, 21 along eastern riverbank

By the mid-17th century German had replaced Czech as the official language of government in Bohemia. The Habsburg policy of Germanisation of their Crown Lands continued apace under Empress and Queen of Bohemia Maria Theresa (1740–80), however this was to change with the accession of her son, the enlightened despot Joseph II (1780–90). As well as abolishing the Jesuits in Prague, through whom much of the Germanisation had been carried out, Joseph also liberated the Jews from their Old Town ghetto. By the late 18th century church sermons were once again being given in Czech and the seeds of a Czech cultural revival had taken root.

The revival continued during the reign of Austrian Emperor and King of Bohemia Ferdinand V (1835–48), which saw the the city's theatres staging patriotic dramas and the publication of František Palacký's groundbreaking *History of the Czech Nation.* Inevitably, Czechs began pushing for equal rights for their language in government and schools, as well as greater autonomy within the Habsburg Empire (see no. 68). Shaken by revolutions erupting across Europe in 1848 Ferdinand prepared to make such concessions but was speedily supplanted by the new Austrian Emperor and King of Bohemia Francis Joseph I (1848–1916). He quickly suppressed any notion of Czech independence and coerced his rebellious dominions back into the Habsburg fold.

Rapid industrialisation in Bohemia since the end of the 18th century led to an exodus of people from the countryside into Prague and the gradual creation of a Czech-speaking, working class majority: Czechs now began slowly forging the political, social and economic infrastructure of their own nation. This period spawned an intellectual and political movement known as the Czech National Revival, whose aim was to reassert both the country's cultural heritage as well as its contemporary achievements.

Although the ultimate dream of Bohemian autonomy from the Habsburg Empire was not achieved, the movement did leave an indelible mark on the city's fabric, most notably in the neo-Renaissance National Theatre (Národní divadlo), constructed by public subscription in 1868–83 on the riverbank at Národní 2 in New Town (Nové Město). It was decorated by the most prominent Czech artists of the day and the theatre's cellar contains foundation stones brought from places of national historical importance. The theatre's architects, Josef Zítek and Josef Schulz, were also responsible for two other proud symbols of the Czech National Revival, namely the National Museum (Národní muzeum), also in the neo-Renaissance style, completed in 1890 at the top of Wenceslas Square (Václavské náměstí), and the Rudolfinum, built in 1876–84 at Alešovo nábřeží 12 in Old Town (Staré Město) and fashioned in an overtly Republican neo-Classical style. Construction of the latter was funded entirely by the Czech Savings Bank as a display of patriotism, a bee representing thrift lodged between the paws of the sphinxes guarding the entrance.

In 1869 it was decided as part of the revival to create a suitably imposing burial ground for Czechs considered important to the movement. The location selected was the rocky outcrop of Vyšehrad, an atmospheric setting already steeped in both legend and real history from the time of the Přemyslids onwards (see no. 75). The Vyšehrad Cemetery, laid out around the Church of Sts. Peter & Paul (kostel sv. Petra a Pavla), has since become the last resting place for many Czech composers, artists, sculptors, writers, intellectuals, singers, politicans and scientists.

The focal point of the cemetery is the so-called Slavín monument, constructed between 1889 and 1893 and designed by Antonín Wiehl as the communal resting place of more than fifty famous Czech personalities; so symbolic is it that sometimes the *entire* cemetery is referred to as the Slavín (meaning 'pantheon'). Typical of those buried here are Alfons Mucha (1860–1939), master of the Czech Art Nouveau (see nos. 56 & 66), František Křižík (1847–1941), inventor and electrical engineer (see nos. 10, 35 & 36), opera singer Emmy Destinn (Ema Destinnová) (1878–1930), and Josef Václav Myslbek (1848–1922), one of the foremost modern Czech sculptors, who spent twenty years creating the famous statue of Přemyslid Duke Wenceslaus (Václav) I (921–935) flanked by four patron saints in Wenceslas Square.

Dotted around the Slavín monument are the graves of many other famous Czechs, whose tombstones are more individually crafted. They include poet and writer Jan Neruda (1834–91) (plot 3-grave 25) (see no. 15), Nobel Prize winning chemist Jaroslav Heyrovský (1890–1967) (13-28), influential Czech National Revival writer Božena Němcová (1820–62) (2-12), and Oscar-winning film director Elmar Klos (1910–93) (9-83) (see no. 83). Of particular interest is the grave of the Romantic poet Karel Hynek Mácha (1810–36) (10-126), which was the assembly point in November 1989 for a demonstration commemorating the 50th anniversary of the closing of Czech universities by the Nazis. It led to more than 50000 people attempting to march on Wenceslas Square, before being broken up by police at Národní třída, and marked the start of the Velvet Revolution (see no. 64).

In terms of the original function of the Vyšehrad Cemetery, namely to celebrate the conscious revival of Bohemian culture, the graves of Czech composers Bedřich Smetana (1824–84) (5-40) and Antonín Dvořák (1841–1904) (14-35) are particularly important, since both produced works that served the Czech National Revival well. Smetana's patriotic cycle of 6 symphonic poems called *Má vlast* (*My Homeland*), for example, cel-

The Slavín monument in the cemetery at Vyšehrad

ebrated Bohemia's history, legends and landscape and were as influential in fostering a sense of Czech national consciousness as his operas *The Bartered Bride* and *Dalibor* (see nos. 20 & 68). However, it was the work *Libuše* that Smetana himself cherished most, written in 1869–1872 and described by him as a "solemn festival tableau" intended only for presentation on special patriotic occasions. It was commissioned for the opening of the National Theatre in 1883 and not surprisingly was banned by the Nazis during the Second World War. Each year on May 12th, the anniversary of the death of the composer, a memorial ceremony is held at his graveside. Afterwards, the concerts of the renowned Prague Spring Music Festival commence with *Má vlast* in the Municipal House (Obecní dům) at Republic Square (náměstí Republiky) 5 in New Town (Nové Město), the building's ceiling suitably decorated with scenes from Czech mythology (see no. 63).

Antonín Dvořák followed Smetana as the leading exponent of Czech musical nationalism and his tomb can be found in the cemetery's Italianate memorial arcade, which was added in 1898 (see no. 73).

Other places of interest nearby: 74, 75

77. Botels, Hotels and Other Unusual Lodgings

Prague 5 (Smíchov), the Admiral Botel moored on Hořejší nábřeží
Metro B to Karlovo náměstí or Anděl; Tram 6, 9 from Národní třída,
12, 20 from Malostranské náměstí

"The River Vltava gives the city life both spiritually and practically. Since 920 a 'free highway on water', it is honoured and celebrated as 'the girdle of Prague, the beautiful'. Even today the view of the town from the deck of a boat has its magic" (*Prague Pilgrim*, Vladislav Dudák).

Prague can boast numerous hotels located in unusual surroundings and top of the list must surely be its fleet of four floating hotels built by the Communists during the 1960s and 70s. It was a time when more hotel beds were needed but there was neither the money nor the inclination to undertake expensive conversions of old buildings.

The oldest of Prague's so-called *Botels* is the Albatros, moored since 1969 at nábřeží Ludvíka Svobody next to the Štefánik Bridge (Štefánikův most). Given originally a life expectancy of 30 years its modest rooms are still available to those desiring a cheap and unusual stay in the centre of Prague. By contrast the Admirál Botel, moored farther upstream at Hořejší nábřeží, just south of the Palacký Bridge, (Palackého most), is quite luxurious, replete with brass fittings and smart green and yellow paintwork.

Those wishing to know more about life on the river should visit the Podskalí Customs House Museum (Podskalská celnice Na Výtoni), on the opposite shore at Rašínovo nábřeží 412. Podskalí, meaning 'under the rock' because it was situated below Vyšehrad, was a riverside settlement founded in the 12th century that made its living by floating timber along the Vltava, mining sand, fishing and selling ice. All that remains today is its Gothic customs house, now the museum, in which duties were once paid for floated timber.

A tour of some other historic hotels in Prague makes landfall on Kampa Island in Lesser Quarter (Malá Strana). Along its cobbled streets stands the U Karlova mostu (At the Charles Bridge) at Na Kampě 15, an old-fashioned riverside tavern from the 1400s, as well as the peaceful Pension Dientzenhofer at Nosticova 2, a 16th century house in which the renowned Baroque architect Kilián Ignáz Dientzenhofer was born.

Moving up towards the Castle there is the Dům U Velké boty at Vlašská 30, a charming family home popular with artists and actors,

The Albatros Botel moored on the Vltava at nábřeží Ludvíka Svobody

and the Hotel U Žluté boty at Jánský vršek 11, a quaint Baroque house from the 1630s with original wood panelling.

On the Nerudova stretch of the Royal Route (Královská cesta), the traditional coronation path of Bohemian kings from Old Town up to Prague Castle (Pražský hrad), there are several more historic hotels, including the 17th century U Červeného lva (House at the Red Lion) at number 41, worth visiting for its painted vaulted ceilings, Hotel Neruda at number 44 dating back to 1348, and Zlatá hvězda (Golden Star) at number 48, more like a museum than a hotel. At the top of Nerudova, where it merges into Úvoz, there is the intimate U Krále Karla at Úvoz 4, once a Baroque Benedictine house, the Hotel Questenberk at number 15 built as a church in the 1660s, and the rustic Romantik Hotel U Raka at Černínská 10, dating back to 1739 and sporting a collection of old millstones outside.

Following the Royal Route back down across Charles Bridge (Karlův most) onto Karlova in Old Town (Staré Město) our tour finishes with the 16th century U Zlaté studny (At the Golden Well) at Karlova 3, named after the ancient well in its cellar, the Iron Gate at Michalská 19, renowned for its superbly renovated Gothic painted ceiling beams, and the Hotel Černý slon at Týnská 1, a 14th century townhouse tucked away on a cobbled backstreet by the Cathedral of the Virgin Mary before Týn (chrám Panny Marie před Týnem).

Other places of interest nearby: 71

78.   The Forgotten Gardens of Prague

Prague 5 (Smíchov), the Kinský Garden (Kinského zahrada) on náměstí
Kinských
Metro B to Anděl then Tram 6, 9, 12, 20

Regarding the historic gardens of Prague, most guidebooks tend to point
the visitor towards those that were established in Lesser Quarter (Malá
Strana) during the Baroque period (see nos. 6 & 23). However, in order to
escape the crowds and discover something rather different, a trip to the
oft-forgotten gardens of southern Prague is highly recommended.

First there is the Kinský Garden on the southern slopes of Petřín Hill,
an area covered in vineyards prior to the Thirty Years War (1618–48).
The garden was laid out by Count Rudolph Kinský in 1825 and includes
a waterfall, ponds and sculptures, as well as the pretty Kinský Summer
Palace. The latter is the work of Viennese architect Jindřich Koch and
remains the purest Empire-style building in Prague (the Empire style
evolved from Classicism and emphasized monumental appearance). In
1905 the Czech folklore collection of the National Museum was installed
in the palace – now called the Musaion Ethnographic Exhibition – as a
result of which several large-scale exhibits were erected in the surrounding garden as part of an unfulfilled plan to create an outdoor museum.
They are still there today and include a wayside shrine, a cross, and the
late-17th century wooden orthodox chapel of St. Michael (sv. Michal), removed from Medvedovce near Mukačevo in Transcarpathian Ukraine.
At the very top of the hill can be found a secret walled garden.

In garden history terms, the Kinský Garden is important because
it is representative of the creation of Prague's so-called English-style
parks during the first half of the 19th century. The city's *bourgeoisie* had
become a significant economic element of society and created a demand
for leafy green spaces open to them. Typical of the times is the Chotko-
vy sady Park adjacent to the Belvedere in Hradčany (see no. 21). It was
established by Count Rudolph Chotek, supreme governor of Bohemia,
on the site of a former timber yard in 1833 and in 1841 was thrown open
to the public as Prague's first municipal park.

Crying out for restoration are the remains of Cibulka Park on Plzeňská
in Košíře (Prague 5). Cibulka is one of Prague's least known garden treas-
ures and reflects the strong Romantic and monumental aesthetics also
prevalent in the early 19th century. The entrance to the park is marked by
a statue of St. John of Nepomuk (sv. Jan Nepomucký) on Nad Hliníkem,

behind which is a ridge topped with a dilapidated belvedere tower. At the far end of the ridge is the abandoned Empire-style summer residence of Bishop Leopold Thun-Hohenstein, who founded the park in 1817. By following the path around to the right a crumbling folly, known as Dante's Hell, is reached, beneath which is a ruined grotto containing a statue of Chronos. In the valley below stood a summerhouse known as Diana's Pavilion from which only a statue of the goddess now remains. Following the stream back to the park entrance a statue of Zeus can be glimpsed amongst the overgrown trees.

A Ukrainian chapel in the Kinský Garden (Kinského zahrada) in Smíchov

During the second half of the 19th century Prague's public parks were developed further. Charles Square (Karlovo náměstí) in New Town, for instance, the largest square in the Czech Republic, was given an English park makeover in the 1870s by the addition of a number of outstanding specimen trees; the Riegrovy sady gardens were laid out in a similar style in neighbouring Vinohrady (Prague 2) between 1904 and 1908. Most impressive of all, however, were the walled Havlíčkovy sady gardens also located in Vinohrady. They are sometimes called Gröbovka after the neo-Renaissance hilltop villa built by factory owner Moric Gröbe in the 1880s. The slopes around the villa now support one of Prague's few remaining vineyards. Just inside one of the main entrances to the gardens on U Havlíčových Sadů can be found a huge ruined grotto and fountain, its artificially created walls riddled with secret passages and stairways.

The slopes of Petřín Hill north of the Kinský Garden comprise old monastic gardens (Seminářská and Strahovská zahrada) and Baroque palace gardens (Lobkovická, Schönbornská and Vratislavská zahrada). The Lobkovická zahrada was the garden of the Lobkowicz Palace (Lobkovický pálac) at Vlašská 19, owned until 1948 by one of Bohemia's major landowners. It later became the West German embassy, where in September 1989 thousands of holidaying East Germans set up a temporary camp demanding West German citizenship, which they received following the fall of the Berlin Wall. Czech artist David Černý commemorated the event with a gold-painted Trabant car on stilts in the embassy garden.

Other places of interest nearby: 8, 9

79. The Plague Cemetery at Smíchov

Prague 5 (Smíchov), the Lesser Quarter Cemetery (Malostranský hřbitov) on Plzeňská
Metro B to Anděl then Tram 4, 7, 9, 10

Stretched out alongside the main road leading westwards out of Prague, in the 5th district of Smíchov, lies an almost forgotten cemetery. This leafy and overlooked corner has an atmosphere all of its own, its Biedermeier-era headstones now mostly abandoned to nature.

The cemetery was founded originally in a vineyard as a makeshift burial ground for victims of the bubonic plague of 1679–80. As with Žižkov's Old Jewish Cemetery and Olšany Cemetery (Prague 3), which were also established as hurried responses to the same epidemic, it was sited at what was then considered a safe distance from the town centre and was used for mass unmarked graves (see nos. 41 & 58). A century later, as a result of Habsburg Holy Roman Emperor and King of Bohemia Joseph II's (1780–90) Funeral Edict, which forbade burials within the city limits on sanitary grounds, these plague cemeteries became permanent graveyards. The Smíchov Cemetery was now used predominantly for the dead of Lesser Quarter (Malá Strana), as well as the castle district of Hradčany, and was referred to thereafter as the Lesser Quarter Cemetery.

In time a wall was erected around the cemetery, which also encompassed a Chapel of St. Rochus (patron saint of plague victims) and a cemetery church of the Holy Trinity. However, by 1910 the rapidly expanding and increasingly industrialised district of Smíchov was encroaching upon the cemetery and plans were drawn up for its removal. Thankfully, a public outcry meant that the cemetery was saved, although its perimeter wall and church were demolished and the area converted into a public park. Today the cemetery is walled once more in order to protect what is now acknowledged to be a very fine, although little-known, collection of funerary monuments. Renowned sculptors such as Jan Ludvík Kranner, Wenceslaus Prachner and Josef and Emanuel Max produced exquisite tombs for the likes of painter Josef Vojtěch Hellich, sculptor Ignác František and engraver Vincenc Morstadt. Another interesting grave is that of the singer Josefína Dušková, which can be found at the back of the cemetery on the lefthand side. She is buried together with her composer husband František Dušek, their headstone recording the fact that they were once the owners of the nearby Villa Bertramka, where Mozart completed the score for his opera *Don Giovanni* (see no. 80). With such strong ties to Mozart it seems fitting that the cemetery retains a similar feel to the St. Marx Cemetery in Vienna, where the composer himself was buried one wintry night in 1791.

Ivy-covered gravestones in Smíchov's Lesser Quarter Cemetery (Malostranský hřbitov)

The bustling district of Smíchov is today a far cry from the community of farmsteads, gardens and vineyards that existed here when the plague cemetery was first established. However, amongst the busy thoroughfares and shopping centres, including the Golden Angel (Zlatý anděl) complex by renowned architect Jean Nouvel, can still be found some older buildings, including a charming neo-Renaissance town hall, a neo-Gothic cloister and the Church of the Heart of Jesus (klášter Sacré Coeur), the neo-Romanesque cloister of St. Gabriel (klášter sv. Gabriela), the neo-Renaissance Church of St. Wenceslaus (kostel sv. Václava), and the Baroque summer palace of Portheim, which belonged to the Jewish textile family of von Portheim (see no. 42).

(Note: many towns across Europe expressed their gratitude to God for having either escaped or survived a visitation of the plague by the erection of plague columns, usually on a market square or busy street. Two good examples exist in Prague, namely the Trinity Column in Lesser Quarter Square (Malostranské náměstí), created in 1715 to a design by Giovanni Battista Alliprandi after the cessation of an epidemic in 1713, and the blackened plague column in Hradčanské náměstí, created sometime between 1726 and 1736 by the Baroque sculptor Ferdinand Maximilian Brokoff and topped with a statue of the Virgin Mary.)

Other places of interest nearby: 80

80. Where Mozart was Happiest

Prague 5 (Smíchov), the Mozart Museum in the Villa Bertramka at
Mozartova 169
Metro B to Anděl then Tram 4, 7, 9, 10

When Johannes Chrysostomus Wolfgangus Theophilus Mozart, better known as Wolfgang Amadeus Mozart (1756–91), drove into Prague
for the first time with his wife Constanze on January 11th 1787 his fame
preceded him. It is said that when he arrived at the city's walls the gate-
keeper asked if he was "the Mr. Mozart who had composed the *Figaro*?"
When Mozart answered in the affirmative he was greeted with a re-
sounding, "You are most heartily welcome!" A little later, as the Mozarts rolled through Old Town (Staré Město) in the carriage of Count
Johann Thun, the composer's first host and most important Prague patron, people in the street could be heard whistling tunes from *Le nozze
di Figaro*. This Italian comic opera, with its libretto by Lorenzo Da Ponte
(1749–1838), had been staged in Prague the previous December and received with greater enthusiasm than in Vienna; when Mozart bade fare-
well to the city four years later he would admit, "My people of Prague
really understand me".

The first eight days of Mozart's stay in Prague were spent in the
magnificent surroundings of the Renaissance Thun Palace at Thunovská 14 in Lesser Quarter (Malá Strana), now the British Embassy.
On the first evening the Mozarts went to a ball at the Bretfeld Palace
at Nerudova 33, where Mozart made the acquaintance of the Italian
adventurer Giacomo Casanova (1725–98), now enjoying his retirement
as librarian to the Count of Waldstein at Duchcov Castle in northern
Bohemia.

On January 18th the Mozarts left the Thun Palace and stayed at
the New Tavern (Nová hospoda) at Celetná 29 (now the House At the
Golden Angel) in order to be near to the Count Nostic National Theatre at Ovocný trh 1 in Old Town. Here Mozart conducted his *Symphony
in D major*, better known as the *Prague Symphony*, as well as a special
performance of *Figaro* the next day. The theatre was named after Count
František Antonín Nostic-Reineck, music lover, patron and Bohemia's
highest-ranking feudal lord, whose palace can still be seen at Maltézské
náměstí 1. The Count built the theatre in 1781–83 for the entertainment
of Prague's large and powerful German community to a design by his
architect Antonín Haffenecker; it remains Prague's finest neo-Classi-

82. The Hollywood of the East

Prague 5 (Barrandov), the Barrandov Film Studios at Kříženeckého
náměstí 5
Metro B to Smíchovské nádraží then Bus 246, 248

South of Smíchov lies the hilltop district of Barrandov, dominated by its film studios and known in cinema circles as the 'Hollywood of the East'. There are even white Hollywood-style letters spelling out the name 'BARRANDE' on the cliffs above the riverbank. This, however, is actually a tribute to the French geologist and palaeontologist Joachim Barrande (1799–1883), tutor to the Comte de Chambord, grandson of the Bourbon King Charles X of France. When the king abdicated during the French Revolution of 1830 Barrande accompanied the royal exiles to Prague, where his attention turned to the fossils of the Lower Palaeozoic rocks of Bohemia. The Barrandov area provided rich pickings for the French fossil hunter, as well as considerable material for the twenty or so books he eventually published: in 1928 the area was named Barrandov after him. An example of the fossil-bearing rocks that would have attracted Barrande can be found at the northern end of Barrandovská, where a plaque bears his name together with a sculpted Trilobite fossil.

The history of the Czech film industry is inextricably linked to the activities of brothers Miloš and Václav Havel, the latter being the father of the former President of the Czech Republic. In 1930 Václav, a civil engineer, came up with a plan for a garden city at Barrandov, and Miloš, already a film distributor, suggested incorporating a modern film studio into the design. Construction of the studio, based on designs by architect-cum-film director Max Urban, began in November 1931 and fourteen months later Barrandov's first Czech film, *Murder on Ostrovní Street (Vražda v Ostrovní ulici)*, was shot there. The studio was soon producing eighty films a year with a permanent staff of three hundred.

During the German occupation of Czechoslovakia in the Second World War the Barrandov studios were enlarged by the addition of three huge interconnecting stages to equal those in Berlin and Munich. Used to produce many Nazi propaganda films they are still in demand today because of their size. After the war Barrandov was nationalised by the Communist regime and remained under state ownership until the beginning of the 1990s. It was during this era that a special effects stage with a back projection tunnel and water tank was constructed.

In terms of films gaining worldwide recognition, the first golden age for Barrandov came during the mid to late 1960s. The period witnessed popular demands for the reform of traditional Communism, culminating in the abortive Prague Spring of 1968 (see no. 4). These political activities were reflected in the so-called Czech New Wave of filmmaking, much of which was undertaken at Barrandov. Classics from the period include *Larks on a String (Skřivánci na niti)* (1969) by Jiří Menzel about political dissidents forced to work in a steel mill by the Communists (banned on release it won an award at the Berlin Film Festival in 1990), *The Ear (Ucho)* (1970) by Karel Kachyňa about state surveillance techniques (again banned by the authorities), and *The Shop on Main Street (Obchod na korze)* (1964) by Ján Kadár and Elmar Klos about a carpenter forced by the Nazis to 'Aryanise' the button shop of an old Jewish woman (it won the 1965 Oscar for Best Foreign Language Film). Less political was *Intimate Lighting (Intimní osvětlení)* (1966) by Ivan Passer, a charming film about the reunion of two old friends after many years, and Menzel's *Closely Observed Trains (Ostře sledované vlaky)* (1966), which won the 1968 Oscar for Best Foreign Film. Another leading light of the Czech New Wave was the director Miloš Forman, whose *Loves of a Blonde (Lásky jedné plavovlásky)* and *The Firemen's Ball (Hoří, má panenko)* both achieved Oscar nominations.

During the 1970s and early 80s Barrandov continued to turn out an average of seventy films a year, particularly comedies, Czech fairytales and programmes for Czech Television. However, a turning point came in the mid-80s as foreign filmmakers started trickling into Prague to avail themselves not only of the excellent facilities at Barrandov but also to use the photogenic city as a backdrop. Major productions included Barbra Streisand's *Yentl* (1983) and, most significantly, Miloš Forman's *Amadeus* (1984). Forman had left Czechoslovakia after Warsaw Pact troops invaded in 1968 and achieved lasting celluloid fame with *One Flew Over the Cuckoo's Nest*, winning five Oscars in the process. Now he returned to his homeland to make a film about Mozart in the city that had so warmly welcomed the composer in 1787; this time the film won eight Oscars.

Shortly after the Velvet Revolution in 1989 Barrandov was privatised and state funding of Czech films declined. However, the resulting decrease in local film production was more than compensated by an increase in foreign production, using both the stages at Barrandov and the streets of Prague for filming (beginning with *Mission Impossible* (1996) directed by Brian de Palma and starring Tom Cruise, such films have included *From Hell*, *The Bourne Identity*, *Blade II*, *The League of*

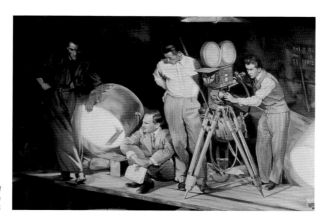

An evocative mural at the Barrandov Film Studios

Extraordinary Gentlemen (see no. 11), *Van Helsing*, *The Brothers Grimm*, Roman Polanski's *Oliver Twist* and the James Bond remake, *Casino Royale*). Meanwhile, Czech films are still making an impact on the outside world, as witnessed by the recent Oscar nomination for *Divided We Fall (Musíme si pomáhat)* (2000) by director Jan Hřebejk about a small Czech village during the Second World War.

Today, Barrandov makes for a fascinating area to explore, from the bustling studio complex itself, with its workshops, film laboratories, back lot and props hire division (boasting over a quarter of a million outfits), to the glitzy, Hollywood-esque villas strung out along nearby Barrandovská, at the end of which stands Max Urban's forlorn, cliff-top Terasa Restaurant (1929), where actors and producers once sunned themselves. At the base of the cliff is an abandoned swimming pool dating from the same period, its multi-decked concrete diving board rising above the encroaching vegetation.

83. The Asian Art Château

Prague 16 (Zbraslav), the Zbraslav Château and Monastery (Zbraslavský zámek a klášter) at Bartoňova 2
Metro B to Smíchovské nádraží then Bus 129, 241, 243, 314, 318, 338, 390 to Zbraslavské náměstí

Zbraslav is one of Prague's more remote districts, lying far to the south at the confluence of the Vltava and Berounka rivers; it was incorporated into Prague in 1974. Although today the area may seem relatively unimportant its intriguing architectural remains tell a different story.

The history of Zbraslav is inextricably tied up with that of its monastery, the first written reference dating back to 1115 when the village belonged to the Kladruby monastery. In 1268 the Přemyslid King Otakar II (1253–78) acquired it and built himself a hunting lodge. More importantly, in 1292 Přemyslid King Wenceslaus (Václav) II (1278–1305) founded the *Aula Regia* ('Royal Hall') monastery here and assigned it over to the Cistercian order. During the early 14th century the monastery became the political centre of the Czech state and its early Gothic Church of the Virgin Mary acted as the new royal burial ground (something the visitor is reminded of when viewing the skulls of the last Přemyslids in caskets, within a stone monument to the legendary Přemysl the Ploughman in the present-day Church of St. Jacob (see no. 75)). Much is known of this golden age from the so-called Zbraslav Chronicle (Zbraslavská kronika) – *Chronicon Aulae Regiae* in Latin – written by two local abbots, Ota and Petr Žitavský.

Unfortunately, in 1420 the monastery and church were damaged by the Taborites during the Hussite Wars (1420–36) and then all but destroyed during the Thirty Years War (1618–48). Things improved during the Baroque period, from 1700 to 1740, when Abbots Wolfgang II Loechner and Thomas Budecius erected fine new buildings to plans by Giovanni Santini and František Maximilian Kaňka, with interior decoration by František Xaver Palko (the abbots also converted a fort in Komořany across the river into a Baroque summer palace for themselves). Such excesses encouraged Habsburg Holy Roman Emperor and King of Bohemia Joseph II (1780–90) to close down the monastery in 1785 as part of his widespread anticlerical reforms. Further ignominy followed when the buildings became the property of Walloon aristocrat Joseph de Souvaige, who built a sugar refinery in the Royal Hall (its

The Zbraslav Château and Monastery (Zbraslavský zámek a klášter) in its lovely riverside setting

walls decorated by master fresco painter Václav Vavřinec Reiner) and a hayloft in the refectory!

Eventually, in 1825 the Zbraslav estates were sold to the Bavarian Prince Friedrich Öttingen-Wallerstein, who adapted the buildings to the needs of a princely residence. Once again the region flourished and in 1850 Zbraslav became the seat of the district council. In 1910 ownership passed to the wealthy industrialist Cyril Bartoň of Dobenín, who in 1912–26 commissioned the architect Dušan Jurkovič to undertake a full restoration of the former monastery into the beautiful riverside château seen today.

In 1940 Bartoň loaned the château to the state and since the end of the Second World War it has been used as an exhibition space by the National Gallery of Prague (Národní galerie v Praze). In 1998 it became the permanent home of the gallery's Asian and Oriental holdings. Chief amongst the exhibits are the Chinese and Japanese collections, although there are also wonderful Indian, Southeast Asian and Islamic artefacts, as well as some lively painted Tibetan wall hangings, called *thangkas*.

The peaceful town of Zbraslav, with its pretty main square, has another claim to fame in that it was once home to Jan Vejvoda. He was the composer of the famous *Beer Barrel Polka (Škoda lásky)*, known more commonly around the world by its refrain of "Roll out the barrel …". He is buried in the graveyard of the Baroque Church of St. Gall (kostel sv. Havla) on Havlín Hill above Zbraslav.)

Other places of interest nearby: 84

84. Prague's Oldest Inhabitants

Prague 16 (Zbraslav), the prehistoric hill-fort above Závist (hradiště nad Závistí)
Metro B to Smíchovské nádraží then Bus 129, 241, 243, 314, 318, 338, 390 to Zbraslavské náměstí, walk south to the river and cross by bridge to the car park beyond the Prague-Zbraslav railway station, and follow the track up into the woods

Man has lived in the environs of Prague since the very dawn of human history, as witnessed by scattered archaeological finds dating back to the Old Stone Age (Palaeolithic). The most ancient of these are over half a million years old. During the 5th millennium BC, Neolithic farmers arrived in the region and created the first cultural landscape of ploughed fields and permanent settlements, in districts such as Dejvice and Bubeneč. The fertile lands at the confluence of the Vltava and Berounka Rivers drew them here, together with the shelter, protection and good vantage points offered by the rocky geology along the riverbanks.

During the 4th and 3rd millennia BC, a period termed the Chalcolithic or Copper Age, the first fortified settlements of Prague appeared, for example in the Šárka Gorge and possibly Vyšehrad (see no. 27). The subsequent Early Bronze Age (1800–1600 BC) saw an artistic flowering too, represented by a cemetery of the Únětice Culture discovered in the northwestern district of Suchdol, containing copper daggers inlaid with gold and amber (see no. 30).

However, in terms of visible prehistoric remains in Prague today, it is the Knovíz Culture of the Middle Bronze Age (1600–1200 BC) that can offer the most dramatic, being responsible for the construction of several important strongholds. The most impressive is on the hill above Závist (Hradiště nad Závistí), on the right bank of the Vltava above the Prague-Zbraslav railway station. It was first fortified around the beginning of the 1st millennium BC and then enhanced during the last four centuries BC, when the Celtic Boii tribe was settling the Prague area. The Boii were the first historical nation to be documented on Bohemian soil, from whom the Latin name 'Bohemia' is derived (the area occupied the western third of what is today the Czech Republic).

By the 1st century BC the hill-fort at Závist had become the biggest fortified settlement in Central Europe, causing Roman Emperor Julius Caesar to coin the term *Oppidum* for such fortified Celtic proto-cities. Archaeologists have shown that the Oppidum at Závist covered well over 150 hectares, that it was connected to the neighbouring prehistoric site of Šance by a series of huge mounds along the Břežany Valley (Břežanské údolí), and most significantly that it had a stone shrine now recognised as the most advanced structure of the La Tène Culture of the Late Iron Age (700–1st century BC). The best time to visit the enigmatic remains is spring, when the wooded slopes of what is now a designated nature reserve are carpeted with wild flowers.

It was also during the 1st century BC that Germanic tribes started filtering into

The hill-fort above Závist (hradiště nad Závistí) was once home to some of Prague's earliest inhabitants

Bohemia and diluting the Celtic presence (there is evidence of a Germanic settlement on Lesser Quarter Square (Malostranské náměstí), for example). It would be two of these tribes, namely the Marcomanni and the Quadi, who eventually took advantage of the decline of the Roman Empire in the 4th century AD and ousted the remaining Celts. The Germanic tribes were themselves seriously troubled by the incursions of Attila the Hun in 451, after which time Slavic tribes (known as *Venedi/Venethi* or *Sklavenoí*), the true ancestors of today's Czechs and Slovaks, gradually settled the area in the 6th and 7th centuries. Their modest archaeological remains include square huts, simple but elegant pottery, and plenty of pig bones.

Although initially ruled over by Turkic Avars, the Slavs staged a successful rebellion in the late 7th century, fuelling numerous 8th century myths relating to the foundation of Prague and the origin of the Přemyslid dynasty, the first documented rulers of Bohemia (see nos. 28 & 75). Being subject to the Great Moravian Empire (today Slovakia) from 830 onwards meant that the Slavs – now called Czechs – were evangelised by Byzantine missionaries, sent in an attempt to stem the political influence of the Franks to the west (see no. 71). Around the same time the first documented Přemyslid ruler, Bořivoj I (c. 870–889), founded Prague Castle (Pražský hrad). Then, in 907 AD the Moravians were conquered by the Magyars, causing Bohemia to ally itself with the Franks and resulting in a political split between Czechs and Slovaks that would last for the next thousand years.

(Note: for a closer encounter with the material remains of Prague's earliest inhabitants a visit to the archaeological collections of both the National Museum (Národní muzeum) on Wenceslas Square (Václavské náměstí) and the Museum of the City of Prague (Muzeum hlavního města Prahy) at Na Poříčí 52 in New Town (Nové Město) is thoroughly recommended.)

Other places of interest nearby: 83

***

Standing on the hill above Závist is the perfect place to finish this odyssey during which some of the more unusual and unsung corners of Prague have been explored. Looking out from these wooded slopes, which were once home to some of the area's earliest inhabitants, northwards along the stately Vltava towards the labyrinthine streets of modern Prague, gives the satisfied explorer the opportunity to reflect on the myriad cultures and characters that have helped shape this uniquely fascinating city in the heart of Central Europe.

Opening times

for museums and other places of interest

(Correct at time of going to press but may be subject to change)

Abaton Club, Prague 8 (Libeň), Na Košince off Povltavská, daily from 8.30 pm

Antikvariát Kant, Prague 1 (Nové Město), Opatovická 26, Mon–Fri 10 am–6 pm, Sat 10 am–3 pm

Antikvariát Galerie Můstek, Prague 1 (Nové Město), Národní třída 40, Mon–Fri 10 am–7 pm, Sat 12 am–4 pm

Antikvariát Karel Křenek, Prague 1 (Staré Město), U Obecního domu 2, Mon–Fri 10 am–6 pm, Sat 11 am–6 pm

Antikvariát Pařížská, Prague 1 (Staré Město), Pařížká 8, Mon–Fri 10 am–7 pm, Sat & Sun 10 am–6 pm

Antonín Dvořák Museum (Muzeum Antonína Dvořáka), Prague 2 (Nové Město), Villa Amerika, Ke Karlovu 20, Tue–Sun Apr–Sep 10 am–1.30 pm, 2–5.30 pm, Oct–Mar 9.30 am–1.30 pm, 2–5 pm

Architecture in Porcelain, Prague 1 (Hradčany), Úvoz 1, daily 9 am–6 pm

Art Deco, Prague 1 (Staré Město), Michalská 21, Mon–Fri 2–7 pm

Au Gourmand, Prague 1 (Staré Město), Dlouhá 10, daily 9 am–5 pm

Baráčnická rychta beer hall, Prague 1 (Malá Strana), Tržiště 23, daily 12 am–1 am

Barrandov Film Studios-Fundus Costume and Props Hire, Prague 5 (Barrandov), Kříženeckého náměstí 322, Mon–Fri 7 am–3 pm

Basilica of St. George (bazilika sv. Jiří), Prague 1 (Hradčany), Prague Castle (Pražský hrad), Jiřské náměstí, see Prague Castle

Bat'a, Prague 1 (Nové Město), Václavské náměstí 6, Mon–Fri 9 am–9 pm, Sat 8 am–8 pm, Sun 9 am–8 pm

Bedřich Smetana Museum (Muzeum Bedřicha Smetany), Prague 1 (Staré Město), Novotného lávka 1 (first floor), Wed–Mon 10–12 am, 12.30–5 pm

Bethlehem Chapel (Betlémská kaple), Prague 1 (Staré Město), Betlémské náměstí, Jan–Mar, Nov–Dec daily 10 am–4.30 pm; Apr–Oct daily 10 am–6.30 pm

Big Ben Bookshop, Prague 1 (Staré Město), Malá Štupartská 5, Mon–Fri 9 am–6 pm, Sat & Sun 10 am–5 pm

Botanical Garden (Botanická zahrada), Prague 2 (Nové Město), Na Slupi 8, Jan–Mar, Sep–Oct daily 10 am–5 pm, Nov–Dec daily 10 am–4 pm, Apr–May daily 10 am–6 pm

Břevnov Monastery (Břevnovský klášter), Prague 6 (Břevnov), Patočkova, guided tours only Apr–Sep Sat 9 am, 10.30 am, 1 pm, 2.30 pm, 4 pm, Sun 10.30 am, 1 pm, 2.30 pm, 4 pm, Oct–Mar Sat & Sun 10 am, 2 pm; Basilica of St. Margaret (bazilika sv. Markéty) Mass Mon–Sat 7 am, 6 pm, Sun 7.30 am, 9 am, 6 pm

Café Imperial, Prague 1 (Nové Město), Na Poříčí 15, daily 9 am–12 pm

Café Louvre, Prague 1 (Staré Město), Národní třída 20, Mon–Fri 8 am–11.30 pm, Sat & Sun 9 am–11.30 pm

Café Montmartre, Prague 1 (Staré Město), Řetězová 7, Mon–Fri 9 am–1 pm, Sat & Sun 12 am–1 am

Capuchin Monastery, Prague 1 (Hradčany), Loretánské náměstí, Mass Sun 8.30 am

Cathedral of St. Nicholas (chrám sv. Mikuláše), Prague 1 (Malá Strana), Malostranské náměstí, daily 10 am–4 pm

Cathedral of St. Vitus (chrám sv. Víta), Prague 1 (Hradčany), Prague Castle (Pražský hrad), Third Courtyard, see Prague Castle; tower closed Jan–Apr, Oct–Dec

Cathedral of the Virgin Mary before Týn (chrám Panny Marie před Týnem), Prague 1 (Staré Město), Staroměstské náměstí 14, Mass Sun 9.30 am, 9 pm, Tue 5 am, Wed–Fri 6 pm, Sat 8 am

Charita Florentinum, Prague 2 (Nové Město), Ječná 4, Mon–Fri 8 am–6 pm, Sat 9 am–1 pm

Charles Bridge Museum (Muzeum Karlova Mostu), Prague 1 (Staré Město), Křižovnické náměstí 3, daily 10 am–6 pm

Church of St Clement (kostel sv. Klimenta), Prague 1 (Staré Město), Karlova, Mass daily 6 pm, Sun 10 am

Church of St. Francis (kostel sv. Františka), Prague 1 (Staré Město), Křižovnické náměstí, daily 10 am–8 pm

Church of St. Giles (kostel sv. Jiljí), Prague 1 (Staré Město), Husova, daily 10 am–4 pm

Church of St. Gall (kostel sv. Havla), Prague 1 (Staré Město), Havelská, Mass Sun 8 am

Church of St. Ignatius (kostel sv. Ignáce), Prague 2 (Nové Město), Ječná, Mass Mon–Fri 6.15 am, 7.30 am, 5.30 pm, Sat 6.30 am, 7.30 am, 5.30 pm, Sun 7 am, 9 am, 11 am, 5.30 pm

Church of St. James (kostel sv. Jakuba), Prague 1 (Staré Město), corner of Malá Štupartská and Jakubská, Mon–Sat 9.30 am–12.30 pm, 2–4 pm

Church of St. John Nepomuk on the Rock (kostel sv. Jana Nepomuckého na Skalce), Prague 2 (Nové Město), Vyšehradská, Mass Sun 11 am

Church of St. Joseph (kostel sv. Josefa), Prague 1 (Malá Strana), corner of Josefská and Letenská, Sun 2–4.30 pm, Mon–Fri 10 am–4 pm

Church of St. Martin in the Wall (kostel sv. Martina ve zdi), Prague 1 (Staré Město), Martinská, Mass Sun 10.30 am

Church of St. Nicholas (kostel sv. Mikuláše), Prague 1 (Staré Město), Staroměstské náměstí, Mon 12 am–4 pm, Tue–Sat 10 am–4 pm

Church of St. Peter (kostel sv. Petra na Poříčí), Prague 1 (Nové Město), Biskupská, Mass Tue, Wed & Thu 6.30 pm, Sun 10.30 am

Church of St. Saviour (kostel sv. Salvátora), Prague 1 (Staré Město), Křižovnické náměstí, Mass Sun 2 pm & 8 pm, Tue 7 pm, Thurs 8 pm

Church of St. Simon and St. Jude (kostel sv. Šimona a Judy), Prague 1 (Staré Město), corner of Dušni and U Milosrdných, box office open one hour before performances

Church of St. Thomas (kostel sv. Tomáše), Prague 1 (Malá Strana), Josefská 8, Mon–Sat 11 am–1 pm, Sun 9–12 am, 4.30–5.30 pm

Church of St. Vojtěch (kostel sv. Vojtěcha), Prague 1 (Nové Město), Vojtěšská, Mass Sun 9.30 am

Church of St. Wenceslaus (kostel sv. Václava na Zderaze), Prague 2 (Nové Město), Dittrichova, Mass Sun 9.30 am

Church of St. Wenceslaus (kostel sv. Václava), Prague 10 (Vršovice), náměstí Svatopluka Čecha, Mass Sun 9 am

Church of Sts. Cyril and Methodius (kostel sv. Cyrila a Metoděje), Prague 2 (Nové Město), Resslova 9, Jan–Apr, Oct–Dec Tue–Sun 10 am–4 pm; May–Sept Tue–Sun 10 am–5 pm

Church of Sts. Peter and Paul (kostel sv. Petra a Pavla), Prague 2 (Vyšehrad), Štulcova, Mon, Wed & Thu 9–12 am, 1–5 pm, Sat 9–12 am, 1–5 pm, Sun 11–12 am, 1–5 pm, Mass Sun 9 am

Church of the Sacred Heart of Our Lord (kostel Nejsvětějšího Srdce Páně), Prague 3 (Žižkov), Vinohradská, Mass Sun 11 am

Church of the Virgin Mary Beneath the Chain (kostel Panny Marie pod řetězem), Prague 1 (Malá Strana), Maltézské náměstí, daily 9 am–5 pm, Mass Sun 9.30 am

Church of the Virgin Mary of the Snows (kostel Panny Marie Sněžné), Prague 1 (Nové Město), Jungmannovo náměstí, Mon–Sat 9 am–3 pm, Mass Sun 9 am, 10.15 am, 11.30 am & 6 pm

Church of the Virgin Mary Victorious (kostel Panny Marie Vítězné), Prague 1 (Malá Strana), Karmelitská 9, Mon–Sat 8.30 am–6 pm, Sun 9 am–7 pm; Museum of the Infant Jesus Mon–Sat 10 am–5.30 pm, Sun 1–5 pm

Clementinum (Klementinum), Prague 1 (Staré Město), Mariánské náměstí 4, Library Mon–Fri 9 am–7 pm, Sat 8 am–7 pm; Chapel of Mirrors (Zrcadlová kaple) during concerts only

Convent of St. Agnes of Bohemia (klášter sv. Anežky České), Prague 1 (Staré Město), U Milosrdných 17, Tue–Sun 10 am–6 pm

Convent of St. George (klášter sv. Jiří), Prague 1 (Hradčany), Prague Castle (Pražský hrad), Jiřské náměstí, Tue–Sun 10 am–6 pm

Czech Museum of Fine Arts (České muzeum výtvarných umění), Prague 1 (Staré Město), Husova 19–21, Tue–Sun 10 am–6 pm

Czech Museum of Music (České muzeum hudby), Prague 1 (Malá Strana), Church of Mary Magdalene, Karmelitská, Wed–Mon 10 am–6 pm

Ďáblice Observatory (Hvězdárna Ďáblice), Prague 8 (Ďáblice), Pod Hvězdárnou 768, Mon 10–12 am, 6–9 pm, Thu 10–12 am, 6.30–8.30 pm, Fri 10–12 am, Sun 2–4 pm

Divadlo Na zábradlí (Theatre on the Balustrade), Prague 1 (Staré Město), Anenské náměstí 5, box office Mon–Fri 2–4 pm, 2.30–8 pm; open 2 hours before performances Sat–Sun

Eco-Technical Museum (Eko-technické muzeum), Prague 6 (Bubeneč), Papírenská 6, guided tours only May–Oct Sat & Sun 10.30 am, 12.30 am, 2.30 pm & 4 pm

Estates Theatre (Stavovské divadlo), Prague 1 (Staré Město), Ovocný trh 1, box office daily 10 am–6 pm

Exhibition of Historical Pharmacies (Expozice historických lékáren), Prague 1, Nerudova 32, Apr–Sep Tue–Sun 11 am–6 pm, Oct–Mar Tue–Sun 10 am–5 pm

Exhibition Palace (Veletržní palác), Prague 7 (Holešovice), Dukelských hrdinů 47, Tue–Sun 10 am–6 pm

Expozice Franze Kafky, Prague 1 (Staré Město), náměstí Franze Kafky 3, Tue–Sat 10 am–6 pm

Fantova kavárna, Prague 1 (Nové Město), Main Station (Hlavní nádraží), Wilsonova, 6 am–11 pm

Flambée Restaurant, Prague 1 (Staré Město), Husova 5, daily 11.30–1.30 am

Former Ceremonial Hall (bývalá Obřadní síň), Prague 1 (Josefov), U starého hřbitova 3B, see the Jewish Museum

Franz Kafka Exhibition (Expozice Franze Kafky), Prague 1 (Staré Město), náměstí Franze Kafky 5, Tue–Fri 10 am–6 pm, Sat 10 am–5 pm

Franz Kafka Museum, Prague 1 (Malá Strana), Cihelná 2b, daily 10 am–6 pm

Galerie Gambra, Prague 1 (Hradčany), Černínská 5, Mar–Oct Wed–Sun 12 am–6 pm, Nov–Feb Sat & Sun 12 am–6 pm

Galerie Mánes, Prague 1 (Nové Město), Masarykovo nábřeží 1, Tue–Sun 10 am–6 pm

Gallery Art Factory, Prague 1 (Nové Město), Václavské náměstí 15, Mon–Fri 10 am–6 pm

Gas Museum (Plynárenské muzeum), Prague 4 (Michle), U Plynárny 500, by appointment only tel. (+420) 267-172-482

Globe Bookstore & Café, Prague 1 (Nové Město), Pštrossova 6, daily 10 am–12 pm

Golden Lane (Zlatá ulička), Prague 1 (Hradčany), Prague Castle (Pražský hrad) Zlatá ulička at the top of Old Castle Steps (Staré zámecké schody), see Prague Castle

Golz-Kinský Palace (palác Golz-Kinských), Prague 1 (Staré Město), Staroměstské náměstí, Tue–Sun 10 am–6 pm

Grand Café Orient, Prague 1 (Staré Město), dům U Černé Matky Boží, Ovocný trh 19, Mon–Fri 9 am–10 pm, Sat 10 am–10 pm, Sun 5–10 pm

Harampádí Antik Bazar, Prague 2 (Nové Město), Pštrossova 22, daily 10.30 am–6 pm

Havelský Market, Prague 1 (Staré Město), Havelská, Mon–Fri 7.30 am–6 pm, Sat & Sun 8.30 am–6 pm

Hergetova Cihelna Restaurant, Prague 1 (Malá Strana), Cihelná 2b, daily 12 am–2 am

Historic Tram 91 (historická tramvají 91), Prague 7 (Holešovice), U Výstaviště, Apr–Nov Sat & Sun on the hour 12 am–6 pm

House at the Stone Bell (dům U Kamenného zvonu), Prague 1 (Staré Město), Staroměstské náměstí 13, Tue–Sun 10 am–6 pm

House of the Black Madonna (dům U Černé Matky Boží), Prague 1 (Nové Město), Celetná 34, Tue–Sun 10 am–6 pm

House of the Lords of Kunštát and Poděbrady (dům pánů z Kunštátu a Poděbrad), Prague 1 (Staré Město), Řetězová 3, currently closed for restoration

Huss Oratory (Husův sbor), Prague 10 (Vršovice), corner of Dykova and U Vodárny, Mass Sun 9 am, Columbarium Sun 8.30–12 am

Jewish Museum (Židovské muzeum), Prague 1 (Josefov), comprising the Old Jewish Cemetery, Former Ceremonial Hall and Klausen Synagogue; also the Maisel Synagogue, Pinkas Synagogue and Spanish Synagogue, Nov–Mar Mon–Fri 9 am–4.30 pm; Apr–Oct Mon–Fri 9 am–6 pm; closed Jewish holidays

Josef Sudek Atelier, Prague 1 (Malá Strana), Újezd 30, Tue–Sun 12 am–6 pm

Josef Sudek Gallery, Prague 1 (Hradčany), Úvoz 24, Wed–Sun 11 am–6 pm

Josef Sudek House of Photography, Prague 1 (Josefov), Maiselova 2, Tue–Sun 11 am–6 pm

Kampa Museum (Muzeum Kampa), Prague 1 (Malá Strana), U Sovových mlýnů 2, daily 10 am–6 pm

Karlov Church (kostel Na Karlově), Prague 2 (Nové Město), Ke Karlovu, Sun 2–4.30 pm

Kavárna Divadla komedie café, Prague 1 (Nové Město), pasáž Vlasty Buriana, Jungmannova 1, Mon–Sat 8.30 am–12 pm, Sun 12 am–12 pm

Kavárna Obecní dům, Prague 1 (Nové Město), náměstí Republiky 5, daily 7.30 am–11 pm

Kavárna Slavia, Prague 1 (Staré Město), Smetanovo nábřeží 2, Mon–Fri 9 am–11 pm

King Solomon Restaurant, Prague 1 (Josefov), Široká 8, Sun–Thu 12 am–11 pm

Klausen Synagogue (Klausová synagóga), Prague 1 (Josefov), U starého hřbitova 3A, see the Jewish Museum

Kubista, Prague 1 (Staré Město), dům u Černý Matky Boží, Celetná 34, daily 10 am–6 pm

Lapidárium, Prague 7 (Holešovice), U Výstaviště, Tue–Fri 12 am–6 pm, Sat & Sun 10 am–6 pm

Le Terroir Restaurant, Prague 1 (Staré Město), Vejvodova 1 (enter via Jilská), daily 11 am–11 pm

Lesser Quarter Cemetery (Malostranský hřbitov), Prague 5 (Smíchov), Plzeňská, daily 9 am–5 pm

Loreto (Loreta), Prague 1 (Hradčany), Loretánské náměstí 7, Tue–Sun 9 am–12.15 pm, 1–4.30 pm

Maisel Synagogue (Maiselova synagóga), Prague 1 (Josefov), Maiselova 10, see the Jewish Museum

Magic Lantern (Laterna Magika), Prague 1 (Nové Město), Nová Scéna, Národní třída 4, box office Mon–Sat 10 am–8 pm

Marold Panorama (Maroldovo panoráma), Prague 7 (Holešovice), U Výstaviště, Apr–Sep Tue–Fri 2–5 pm, Sat & Sun 10 am–5 pm

Maso Tomáš Turek, Prague 1 (Nové Město), Jindřišská 23, Mon 8 am–6 pm, Tue, Wed & Fri 7 am–6 pm, Thu 7 am–6.30 pm, Sat 8 am–12.30 pm

Matrix Club, Prague 3 (Žižkov), Koněvova 13, daily from 8.30 pm

Mecca Club, Prague 7 (Holešovice), U Průhonu 3, club Fri & Sat 10 pm–6 am; restaurant Mon–Thu 10 am–11 pm, Fri 10 am–6 am, Sat 8 am–6 am

Military Antique Army Shop, Prague 1 (Nové Město), Křemencova 7, Mon–Fri 11 am–5 pm

Military Museum (Armádní muzeum), Prague 3 (Žižkov), U Památníku 2, Tue–Sun 9.30 am–6 pm

Miniatures Museum (Muzeum miniatur), Prague 1 (Hradčany), Strahovské nádvoří 11, daily 9 am–5 pm

Mirror Maze (zrcadlové bludiště), Prague 1 (Malá Strana), Petřín Hill, Jan–Mar, Nov–Dec daily 10 am–4.30 pm; Apr–Oct daily 10 am–6.30 pm

Mozart Museum, Prague 5 (Smíchov), Villa Bertramka, Mozartova 169, Jan–Mar, Nov–Dec daily 9.30 am–4 pm; Apr–Oct daily 9.30 am–6 pm

Mucha Museum (Muchovo muzeum), Prague 1 (Nové Město), Kaunický palác, Panská 7, daily 10 am–5 pm

Municipal House (Obecní dům), Prague 1 (Nové Město), náměstí Republiky 5, box office Mon–Fri 10 am–6 pm

Musaion Ethnographic Exhibition, Prague 5 (Smíchov), Kinského zahrada 98, Tue–Sun Oct–Apr 9 am–5 pm, May–Sep 10 am–5 pm

Museum of Communism (Muzeum komunismu), Prague 1 (Nové Město), Na příkopě 10 (1st floor), daily 9 am–9 pm

Museum of the City of Prague (Muzeum hlavního města Prahy), Prague 1 (Nové Město), Na Poříčí 52, Tue–Sun 9 am–6 pm

Museum of Decorative Arts (Uměleckoprůmyslové muzeum), Prague 1 (Staré Město), 17. listopadu 2, Tue–Sun 10 am–6 pm

Náprstek Museum (Náprstkovo muzeum), Prague 1 (Staré Město), Betlémské náměstí 1, Tue–Sun 10 am–6 pm

National Museum (Národní muzeum), Prague 1 (Nové Město), Václavské náměstí 68, daily May–Sep 10 am–6 pm, Oct–Apr 9 am–5 pm; closed first Tue of the month

National Museum of Agriculture (Národní zemědělské muzeum), Prague 7 (Holešovice), Kostelní 44, Tue–Sun 9 am–5 pm

National Technical Museum (Národní technické muzeum), Prague 7 (Holešovice), Kostelní 42, the museum is closed for renovation until 2010

National Theatre (Národní divadlo), Prague 1 (Nové Město), Národní 2, box office daily 10 am–6 pm

Nedělní Cukrárna Canteen, Prague 6 (Střešovice), Vítězné náměstí 3, daily 6 am–8 pm

Novoměstský pivovar Brew-Pub, Prague 1 (Nové Město), Vodičkova 20, Mon–Fri 10 am–11.30 pm, Sat 11.30 am–11.30 pm, Sun 10 am–10 pm

Observatory Tower (hvězdárenská věž) and Baroque Library, Prague 1 (Staré Město), Carolinum, Karlova, guided tours only on the hour Mon–Fri 2–6 pm, Sat & Sun 11 am–6 pm

Old Jewish Cemetery (Starý židovský hřbitov), Prague 1 (Josefov), U starého hřbitova 3, see the Jewish Museum

Old-New Synagogue (Staronová synagóga), Prague 1 (Josefov), Červená 2, Jan–Mar, Nov–Dec Mon–Thu, Sun 9.30 am–5 pm, Fri 9 am–2 pm; Apr–Jun Mon–Thu, Sun 9.30 am–6 pm, Fri 9.30 am–5 pm

Old Royal Palace (Starý královský palác), Prague 1 (Hradčany), Prague Castle (Pražský hrad), Third Courtyard, Jiřské náměstí, see Prague Castle

Old Town Bridge Tower (Staroměstská mostecká věž), Prague 1 (Staré Město), Křižovnické náměstí, Jan–Mar, Nov–Dec daily 10 am–5 pm; Apr, May, Oct daily 10 am–7 pm; Jun–Sept daily 10 am–10 pm

Old Town Hall (Staroměstská radnice), Prague 1 (Staré Město), Staroměstské náměstí, Tue–Sun 9 am–6 pm

Olšany Cemetery (Olšanské hřbitovy), Prague 3 (Žižkov), Vinohradská, daily dawn–dusk

Olšany New Jewish Cemetery
(Nový židovský hřbitov), Prague 3
(Žižkov), Izraelská, Sun–Thu
9 am–5 pm, Fri 9 am–2 pm

Pálffy palác Restaurant, Prague 1
(Malá Strana), Valdštejnská 14, daily
11 am–11 pm

Palatial Gardens (Palácové
zahrady), Prague 1 (Malá
Strana), Valdštejnské náměstí 3/
Valdštejnská 12–14, Apr–Oct daily
10 am–4 pm

**Pedagogical Museum of J. A
Comenius** (Pedagogické muzeum
J. A. Komenského), Prague 1 (Malá
Strana), Valdštejnská 20, Tue–Sun
10–12.30 am, 1–5 pm

Peklo Restaurant, Prague 1
(Hradčany), Strahovské nádvoří 1,
daily 11 am–11 pm

Petřín Funicular Railway (lanová
dráha na Petřín), Prague 1 (Malá
Strana), from lower station on U
Lanové dráhy off Újezd to upper
station at Petřín, daily 9.15 am–
8.45 pm, every 10–15 minutes

Petřín Observation Tower
(Petřínská rozhledna), Prague
1 (Malá Strana), Petřín Hill,
Jan–Mar, Nov–Dec Sat & Sun
10 am–4.30 pm; Apr–Oct daily
10 am–7 pm

Pinkas Synagogue (Pinkasova synagóga), Prague 1 (Josefov), Široká 3,
see the Jewish Museum

Pivovarský klub, Prague 8 (Karlín),
Křižíkova 17, daily 11 am–11.30 pm

Planetarium, Prague 7 (Holešo-
vice), Královská obora 233,
Mon–Thu 8.30–12 am, 1–8 pm, Sat
& Sun 9.30–12 am, 1–8 pm

**Plavecký Stadion Podolí swim-
ming centre,** Prague 4 (Podoli),
Podolská 74, Mon–Fri 6 am–9 pm,
Sat & Sun 8 am–7 pm

Podskalská Customs Museum
(Podskalská celnice na Výtoni),
Prague 2 (Nové Město), Rašínovo
nábřeží 412, Tue–Sun 10 am–6 pm

Police Museum (muzeum policie
CR), Prague 2 (Nové Město), Ke
Karlovu 1, Tue–Sun 10 am–5 pm

Postal Museum (Poštovní muzeum), Prague 1 (Nové Město), Nové
Mlýny, Tue–Sun 9 am–5 pm

Postcards Family Museum
(Muzeum pohledů), Prague 1
(Staré Město), Liliová 4, Tue–Sun
11 am–7 pm

Powder Gate (Prašná brána),
Prague 1 (Staré Město), U prašné
brány, Apr–Oct daily 10 am–6 pm

Powder Tower (Prašná věž),
Prague 1 (Hradčany), Prague Castle
(Pražský hrad), Third Courtyard, off
Vikářská, see Prague Castle

Prague Botanical Gardens
(Botanická zahrada Praha), Prague 7
(Trója), Nádvorní 134, Apr–Oct
9 am–6 pm

Prague Castle (Pražský hrad),
Prague 1 (Hradčany), Hradčanské
náměstí, Apr–Oct grounds
5 am–12 pm, buildings 9 am–5 pm,
gardens 8 am–6 pm, Nov–Mar
grounds 6 am–11 pm, buildings
9 am–4 pm, gardens closed except
Gardens on the Bastion

Prague Castle Picture Gallery
(Obrazárna Pražského hradu),
Prague 1 (Hradčany), Prague Castle
(Pražský hrad), Second Courtyard,
see Prague Castle

Prague Jewellery Collection
(Pražský kabinet šperku), Prague 1
(Malá Strana), Cihelna 28, daily
10 am–6 pm

**Prague Public Transport
Museum** (Muzeum městské hro-
madné dopravy v Praze), Prague 6
(Střešovice), Patočkova 4, Apr–mid
Nov Sat & Sun 9 am–5 pm

Prague Steamship Company
(Pražská paroplavební společnost),
Prague 2 (Nové Město), Rašínovo
nábřeží, all year round

Prague Waterworks Museum
(muzeum pražského vodárenství),
Prague 4 (Podolí), Podolí Waterworks (Podolská vodárna), Podolská
17, by appointment only tel. (+420)
272-172-344

Prague Zoo (Zoo Praha), Prague 7
(Troja), U Trojského zámku 3, Jan,
Feb, Nov, Dec daily 9 am–4 pm; Mar
daily 9 am–5 pm; Apr–May daily
9 am–6 pm; Jun–Aug 9 am–7 pm;
Sept–Oct daily 9 am–6 pm

Prague Zoo Chairlift (sedačková
lanovka), Prague 7 (Troja), Prague
Zoo (Pražská zoologická zahrada),
U Trojského zámku 3, Apr–Oct
Tue–Thu, Sat & Sun 10 am–6 pm;
only runs if sufficient users

Radegast beer hall, Prague 1
(Staré Město), Templová 2, daily
11 am–12.30 am

Restaurace U Rotta, Prague 1
(Staré Město), Malé náměstí 3, daily
12 am–11 pm

Restaurant Svatá Klára, Prague 7
(Troja), U Trojského zámku 35, daily
6 pm–1 am

Rotunda of St. Martin (rotunda
sv. Martina), Prague 2 (Vyšehrad),
V Pevnosti, Mass Sun evening

Rotunda of the Holy Cross
(rotunda sv. Kříže), Prague 1 (Staré
Město), corner of Konviktská and
Karoliny Světlé, Mass Sun 5 pm,
Tue 6 pm

Rudolfinum, Prague 1 (Josefov),
Alešovo nábřeží 12, box office
Mon–Fi 10a–6 pm; closed mid
July–mid Aug

Schwarzenberg Palace
(Schwarzenberský palác), Prague 1
(Hradčany), Hradčanské náměstí,
Tue–Sun 10 am–6 pm

Sea World (Mořský svět), Prague 7
(Holešovice), U Výstaviště, daily
10 am–7 pm

Shakespeare & Sons Bookshop,
Prague 10 (Vršovice), Krymská 12,
daily 12 am–12 pm

Slavonic Monastery (kláster Na
Slovanech), Prague 2 (Nové Město),
Na Slovanech, Mon–Fri 9 am–4 pm

Spanish Synagogue (Španelská
synagóga), Prague 1 (Josefov),
Vězeňská 1, see the Jewish
Museum

Star Palace (letohrádek Hvězda),
Prague 6 (Liboc), obora Hvězda
game park off Bělohorská, daily
Apr–Oct Tue–Sun 10 am–5 pm

Štefánik Observatory (Štefánikova
hvězdárna), Prague 1 (Malá Strana),
Petřín Hill, Jan, Feb, Nov–Dec Tue–
Fri 6–8 pm, Sat & Sun 10–12 am,
2–8 pm; Mar Tue–Fri 7–9 pm, Sat
& Sun 10–12 am, 2–6 pm, 7–9 pm;
Apr–Aug Tue–Fri 2–7 pm, 9–11 pm,
Sat & Sun 10–12 am, 2–7 pm,
9–12 pm; Sep Tue–Fri 11 am–6 pm,
8–10 pm, Sat & Sun 10–12 am,
2–6 pm, 8–12 pm; Oct Tue–Fri
7–9 pm, Sat & Sun 10–12 am,
2–6 pm, 7–9 pm

Sternberg Palace (Šternberský
palác), National Gallery Collection
of European Old Masters, Prague 1
(Hradčany), Hradčanské náměstí 15,
Tue–Sun 10 am–6 pm

Strahov Monastery Library
(Strahovský kláster), Prague 1
(Hradčany), Strahovské nádvoří 1,
daily 9–12 am, 1–5 pm

Troja Chateau (zámek Troja),
Prague 7 (Holešovice), U trojského
zámku 1, Apr–Oct Tue–Sun
10 am–6 pm; Nov–Mar Sat & Sun
10 am–5 pm

Týnská literární kavárna,
Prague 1 (Staré Město), Týnská 6,
Mon–Fri 9 am–11 pm, Sat & Sun
10 am–11 pm

U Bakaláře (At the Bachelor) Canteen, Prague 1 (Staré Město), Celetná 13, Mon–Fri 9 am–7 pm, Sat–Sun 11 am–7 pm

U Buldoka (At the Bulldog) beer hall, Prague 5 (Smíchov), Preslova 1, Mon–Thu 11 am–12 pm, Fri 11 am–1 pm, Sat 12 am–12 pm, Sun 12 am–11 pm

U Černé lišky (At the Black Fox) Restaurant, Prague 1 (Staré Město), Mikulášská 2, daily 10 am–10 pm

U Černého vola (At the Black Ox) beer hall, Prague 1 (Hradčany), Loretánské náměstí 1, daily 10 am–10 pm

U Fleků beer hall, Prague 1 (Nové Město), Křemencova 11, daily 9 am–11 pm; Brewing Museum (Pivovarské muzeum) daily Mon–Fri 10 am–5 pm, Sat & Sun 10 am–4 pm

U Hudků Herna Bar, Prague 3 (Žižkov), Bořivojova 110, daily, all hours

U Knihomola (Bookworm) International Bookstore, Prague 2 (Vinohrady), Mánesova 79, Mon–Sat 9 am–1 pm, Sun 11 am–6 pm

U Maltézských rytířů (Knights of Malta) Restaurant, Prague 1 (Malá Strana), Prokopská 10, daily 11 am–11 pm

U Medvídků (At the Little Bears) brewery & beer hall, Prague 1 (Staré Město), Na Perštýně 7, Mon–Sat 11.30 am–11 pm, Sun 11.30 am–10 pm

U Modré růže (At the Blue Rose) Restaurant, Prague 1 (Nové Město), Rytířská 16, daily 11.30 am–11.30 pm

U Pinkasů beer hall, Prague 1 (Nové Město), Jungmannovo náměstí 16, 9 am–11 pm

U Rozvařilů Canteen, Prague 1 (Nové Město), Na Poříčí 26, Mon–Fri 7.30 am–8.30 pm, Sat 8 am–6 pm, Sun 10 am–6 pm

U Ševce Matouše (At the Shoemaker Matthew) Restaurant, Prague 1 (Hradčany), Loretánské náměstí 4, daily 11 am–4 pm, 6–11 pm

U svatého Tomáše (At the Holy Thomas), Prague 1 (Malá Strana), Letenská 12, currently being renovated

U Tří housliček (At the Three Fiddles) Restaurant, Prague 1 (Malá Strana), Nerudova 12, daily 11.30 am–12 pm

Včelařské potřeby, Prague 1 (Nové Město), Křemencova 8, Mon & Wed 9 am–5 pm, Tue & Thu 9 am–6 pm, Fri 9 am–2 pm

Villa Bílek (Bílkova vila), Prague 1 (Hradčany), Mickiewiczova 1, the villa is closed for renovation until 2009

Villa Müller (Müllerova vila), Prague 6 (Střešovice), Nad Hradním vodojemem 14, guided tours only Tue, Thu, Sat & Sun 10 am, 12 am, 2 pm & 4 pm

Vrtba Garden (Vrtbovská zahrada), Prague 1 (Malá Strana), Karmelitská 25, Apr–Oct daily 10 am–6 pm

Vyšehrad Cemetery, Prague 2 (Vyšehrad), Štulcova, Apr–Oct daily 9.30 am–6 pm, Nov–Mar 9.30 am–5 pm

Výstaviště, Prague 7 (Holešovice), U Výstaviště, Tue–Fri 2–9 pm, Sat & Sun 10 am–9 pm

Wallenstein Garden (Valdštejnská zahrada), Prague 1 (Malá Strana), Letenská, Apr–Oct 10 am–6 pm

Wallenstein Riding School (Valdštejnská jízdárna), Prague 1 (Malá Strana),Valdštejnská, Tue–Sun 10 am–6 pm

Zbraslav Chateau and Monastery (Zbraslavský zámek a klášter), Prague 16 (Zbraslav), Bartoňova 2, Tue–Fri 10 am–6 pm

Zvonice (Belfry) Restaurant, Prague 1 (Nové Město), Jindřišská Věž, Senovážné náměstí, daily 11.30 am–12 pm

The world's only Cubist street lamp, on Jungmannovo náměstí (see no. 46)

Bibliography

GUIDEBOOKS

Time Out Prague 7th ed. (Various), Penguin Books, 2006

Globetrotter Prague (Brigitte Lee & Jack Messenger), New Holland Publishers (UK) Ltd., 2008

Blue Guide Prague, (Jasper Tilbury), W. W. Norton Ltd., 2004

Eyewitness Travel Guide Prague (Vladimír Soukup & Marianne Petrou), Dorling Kindersley, 2008

The Rough Guide to Prague (Rob Humphreys), Penguin Books, 2008

Lonely Planet Prague (Neil Wilson), Lonely Planet Publications, 2007

AA Essential Spiral Guide Prague (Various), AA Publishing, 2007

ILLUSTRATED BOOKS

Wonders of Prague (Petr David, Vladimír Soukup & Zdeněk Thoma), Euromedia Group, k. s. – Knižní klub, 2004

Prague Magic (Eva Veselá), e.v. art publishing, 2005

Prague Detailed Picture Guide (Jana Švábová & Tomáš Rygl), ATP Publishing, 2005

ARCHITECTURE AND MONUMENTS

Prague: A Guide to Twentieth Century Architecture (Ivan Margolius), Konemann, 1997

Prague Castle (Jiří Podrazil), Baset Publishing House, 2001

Prague Castle – Hradčany (Vladislav Dudák), Baset Publishing House, 1998

Prague Castle – Golden Lane (František Kadlec), Prague Castle Administration, 1999

Charles Bridge (Vladislav Dudák & Jiří Podrazil), Baset Publishing House, 2003

Prague Gardens (Eduard Škoda), Prague Publishing House of Jiří Poláček, 2001

CHURCH, CEMETERY AND MUSEUM GUIDEBOOKS

The Cathedral of St. Vitus in Prague (Ivo Hlobil), Opus Publishing Ltd., 2006

The Prague Loreto – A Guide for the Pilgrimage Site (Markéta Baštová & Teresie Cvachová), Order of the Friars Minor Capuchin, 2005

Jewish Prague (Jindřich Lion), Mandelbaum Verlag, 2005

The History of the Prague Sewage System with Special Regard to the Prague-Bubeneč Sewage Works (Jan Palas, Tomáš Just, Michal Martinek & Jiří Wanner), Ekotechnické museum Praha, 2004

National Museum (Various), National Museum Publications, 2006

Náprstek Museum (Various), National Museum Publications, 2006

FICTION

Utz (Bruce Chatwin), Penguin Books Ltd., 1989

The Good Soldier Svejk and his Fortune in the World War (Jaroslav Hašek), trans. Cecil Parrott, Penguin Books Ltd., 2005

The Castle (Franz Kafka), trans. J. Underwood, Penguin Modern Books, 2000

Metamorphosis (Franz Kafka), trans. Malcolm Pasley, Penguin Modern Books, 2000

The Trial (Franz Kafka), trans. Idris Parry, Penguin Modern Books, 2000

Severin's Journey into the Dark (A Prague Ghost Story) (Paul Leppin), Twisted Spoon Press, 2001

The Angel of the West Window (Gustav Meyrink), trans. Mike Mitchell, Dedalus, 1991

The Golem (Gustav Meyrink), trans. Mike Mitchell, Dedalus, 1995

Tales of the Little Quarter (Jan Neruda), trans. E. Pargeter, Greenwood Press, 1977

Prague Tales (Jan Neruda), trans. Michael Henry Heim, Central European University Press, 2000

HISTORY

Magic Prague (Angelo Maria Ripellino), Picador, 1995

Prague in Black and Gold: The History of a City (Peter Demetz), Penguin Books Ltd., 1998

A Brief History of the Czech Lands to 2004 (Petr Čornej & Jiří Pokorný), Práh Press, 2003

Prague Pilgrim: Prague from Every Side (Vladislav Dudák), Baset, 1995

In Strangest Europe (Peter Ratazzi), The Mitre Press, 1968

The Cooking of Vienna's Empire (Joseph Wecksberg and Fred Lyon), Time Life Books, 1979

WEBSITES

www.praha-mesto.cz (Prague City Hall)

www.pis.cz (Prague Information Service)

www.praguer.com (Prague Tours, Walks & Excursions)

www.walks.cz (Daily Walks of Prague)

www.praguetravel.cz (Prague Walking Tours)

www.praguewalks.com (Prague Walks)

www.legacytours.cz (Prague Jewish Information & Travel Bureau)

www.heartofeurope.cz (Prague Culture)

www.dpp.cz (Prague's public transport system)

www.praguepost.com (English language online newspaper)

www.czechtourism.com (Czech Republic Tourism)

www.travel.cz (Czech Republic accomodation)

Acknowledgements

First and foremost I would like to thank the staff of my Viennese publisher Christian Brandstätter Verlag, not only for their continued belief in my work but also their professionalism, enthusiasm and good humour in bringing it to the bookshop shelves. In this respect I am especially
grateful to Christian Brandstätter, Elisabeth Hölzl and Clemens Hutter. My especial thanks also
to Matthias Goldmann, for his excellent translation of my English manuscript for the German-
language edition, and to Ekke Wolf for designing the layout. I am also grateful to Juraj Heger of
Slovart in Bratislava for distribution of the book in the Czech and Slovak Republics.

My thanks also go to Dr. Jan Jungmann, Helena Nejedlá, and Andreas Deppe for their tireless
proof-reading of my manuscript, and for checking grammar and punctuation. Any remaining
errors are entirely my own.

For kind permission to take photographs, as well as arranging for access and the provision of
information, the following people are very gratefully acknowledged:

Kristina Alda (Prague Post), Architecture in Porcelain (Úvoz 1), Ladislav Beneš, Big Ben Bookshop, Karel Bulva (Peklo Restaurant), Nadia Černíková and Radek Janata (U Maltézských
rytířů Restaurant), Czech Museum of Fine Arts, Ekaterina Dotcheva (Hotel Vinárna), Eva
Effenbergerová (Gambra Gallery), Hotel Rezidence Lundborg, Josef Sudek Atelier, Jiří Kalina
and Vit Bavtošek (Restaurant Svatá Klára), Rudolf Kaválek and Zdeněk Laňka (National Technical Museum), Jana Kolářová (Expozice Franze Kafky), Magdalena Kordová and Petra Čeperová
(Czech Centre for Tourism, Vienna), Nenad Kralev (Czech Orthodox Church of SS. Cyril and
Methodius), Evžen Kůs (Prague Zoo), Marie Linkášová (Marold Panorama), Irena Lehkoživová
and Lída Egerová (Church of St. Francis), Lucerna Cinema, Michal Motyčka (Globe Bookstore
& Café), Museum of the City of Prague, Na Ryknu Souvenir Shop (Malé náměstí), František
Novák (House of the Lords of Kunštát and Poděbrady), the caretaker at the Old Lesser Town
Cemetery in Smíchov, Olšany Cemetery, Martin Opatrný (Loreto), Pedagogical Museum of
J. A. Comenius, Father Petr (Church of the Virgin Mary Victorious, Lesser Quarter), Prague Infor-
mation Service (Pražská informační služba), Blanka M. Remešová (Gallery Art Factory), Tomáš
Rygl (ATP Publishing), Restaurace U Rotta, Magdalena Ševčíková (Hotel Residence Řetězová),
Martin Slavíc (Eco-Technical Museum), Antonín Štefka (Powder Tower), Jaroslav Ullmann (Na
Slupi Botanical Gardens), Ladislav Veselý (Minipivovar U Medvídků), and Tom and Marie Zahn
(P.A.T.H. Ways, Prague).

For the supply of film, high-quality processing and
technical advice my thanks go to Franz and Veronika
Schieder, Robert Kopetzky and Josef Slavik, formerly
of Foto Wachtl (Vienna).

The following Prague acquaintances are much appreciated for their friendship and assistance:

Gloria Bisiani and Ivan Falta (B.F. Welcome), Lucie
Jiraskova, Kit Knotts, Alper Meranezlioğlu, Gordon
Pleasant, Steinthor Sigurdarson, Michael Stavaric, Kelly
Wulf, Dagmar Žáková (for the excellent accommoda-
tion), and Joy Kadečková – may she rest in peace.

Finally, very special thanks to my father Trevor, for inspiring me to track down unusual locations in the first
place – thanks Dad for making it all such fun!

1ˢᵗ Edition

Graphic Design: Beatrix Kutschera, Atelier 21, Vienna
Typesetting: Ekke Wolf, typic.at
Reprographics: Grasl Druck & Neue Medien, Bad Vöslau
Printing/*Tisk*: DELO tiskarna, Slovenia

All illustrations © 2008 Duncan J. D. Smith except:

Maps: APA, Wien

ISBN 978-3-85033-155-5
For the Czech books: 978-80-7391-149-2

Christian Brandstätter Verlag
GmbH & Co KG
A-1080 Wien, Wickenburggasse 26
Telefon (+43-1) 512 15 43-0
Telefax (+43-1) 512 15 43-231
E-Mail: info@cbv.at
www.cbv.at

10 9 8 7 6 5 4 3 2 1
www.slovart.cz

A humorous detail on a Renaissance doorway in Josefov